INTELLECTUAL PROPERTY RIGHTS AND HUMAN DEVELOPMENT IN INDIA

INTELLECTUAL PROPERTY RIGHTS AND HUMAN DEVELOPMENT IN INDIA

TALWAR SABANNA

SERIALS PUBLICATIONS
NEW DELHI (INDIA)

First Published – 2009

ISBN: 978-81-8387-227-0

Published by

SERIALS PUBLICATIONS
4830/24, Prahlad Street, Ansari Road
Darya Ganj, New Delhi-110002 (India)
Phone: 23245225 Fax: 91-11-23272135
E-mail: serials@satyam.net.in

CONTENTS

	Preface		*vii*
1.	Preserving Bio-diversity Versus Protecting Intellectual Property Rights: Can the Conflict Be Resolved?	*Sabyasachi Ghosh, Moiz & Tundawala*	1
2.	Information Technology Law and Intellectual Property Rights	*S.B. Somannavar*	17
3.	Implementation of Intellectual Property Rights in Current Political System	*Ujjwal Kacker*	49
4.	Nutraceuticals; Need for Patenting in India	*B.N. Nimbur & D.S. Naik*	69
5.	Patent Law in India– A Perspective	*Preethi Venkataramu & Srinivasulu N. S.*	79
6.	WTO and Agricultual Issues	*Lakshya Pal S. Shekawat & Prashant Kumar*	95
7.	Geographical Indications: Feasibility of Extending Protection under the TRIPS Regime	*Shouvik Kumar Guha*	113
8.	Controversies in a Harmonized Global Patent System: A Study of the WIPO Patent Agenda	*Debosmita Nandy*	133
9.	Intellectual Property Disputes and Arbitration	*Mallika Tasly & Sidharth A Menon*	147
10.	Understanding Originality in Copyright Law and the Development of an Indian Position on the Protection of Compilation of Facts	*Swayambhu Mukherjee*	159

11.	Unemployment and Jobless Growth in India under the Era of Globalisation	*V. S. Adigal*	177
12.	Health Infrastructure in India: Present Challenges and Future Prospects	*Dinesh P. T., Jayasheela & V. Basil Hans*	191
13.	Social Sector and Dalits in India: A Review	*P. S. Kamble, B.J. Kadam & J. P. Patil*	201
14.	Service-led Growth in India: An Analysis	*Debesh Bhowmik*	213
15.	Gender Discrimination and Wage Discrimination of Agricultural Labourers: A Study in Gulbarga District of Karnataka	*Vithob B., Y. S.Vaggi & N. Mallikarjun*	229
16.	Socio-economic and Health Problems of the Elderly People in Rural Areas	*Basalingamma Halemani & S.A. Kazi*	241
17.	Contesting Modernity and Globalisation: Multiculturalism or Polarization; A Comparitive Analysis of the Indian and the British Experience	*Ravi Dalwai*	251
18.	"Scheduled Caste Women in Higher Education and Policies: A Study of Karnataka"	*Sindhe Jaganath R. & V. Rama Krishna*	259
19.	Urban Solid Waste Management A Case Study of Belgaum Muncipal Corporation	*Abhay M.Patil*	273
20.	Microfinance: An Effective Tool for Financial Inclusion	*Dinesh P. T. & Jayasheela*	289

PREFACE

The push for strong international IPRS has come primarily from governments of developed countries that have made knowledge economy innovation a central pillar of their industrial strategies. These Governments are not, how ever, only seeking to enhance the interests of their domestic terms. They have recognized the importance of private capital in producing innovations which improve the overall well–being of society and that in a market economy, IPRS are required to induce these investments. There is significant potential for improving the lives of many people in developing countries through improved medicines and agricultural crops.

India is a country having large amount of natural resources and many people and community with intellectual property to make use of them. However, people are faraway from formal, scientific and legal right. Further, it is a country with largest democracy in the world. There is open society. Indian gates are opened to the formal and informal invitation to the people of other countries. After the departure of British, particularly in the recent years, people of many countries thronging in India and getting acquainted with the intellectual properties informally mixing with people and community. In this issue an attempt is made to look at the IPRS and human development with special reference to India.

Preserving Biodiversity Versus Protecting Intellectual Property Rights: Can the Conflict Be Resolved?

Sabyasachi Ghosh & Moiz Tundawala**

INTRODUCTION

While it is imperative to encourage the creative innovative zeal by endowing the inventor with adequate incentives, the ultimate collective objective of good for the larger society must not be lost sight of. Commercialization of rights in favour of individuals and body corporate perpetuates the hierarchical divide between those with access to resources and those who remain confined to their own spheres without any means of communication owing to a lack of common understanding with regard to the modes of existence. Thus, one must take the initiative to protect the interests and aspirations of indigenous communities owning and controlling the traditional biological resources collectively for centuries. Traditional knowledge, which encompasses information about the agronomic or culinary characteristics of crops or the medicinal qualities of native species, comprises insights and understandings developed through generations, thereby forming an integral aspect of an indigenous group's cultural survival. Seeking to derive commercial benefits from the use of these resources without accommodating their grievances constitutes an act of biopiracy that is heinous in its sheer audacity. Biopiracy is thus a performance entirely different from bioprospecting as the latter is concerned merely with exploration of wild plants and animals for commercially valuable genetic and biochemical resources.

There appears to exist an apparent contradiction in scholarly opinion on the said distinguishing features on a global scale. On one hand, the

* The West Bengal National University of Juridical Sciences, Dr. Ambedkar Bhavan , 12 LB Block, Sector-III, Salt Lake City, Kolkata-700098.

Email Correspondence:ghose.sabyasachi@gmail.com & moiztundawala@gmail.com

Trade Related Intellectual Property Rights (TRIPs) Agreement endeavours to promote a strong intellectual property rights regime, while at the other end of the spectrum, the Convention on Biological Diversity (CBD) is concerned with the protection and preservation of bio diversity and biological resources, with its commitment being concentrated on the protection of the traditional rights of indigenous people. However, alternative constructions of the existing framework can be envisaged which offer more balanced solutions to the seeming disconnect. This paper will endeavor to explore such alternative constructions and will examine the various Indian laws- the Biological Diversity Act, 2002 the Plant Varieties and Protection of Farmers' Rights Act, 2001 and the Patent (Amendment) Act, 2005 to ascertain whether they are capable of upholding the balance.

IPR AND BIOLOGICAL RESOURCES: WHEREIN DOES THE CONFLICT LIE?

Trouble Brewing in the Turmeric Case

In 1995, two U.S. based Indians were granted U.S. Patent 5,401,504 on use of Turmeric in Wound Healing (popularly known as the Turmeric patent), which was assigned to the University of Mississippi Medical Centre, U.S. The invention claimed under the patent was the use of turmeric at the site of an injury and/or its oral intake to promote the healing of a wound[1].

The news was greeted with disbelief and surprise by most people in India. Turmeric has been traditionally used in India for its many special properties in wound-healing. For instance, it is used as a blood purifier, in treating the common cold, and as an anti-parasitic for many skin infections. It is also used as an essential ingredient in cooking many Indian dishes. How could someone obtain a patent i.e., an exclusive right to sell and distribute something that was so commonly known; was the disturbing question[2]. The media coverage of the patent generated debate and discussion on the issue and the Centre for Scientific and Industrial Research (CSIR), an autonomous institution under the Department of Science and Technology, Government of India, decided to file for re-examination of the patent at the United States Patent and Trademark Office (USPTO).

The challenges before them were many, since the patent had to be challenged in accordance with the specific requirements under U.S. law. The claimed subject matter was the use of "turmeric powder and its administration", both oral as well as topical, for wound healing. As per the requirements of U.S. law, it was necessary to find adequate evidence in the form of printed and published information that would establish that the manner of use of turmeric as in the claimed invention, was known before the patent was claimed and, therefore, the patent was invalid. Despite the fact that the use of turmeric was known to every Indian household for ages, finding published information on the use of turmeric powder through oral as well as topical route for wound healing was a difficult task. Fortunately, after an extensive search, 32 references were located, some of which were more than 100 years old, and in the languages of Sanskrit, Urdu and Hindi. The USPTO revoked the patent, stating that the claims made in the patent were obvious and anticipated, and agreeing that the use of turmeric was an old art of healing wounds.

The patent on the "use of turmeric in wound healing" is but one of the many examples of how patents are being sought over various aspects of biological resources and products derived from the same. The various useful properties and knowledge regarding biological resources have been identified and preserved through consistent skill, observation and usage by various local and indigenous communities through the world. But since these do not meet the modern 'innovation' criteria of patent law, access to them is assumed to be 'free'[3]. This case and many others like it bring into prominence certain important legal issues relating to control and ownership of biological resources and their patentability. A brief examination of these issues will serve a useful purpose for our subsequent enquiries and explorations.

Patents: What do they Mean Anyway?

Patents are a form of intellectual property rights, rights to intangible property. A patent seeks to reward the inventor for the information embodied in his/her invention, but not for the physical product itself. The patent laws aim at ensuring a fair return to the inventor, while at the same time encouraging innovation and making new inventions available to the public. After the patent period is over, the invention passes into the public domain, and is then available to all. Thus, the patent system endeavours to strike a fine balance between private and public interests[4].

A patent can be granted only when the three fundamental conditions of 'novelty', 'inventive step' and 'industrial application' are fulfilled. With the coming into force of the Agreement on Trade Related Aspects of Intellectual Property Rights, these requirements have concretized into mandatory prescriptions[5].

PROTECTION OF BIOLOGICAL DIVERSITY: TO REGULATE OR NOT TO REGULATE?

Biological diversity or biodiversity encompasses all species of plants, animals and micro-organisms and the variations between them, and the eco-systems of which they form a part. There are almost infinite number of plant, animal, and microorganism varieties in the world today. We largely remain ignorant of all the species that are living on this planet and new species keep getting discovered[6].

Traditional knowledge associated with such biological resources is an intangible component of the resource itself. It encompasses information about the agronomic or culinary characteristics of crops or the medicinal qualities of native species[7]. Normally, traditional knowledge comprises insights and understandings developed through generations. As a result, it forms an essential aspect of an indigenous group's cultural survival[8]. But with rapid advances in science and technology, such knowledge has the potential of being translated into commercial benefits by providing leads for the development of useful products and processes[9].

Today biological diversity provides the feedstock to the biotechnology industry. Primarily concentrated in the tropics-the developing world, it is basic to the progress in improving the productivity of plants, animals and all other living organisms[10].

BIO-PIRACY AND BIO-PROSPECTING: BROTHERS UNDER DIFFERENT GARBS?

The commercial potential involved in biological resources and the associated traditional knowledge has assumed enormous magnitude in the last couple of decades with the tremendous proliferation of the biotechnology industry. Given that most of the world's biodiversity-rich countries are developing countries located in the tropics, these nations should have been in a strong position to benefit substantially by trading in such bio-resources and the associated traditional knowledge. Unfortunately, this is far from the case. More often than not it is the giant corporations of the developed world who are instrumental in appropriation of the precious bio-resources and the allied traditional knowledge of the South, without the prior informed consent (PIC) of the legitimate holders of such resources, thereby bypassing any benefit-sharing arrangement with them[11].

Thus, biopiracy[12] occurs when corporations use the folk wisdom of indigenous people to locate and understand the use of medicinal plants and then exploit this knowledge commercially[13]. It refers to the appropriation and monopolization of a traditional population's knowledge and biological resources, including the smuggling of diverse forms of plants and animals[14]. Bio-piracy results in traditional population losing control over their resources[15].

However, notwithstanding unscrupulous practices by corporations in the developed world, the argument in favour of intellectual property protection still remains- further research and development requires incentives[16]. Let us hypothesize that a drug company discovers a complex chemical compound having pharmacologically interesting characteristics in a rainforest. Such a discovery would be potentially beneficial to all concerned, but unless the essential follow-up work of purifying the compound, reproducing it either synthetically or otherwise, and clinically proving its safety and efficacy for human medicinal use— unless those three extremely expensive but essential efforts are protected by intellectual property-there would be no incentive to undertake the efforts[17].

Facilitative access to resources is envisaged by the concept of bio-prospecting. It can be defined as the "exploration of wild plants and animals for commercially valuable genetic and biochemical resources[18]". Bio-prospecting is a fair enterprise based on certain legal conditions and benefit sharing[19]. It can help medical and other scientific research by collecting biological samples[20].

Any legal mechanism must take cognizance of these rival contestations. While it is essential to grant incentives to promote research and development, the appropriation and abuse of existing biological resources to the detriment of indigenous communities cannot be justified.

INTERNATIONAL SCENARIO: THE DEBATE CONTINUES

The current debate surrounding biotechnology is centered on the ownership or control over biological resources. On one hand, are developed countries such as the United States who are pressing for strong intellectual property protection, whether it is patent protection or a *sui generis* regime. On the other hand are the developing countries which are the primary storehouses of the biological resources. They are demanding a share in the profits made from the use of such resources and are asserting sovereign control over these resources. Involved in this scenario are two instruments of immense importance, the Agreement on Trade Related Aspects of Intellectual Property Rights and the Convention on Biological Diversity-two documents seemingly at cross-purposes.

TRIPs: A Commendable Effort or An Exercise in Futility?

The traditional paradigm that biological resources formed part of a global commons was eroded by the extension of patents to living organisms[21]. In most developed countries, patents are issued for microorganisms, genetically modified plants and animals, and isolated and purified genes and genetic sequences[22]. This traditional paradigm was further upset by the increased assertion and expansion of other forms of intellectual property rights over plants, known as plant breeders' rights[23]. By the early 1990s biological goods were subjected to a range of intellectual property rights, but developing countries were facing pressure, particularly from the United States, to extend intellectual property protection to such goods in their own countries[24].

Recognizing that nations were becoming part of an increasingly dependent world economy, industrialized countries turned to the Uruguay Rounds Agreement of the GATT in an attempt to secure minimum standards of intellectual property protection. GATT had a distinct advantage over existing forum for multilateral negotiations, since an intellectual property agreement concluded in GATT would commit all GATT members to minimum intellectual property rights standards. The conclusion of the Uruguay Rounds Agreements in 1994 established the WTO and ushered in the TRIPS Agreement under its auspices. The purpose of TRIPS is to harmonize differing national laws on intellectual property rights. Some have regarded this treaty as a breakthrough in the field of international trade and cooperation. Others have severely criticized the single-mindedness with which the developed countries pursued trade issues to the detriment of developing countries[25]. TRIPS adopts the long-established, minimum substantive norms established in the Berne Convention for the Protection of Literary and Artistic Work, governing copyrights, and the Paris Convention for the Protection of Industrial Property, governing patents and trademarks[26]. TRIPS includes provisions protecting a broad range of intellectual property rights, including patents, copyrights, trademarks, geographical indications, and industrial designs[27]. Patent protection is available for a period of twenty years from the time of filing, and patentable subject matter has been defined as any new development that involves an inventive step and an industrial application[28]. In addition, TRIPS strengthens international patent protection by prohibiting discrimination against foreign patents[29]. TRIPS includes provisions that exclude certain subject matter from patentability for a limited time, such as products that protect human, plant or animal life and health, or products that are harmful to the environment[30].

In addition to requiring relatively high standards of intellectual property rights protection, TRIPS triggers the application of various dispute resolution mechanisms when its provisions are violated by WTO member states[31]. TRIPS benefits from strengthened dispute resolution procedures because it falls under the auspices of the WTO. Prior to the creation of the WTO, a panel decision was not binding unless it was agreed to by all member states. The Dispute Settlement Body (DSB) now provides that all decisions are automatically binding unless there is consensus among the member states to block the decision[32]. A member state's failure to abide by a DSB decision can be enforced by sanctions in the form of a withdrawal of trading concessions[33]. The high stakes implicit in this unprecedented linkage between trade and intellectual property has placed great pressure on India and other developing countries[34].

CBD: The Future Beckons

The CBD was first presented at the United Nations Conference on Environment and Development (UNCED), which took place in Rio de Janeiro in 1992. It came into force in 1993 and has 182 contracting parties[35]. According to international environmental concerns at UNCED, the CBD specifically focused on conservations about the Earth's biological diversity and its sustainability through national strategies, plans, and programs[36]. In the CBD, intellectual property rights were addressed in three separate articles relating to indigenous people[37]. The Convention came into force with the following three objectives: the conservation of biological diversity; the sustainable use of its components; and fair and equitable sharing of benefits arising out of the utilization of genetic resources.

In particular, three articles of the CBD are the locus of importance in the ongoing debate over the protection of biological resources. The Convention begins its discussion by proclaiming not the common heritage of the biological resources but, rather, the sovereignty of nations over them[38]. Article 15 focuses on the rights of the State, evidently assuming that the various stakeholders in a given society work together as one unit. It is essentially concerned with the movement of biological resources across the territorial limits of States. Such access is not only subject to the national legislations of the governments, but also to the "prior informed consent" of the contracting parties providing such resources, it must be based on "mutually agreed terms" and requires "benefit sharing."

Article 8(j) provides for the concerns of local and indigenous communities. Included are requirements for the state to identify and document the knowledge, innovations, and practices (KIPs) of such communities in an effort to determine what constitutes conservation and sustainable use of biological diversity. States are also required to seek the approval and involvement of communities when promoting the wider application of KIPs. Finally, Article 8(j) calls for an equitable sharing of benefits that rise from the utilization of KIPs between the state and local and indigenous communities.

Thus the TRIPs is informed by the individual private rights protection approach. On the other hand, the Convention on Biological Diversity seeks to conserve biodiversity and is hence accommodative of the public rights approach. It specifically provides that any intellectual property rights regime cannot run contrary to its provisions[39].

THE INDIAN RESPONSE: TAKING ADVANTAGE OF THE LOOPHOLES IN THE INTERNATIONAL LEGAL REGIME

India is a signatory to the Convention on Biological Diversity and is at the same time an essential component of the developing block at the World Trade Organizations trade negotiations. Its laws do seek to give effect to its TRIPS obligations, but at the same time are in a way reflective of its core commitments. India presents a unique model, which if emulated with suitable modifications, can go a long way in resolving the apparent conflict.

The Biological Diversity Act: The Indian Rejoinder

In December 2002 India passed a comprehensive legislation restricting access to biological material in its territory[40]. The Act aims to promote conservation, sustainable use and equitable sharing of benefits of India's biodiversity resources, including habitats, cultivars, domesticated stocks and breeds of animals and micro-organisms[41]. With this in view it provides for the establishment of a National Biodiversity Authority[42], State Biodiversity Boards[43] and Biodiversity Management Committees at the level of Panchayats (village committees) and Municipalities[44]. The law broadly prohibits any foreign person[45], or foreign corporation[46] from "obtaining any biological resource[47] occurring in India or knowledge associated thereto" for research, survey or commercial utilization[48] without the prior approval of the National Biodiversity Authority[49]. Regulation of bio-prospecting by Indian resident citizens and Indian corporations is left to subnational (state) biodiversity boards. The statute further prohibits any foreign person or corporation from "transfer[ring] the results of any research relating to biological resources occurring in, or obtained from, India" without the prior approval of the National

Biodiversity Authority[50]. Moreover, even if the National Biodiversity Authority approves the obtainment or transfer of any such resource or information, the applicant may not subsequently transfer that resource or information without the authority's consent[51].

The law, in turn, requires the National Biodiversity Authority to secure equitable benefit sharing for the use of "accessed biological resources, their by-products...and knowledge relating thereto[52]". Where a biological resource or associated knowledge has been acquired from a specific individual, group, or organization, the authority may, but need not, direct payment of moneys collected to such individuals, groups, or organizations[53]. The law does not require bio-prospectors to obtain the consent of affected individuals or groups before obtaining biological resources. However, the National Biodiversity Authority must consult with specially created local committees when making decisions "relating to the use of biological resources" and associated knowledge[54]. Finally, the law prohibits any person, whether foreign or Indian, from applying for any intellectual property right in or outside India "for any invention based on any research or information on a biological resource obtained from India" without the prior approval of the National Biodiversity Authority[55].

However, it is not short of loopholes. It exempts from its protection, plants registered under the Protection of Plant Varieties and Farmers' Rights Act, 2001[56]. It is unjustifiably soft to Indian corporate and other entities, requiring them only to make "prior *intimation*" to a State Biodiversity Board for the commercial use of bioresources, rather than seek *permission* from the National Biodiversity Authority as in the case of foreigners[57]. The Act fails to fully empower local communities to protect their resources and knowledge from being misused, or to generate benefits (except charging collection fees). It has very weak or no representation of local community members on the State Biodiversity Boards or National Biodiversity Authority. Further, State Governments are provided with the power to declare biodiversity heritage sights without consultation and consent of affected communities[58]. Finally, citizens cannot directly approach the courts. They can only prefer an appeal to the High Court against any order by the National Biodiversity Authority or State Biodiversity Boards[59].

According to many, the acceptance of the intellectual property rights paradigm is in itself the fundamental flaw inherent in the legislation. But many others believe that if necessary changes are incorporated, it can be a potent tool to ensure preservation of biological diversity and associated traditional knowledge against misappropriation and abuse.

1970 Amendments to the Patent Act: The Old Order Changeth

This Act, which is an amendment to the Patent Act, 1970, is significant in the sense that it stipulates disclosure of the 'source and geographical origin of the biological materials in the specification, when used in an invention'. This issue of disclosure is a contentious one being pushed by the less-developed countries in the TRIPS.

The 2005 amendment has introduced important provisions relating to pre-grant and post-grant opposition. The revised section 25(1) which deals with pre-grant opposition provides as follows:

"Where an application for a patent has been published but a patent has not been granted, any person may, in writing, represent by way of opposition to the Controller against the grant of patent within the prescribed period on the grounds of (a) patentability including novelty, inventive step and industrial applicability, or (b) non-disclosure or wrongful mentioning in complete specification, source and geographical origin of biological material used in the invention and anticipation of invention by the knowledge, oral or otherwise available within any local or indigenous community in India or elsewhere, and the Controller shall if requested by such person for being heard, hear him and dispose of the representation in such manner and within such period as may be prescribed".

Section 25(3) dealing with post-grant opposition further stipulates that at any time after the grant of patent but before the expiry of a period of one year from the date of publication of grant of a patent, any person interested may give notice of opposition to the Controller in the prescribed manner on certain specified grounds. The eleven grounds stipulated for such post-grant opposition include the following two grounds:

- That the complete specification does not disclose or wrongfully mentions the source and geographical origin of biological material used for the invention;
- That the invention so far as claimed in any claim of the complete specification was anticipated having regard to the knowledge, oral or otherwise, available within any local or indigenous community in India or elsewhere.

After the 2002 amendment, section 64(1) now allows revocation of patents on grounds of:

(1) Non-disclosure or wrongful mentioning in the patent application of the source or the geographical origin of biological material used for the invention concerned.

(2) Knowledge, oral or otherwise, available within any local or indigenous community in any country as anticipation of the invention concerned[60].

These two provisions enable recognition and reward of source countries and traditional knowledge holders[61]. There however is no requirement for providing information about the prior informed consent in the Act itself. Neither does the Act have stipulations on benefit sharing agreements. However, these are provided for under the Biological Diversity Act, 2002.

CONCLUSION: THE ROAD AHEAD

A patent can be granted to an invention only if it is a new product or process, and involves an inventive step and is capable of industrial application. But what exactly does 'novelty' mean? Can an invention, if anticipated on the basis of a traditional knowledge of any country, be at all regarded to be 'novel'?

The TRIPs Agreement no where provides for a definition of the concept of 'novelty' or 'newness'. Member states are therefore free to define and interpret the term in their own ways.

As noted above, in India, if some traditional knowledge, oral or otherwise, is used for anticipating an 'invention' then the patented subject matter does not satisfy the criterion of 'novelty' according to the Indian interpretation of the term 'new'. Further, section 2(l) of the amended Patents Act defines 'new invention' as 'any invention or technology which has not been anticipated by publication in any document or used in the country or elsewhere in the world before the date of filing of patent application with complete specification, i.e. the subject matter has not fallen in public domain or that it does not form part of the state of the art.' Indian law makes no distinction between the home country and a foreign country when it comes to the determination of novelty of an invention. However, since the TRIPS Agreement has no binding prescriptions relating to 'novelty', the laws of countries like the US do not consider that the 'novelty' requirement has been lost when an invention has been divulged outside the United States by 'non-written' means such as public use and sale[62]. Only existence of a patent or a published description of the invention is considered to be part of 'prior art' in case of a foreign country.

The newly incorporated provisions in the Patents Act and the requirements of 'prior informed consent' and 'benefit sharing' in the Biological Diversity Act, 2002 subject to certain modifications go a large way in protecting Indian bioresources from threats of bio-piracy domestically. But as we move to an increasingly globalized economic order, it is imperative to institutionalize such a protective shield for the preservation of biological resources and the associated traditional knowledge at the international level. The TRIPS Agreement, in its present form does not include provisions for the protection of the same. The block of developing countries is thus calling for amendments to the Agreement in line with the Convention on Biological Diversity to safeguard the rights and interests of indigenous communities. They call for specific provisions ensuring that an applicant for a patent relating to biological material or traditicnal knowledge specifically provide, as a condition for acquiring patent rights, disclosure of the source and country of origin of the biological resources and of the traditional knowledge used in the invention, evidence of prior informed consent through approval of authorities under the relevant national regimes, and evidence of fair and equitable benefit sharing under the national regime of the country of origin[63].

The road ahead may not be smooth for those negotiating for the inclusion of these safeguards in TRIPS. But it would be imperative for all parties not to rigidly cling on to their principled positions. A complete exclusion from the multilateral trading arrangement of patents on products and processes derived from biological resources and information associated with them may not be a feasible idea. At the same time, the international community as a whole must also recognize the legitimate hopes and aspirations of indigenous groups and communities who have held and preserved these resources since time immemorial. Only then can we dream to elevate to a higher level of economic progress which is inclusive of all constituents of the human fraternity.

NOTES

1. United States Patent Application No. 174363.
2. R.A. Mashelkar, *Curr. Sci.*, 2001, 81, 955–965.
3. Sangeeta Udgaonkar, *The Recording of Traditional Knowledge: Will it Prevent Bio-Piracy?, Cur. Sci.*, Vol. 82, No. 4, 25 February, 2002.
4. Salil K. Roy Chowdhry and H.K. Saharay, Law Relating to Trade Marks Copyrights Patents and Designs, Kamal Law House, 1996.
5. Article 27 of the Agreement on Trade Related Aspects of Intellectual Property Rights, 1994 states: 'Patentable Subject Matter– 1. Subject to the provisions of paragraphs 2 and 3, patents shall be available for any inventions, whether products or processes, in all fields of technology, provided that they are new, involve an inventive step and are capable of industrial application'.

6. Manju Sharma, New Biosciences: Opportunities and Challenges as we Move into the Next Millennium, Indian Science Congress Association, 1999.
7. See Paul Gepts, Who owns Biodiversity, and How Should the Owners Be Compensated?, 134 Plant Physiology, 1295, 1303 (2004).
8. *Ibid.*
9. Kasturi Das, Combatting Biopiracy, the Legal Way, 6 May 2005, retrieved from *http: / / www.indiatogether.org /* 2005/may/env-biopiracy.htm on 14th February, 2008.
10. See S.K. Verma, Access to Biological and Genetic Resources and their Protection, 43 JILI 1, 2 (2001).
11. See Paul Gepts, Who owns Biodiversity, and How Should the Owners Be Compensated?, 134 Plant Physiology, 1295, 1303 (2004).
12. Bio-piracy is defined as: 1. unauthorized use of biological resources, such as plants, animals, organs, microorganisms or genes; 2. unauthorized use of traditional communities 'knowledge on biological resources; 3. unequal share of benefits between a patent holder and the indigenous community whose resource and/or knowledge has been used; or 4. patenting of biological resources with no respect to patentable criteria (novelty, non-obviousness and usefulness)—Wikipedia, Bio-piracy, at *http: / / en.wikipedia.org / wiki / Bio-piracy* (last visited on 14th February, 2008).
13. See Andrew Kimbrell, Replace Bio-piracy with Biodemocracy, (July 23, 1996), at *http: / / www.ratical.org / co-globalize / ReplaceBPwBD.html* (last visited 14 February, 2008).
14. Ethical Boundaries, Bio-piracy in the Amazon—Introduction, retrieved from *http: / / www.amazonlink.org / biopiracy / (n.d.)* on 14th February, 2008.
15. *Ibid.*
16. Gerald J. Mossinghoff, The Biodiversity Convention And Intellectual Property Rights: Conflict Or Harmony?, May 1998, retrieved from *http: / / www.oblon.com / media / index.php?id=203* on 14th February, 2008.
17. *Ibid.*
18. See Sudhir Ghatnekar & Mandar Ghatnekar, Bio-prospecting or Bio-piracy?, Indian Express, Feb. 8, 1999, at *http: / / www.expressindia.com / fe / daily / 19990208 / fec0801.html.* (last visited 14th February 2008).
19. Vandana Shiva, Bio-Piracy: The Blunder of Nature and Knowledge 19-24 (1997), p. 72.
20. See Michael A. Gollin, Bio-piracy: The Legal Perspective, February 2001, at *http: / / www.actionbioscience.org / biodiversity / gollin.html* (last visited 14th February 2008).
21. See Diamond v. Chakrabarty, 447 U.S. 303 (1980) (allowing a patent on a genetically engineered bacterium and holding that patents could issue on living things).

22. See Sabrina Safrin, Hyperownership in a time of Biotechnological Promise: The International Conflict to Control the Building Blocks of Life, 98 AJIL 641, 645 (2004). See also Colin Macilwain, When Rhetoric Hits Reality in Debate on Bioprospecting, 392 Nature 535 (1998).
23. See Laurence R. Helfer, Intellectual Property Rights in Plant Varieties: International Legal Regimes and Policy Options for National Governments 14-21 (UN Food and Agricultural Organization, 2004). See also Kal Raustiala & David G. Victor, The Regime Complex for Plant Genetic Resources, 58 Int'l. Org. 277, 286-93 (2004).
24. See Sabrina Safrin, Hyperownership in a time of Biotechnological Promise: The International Conflict to Control the Building Blocks of Life, 98 AJIL 641, 646 (2004).
25. See Shukla, Amendment of Patents Act: Why Parliament must Defeat it?, *Econ. & Pol. Weekly*, Dec. 10, 1994, pp. 3128.
26. See Doris Estelle Long, The Impact of Foreign Investment on Indigenous Culture: An Intellectual Property Perspective, 23 N.C.J. Int'l. L. & Com. Reg. 229, 235 (1998).
27. *Ibid,* p. 250.
28. See Amy E. Carroll, A Review of recent decisions of the United States Court of Appeals for the Federal Circuit: Not Always the Best Medicine—Biotechnology and the Global Impact of U.S. Patent Law, 44 Am. U. L. Rev. 2433, 2460 (1995).
29. *Ibid.*
30. *Ibid.*
31. See Robert J. Gutowski, The Marriage of Intellectual Property and International Trade in the TRIPS Agreement: Strange Bedfellows or a Match made in Heaven?, 47 Buff. L. Rev. 713, 737-38 (1999).
32. See Robert J. Gutowski, The Marriage of Intellectual Property and International Trade in the TRIPS Agreement: Strange Bedfellows or a Match made in Heaven?, 47 Buff. L. Rev. 713, 737-38 (1999).
33. *Ibid.*
34. See Michael Woods, Food for Thought: The Biopiracy of Jasmine and Basmati Rice, 13 Alb. L. J. Sci. & Tech. 123, 132 (2002).
35. See Amy E. Carroll, A Review of recent decisions of the United States Court of Appeals for the Federal Circuit: Not Always the Best Medicine—Biotechnology and the Global Impact of U.S. Patent Law, 44 Am. U. L. Rev. 2433, 2461-62 (1995).
36. See Graham Dutfield, Intellectual Property Rights and the Life Science Industries: A Twentieth Century History 212 (2003).
37. See Amy E. Carroll, A Review of recent decisions of the United States Court of Appeals for the Federal Circuit: Not Always the Best Medicine—

Biotechnology and the Global Impact of U.S. Patent Law, 44 Am. U. L. Rev. 2433, 2462 (1995).

38. Convention on Biological Diversity (hereinafter referred to as CBD), June 5, 1992, Article 15(1), 31 I.L.M. 818, 823 (1992).
39. Convention on Biological Diversity (hereinafter referred to as CBD), June 5, 1992, Article 15(1), 31 I.L.M. 818, 823 (1992), Art. 16.5.
40. Biological Diversity Act, 2002, No. 18, Feb. 5, 2003, at *http://envfor.nic.in/divisions/biodiv/act/bio_div_act.htm* (last visited February 16, 2008).
41. *Ibid*, see Preamble.
42. *Ibid*, see Section 8.
43. Section 22 of the Biological Diversity Act, 2002.
44. *Ibid*, Section 41.
45. *Ibid*, §3(2)–this refers to any person not resident in India.
46. *Ibid*, Foreign Corporation refers to any "body corporate, association or organization...not incorporated or registered in India" or "which has any non-Indian participation in its share capital or management."
47. *Ibid*, "Biological resource" broadly encompasses "plants, animals and micro organisms or parts thereof, their genetic material and by-products...with actual or potential use or value"— §2(c). Biological resources do not include "products which may contain portions or extracts of plants and animals in unrecognizable and physically inseparable form"— §2(c).
48. Biological Diversity Act, 2002, No. 18, Feb. 5, 2003, at *http://envfor.nic.in/divisions/biodiv/act/bio_div_act.htm* (last visited February 16, 2008), §3(1). "Commercial utilization" refers to end uses of biological resources for commercial purposes, such as for drugs, food flavours, cosmetics, colours, and "genes used for improving crops and livestock through genetic intervention."-§2(f).
49. *Ibid*, §3. The National Biodiversity Authority is a national interagency body-§8.
50. *Ibid*, §§4. 19(1).
51. *Ibid*, §20(1).
52. Section 21 of the Biological Diversity Act, 2002.
53. *Ibid*, §21(3).
54. *Ibid*, §41(2).
55. *Ibid*, §6(1).
56. Ibid, Section 6(3).
57. *Ibid*, Section 7.
58. Biological Diversity Act, 2002, No. 18, Feb. 5, 2003, at *http://envfor.nic.in/divisions/biodiv/act/bio_div_act.htm* (last visited February 16, 2008), Section 37.

59. *Ibid*, Section 52.
60. The TRIPS Agreement has no specific stipulations on revocations. Article 32 only lays down that patents are judicially reviewable.
61. *Ibid*, at 447-48.
62. Section 101, U.S.C. provides: A person shall be entitled to a patent unless: A. The invention was known or used by others in this country or patented or described in a publication in this or a foreign country before the invention thereof by the applicant for patent.-or–B. The invention was patented or described in a trade publication in this or a foreign country or in public use or on sale in this country more than one year prior to the date of the application for patent in the United States.

    It may be a difficult road ahead for those negotiating for the inclusion of such safeguards in the TRIPS Agreement. But it may be the only way out to progress to an equitable world order which honours its inventors, while at the same time cherishing its biodiversity and the legitimate aspirations of communities owning and controlling them.
63. See S.K. Verma, Access to Biological and Genetic Resources and their Protection, 43 JILI 1, 2 (2001).

Information Technology Law and Intellectual Property Rights

*S.B. Somannavar**

I

INTRODUCTION

Information Technology Law-Meaning

"A group of laws relating to the activity using the domain of information technology which includes communication, digital electronics and computer systems" are called IT Laws. [*N. Vidyashankar, 2006*].

In fact, the IT has bestowed immense benefits to the mankind; but not everyone is using them for the good of the society. The criminal activities in the virtual cyber space are collectively called 'Cyber Crimes'. The menace of the cyber crime, the world over, is threatening the very existence of organizations. Cyber crime is affecting everyone individuals, organizations and even the governments. However, the biggest hurdle in dealing with this type of crime is that most of the people affected by this crime are not even aware of its existence. [*Col. R.S. Prasad, 2004*].

Broadly speaking, computer-related crimes are of two categories:

(i) Computer as a target of the crime.

(ii) Computer as an instrument of the crime.

Computer as a Target of the Crime

Some of the important crimes where the computer is the target of the crime or

* Department of Economics KLE Society's Lingaraj (Autonomous) College Belgaum Karnataka, INDIA., *Email: sbsomannavar@sify.com*

(i) Sabotage of computer systems or computer networks.

(ii) Sabotage of operating systems and programmes.

(iii) Theft of Data/Information (fastest growing computer-related crime).

(iv) Theft of Intellectual Property, such as computer software.

(v) Theft of marketing information and

(vi) Blackmail based on information gain from computerized files such as medical information, personal history, sexual preferences, financial data, etc.

Computer as an Instrument of the Crime

Here the computer is used as an instrument facilitating crime. The recent attack on the Indian Parliament where computer and internet was used in variety of ways to perpetrate the crime is a vivid example of this type of crime. The terrorists and criminals are using internet methods such as email to flash encrypted messages around the globe. Frauds related to electronic banking or e-commerce are other examples. In these crimes, computer programmes are manipulated to facilitate the crimes namely:

(i) Fraudulent used of ATM cards and accounts.

(ii) Credit card frauds.

(iii)Frauds involving electronic funds transfers.

(iv)Telecommunication Frauds and

(v) Frauds relating to e-Commerce and Electronic Data Interchange.

Theft of IPRs is also a part of cyber burglars. In the USA alone, the Fortune 1000 companies suffer a loss of about 300 billion dollars on this account. Their targets are computer software, semiconductor and pharmaceutical units. [*Atul Kumar, 2004*].

IPRs–Meaning

Intellectual Property is a set of rights conferred by law on an individual because of the ownership and possession of an object.

Ownership implies the right to posses, use and dispose of the property and excludes others from the same.

As modern science and technology is making fast progress, human ingenuity is putting up with new ideas and products, to control the market. New areas have emerged with claims for recognition as Intellectual Property.

The human intellectual creativity has lead to the production of works in the industrial, scientific, literary and artistic domain. These works can be in the form of an invention, a manuscript, a suite of software or business name. The traditional principal IPRs are copyright, patent, design rights and the law of confidential information.

[IGNOU and WIPO Study Material, MIP 001, General Overview of Intellectual Property, 2004].

IT Law & IPRs

In the information technology domain, the need for IPRs has become essential with a large number of business activities carried out by using the various tools of information technology.

The use of internet to send a message (email) or to obtain, the Domain Name System (DNS) has to be used through the Internet Protocol (IP) address. The Domain Name System helps people to navigate the Internet by matching the IP address numbers to user-friendly names. With the huge amount of money involved in transactions using the internet, it is essential to register the internet domain names. There have been 33000000 internet domain names registered with the United States Patent and Trademark Office. This signifies the importance of domain name business using the internet.

Disputes have cropped up in the use of domain name systems. Because of:

(i) Individuals or organizations registering a website with no rights.

(ii) Conflict between equally entitled persons to register the domain names.

(iii) Misspelling of popular brand names like *www.pesi.com and www.rediff.com*

Some of the domain name disputes which have reached the courts are The Comp Examiner Agency, INC., Vs. Juris, INC., MTV Networks Vs. Adam Curry, Hasbro, INC. Vs Internet Entertainment Group Ltd. and Prince Sports Group Vs Prince PLC, *et al.*

The domain name dispute reaching Indian courts are Yahoo INC. Vs. Akaṣh Arora and Anr, Rediff Communication Ltd. Vs. Cyber Booth and Anr, Aqua Minerals Ltd. Vs. IT Company and Bennett Coleman and Co. Ltd. Vs. Steven S Lalwani.

In the above cases, the domain name was identical and confusingly similar to the complainant's trademark or service mark. It was to be proved that the domain name holder has not rights or legitimate interests in the domain name and such domain names and registered and being used in bad faith.

II

OBJECTIVES OF THE STUDY

The present study aims at following objectives:

(1) To establish the relevance of IT Law in IPRs.

(2) To understand the IT Law in India.

(3) To study the IPRs in India.

(4) To analyze the IT Law Cases abroad and in India.

(5) Conclusion.

III

METHODOLOGY

A. The study has obtained the essential information from

(i) Books (ii) Internet.

B. The study analyses the IT Law cases in India and Abroad.

C. Draw the conclusions.

IV

RELEVANCE OF IT LAW IN IPRS

The increasingly fast evolution of information and communications technologies has placed enormous pressure on Intellectual Property legal regime throughout the world. Infringement of intellectual property rights over the internet has grown to unprecedented level. The traditional schemes of protection of copyrights, trademarks, patents, software, databases and so forth seem less well suited to solve many of the problems face today by governments, business and citizens throughout the world. This is true especially when virtually every act makes a copy, where innovation is happening at a rapid pace, and in an environment where sharing of information is nearly instantaneous and costless. Today, every country is faced with tricky issues related to whether and how to implement international, regional or national reforms to its intellectual property laws. In the context of the developing countries, these issues frequently raise fears for a new form of structurally-enforced imperialism, grounded in property rights and enforced by the most powerful, intellectual property–exporting countries.

There have been tremendous pressures upon the traditional system of *copyright* in Europe. Asia and elsewhere in the world. For example, a simple shift of format–the transition from hard copy objects like vinyl records to dignitized bits of information like MPSs–has prompted an upheaval of business models, legal principles and social practices associated with the use, distribution and control of media. This upheaval has created a void in the digital media world, a void that policy makers, industry representatives and consumers are scrambling to fill with new laws and technological solutions. While the transition to digitization has raised plenty of questions about what is legal, lucrative and beneficial for advancing the arts and production of creative works, the answers are far from clear. And the implications of the outcome of this crisis range far beyond the entertainment goods at issue today.

A series of essentially peer to peer technologies–Napster, Grokster, Kazaa, Morpheus, eDonkey and others–have brought with them extraordinary promise for creative, lawful acts. But these technologies also present unprecedented challenges to the music and movies distribution business, which is turn has applied pressure to policy makers. Many countries are considering ways that new equilibrium the divergent interests of artists, performer, producers and consumers can be achieve. Research reveals that there are at least five plausible future scenarios for resolving this crisis .Four of the five possible scenarios would require substantial changes to national and international intellectual property law, business models and social norms [*Stanford, 2004*].

In response to this crisis, some advocate expanding the scope of intellectual property law in order to provide additional protection of digital asses, such a as music, movies and text. This goal can be accomplished through the enactment of new legislation and the expansion of 'conventional' doctrines to digital rights disputes. Others endeavour to use new legislation to shore up technological shields developed by private industry. This approach might involve mandating or simply suppurating the deployment of protective technologies and criminalize the efforts to circumvent them. Last, some observers think that intellectual property law as applied to the Internet is already over protective and ought to be substantially reformed. The legal and technologies environments should be adjusted in such as manner as to take advantage of the opportunities presented by the digital technologies and the Internet in particular. Legal reform ought to reform on the development of a robust public domain, particularly with respect to digital materials, to encourage new form of creativity and reuse of ideas and expressions.

The Internet provides ample opportunity for new means of *trademark* infringement. Trademarks can now be infringed in ways that reach markets through the world in seconds. At the same time, the Internet has created enormous potential to build international brands online and for new forms of non-commercial communication. One of the solutions proposed by the international community includes the application of ICANN's Uniform Dispute Resolution Policy to solve conflicts between trademark rights and domain names in the Internet context. The UDRP and Associated National Laws raise issues as to fairness, enforceability of decisions and interaction with traditional domestic trademark law and civil procedure.

The *software industry* is also facing new challenges. Law makers have passed a series of reforms that provide for greater protection for software, especially through the patent regime and through database protection legislation. The scope of these projections is important in decision making about how to develop, distribute and use software in the digital ear. Successful software development projects have adopted a broad range of approaches to intellectual property, from the most locked-down, proprietary model to the most determinedly 'open' or 'free software' modes. Key issues at present include the controversial move to extend subject matter coverage to allow the patenting of software, the patenting of business models and protections extended to database's These protections afford software developers the ability to profit more handsomely from their work in the near-term, but may act to restrict innovation in the process. These patents likewise pose problems for the extension of the open source software movement, which offers a vibrant alternative to the dominant proprietary development model.

These doctrinal area–copyright, trademark. Patent, database protection and so forth- present extremely important issues, especially for developing countries, related to the control of knowledge necessary to compete in the global economy. *(cyber.law.harvard.edu / ilaw / eurasia_2004].*

V

THE IT LAW IN INDIA

The United Nations Commission on International Trade Law (UNCITRAL) adopted a Model Law on electronic commerce in 1996. The General Assembly of the United Nations by its Resolution No. 51/162, dated 30th January 1997, recommended that all States should give favourable considerations to the said Model Law when they enact or revise their laws. The Model Law provides for equal legal treatment of users of electronics communication and paper based communication.

The WTO is likely to form a work program for the possible creation of multilateral trade deals through the medium of electronic commence.

The Information Technology Act 2000 (Act No. 21 of 2000) came into force in India on 17th October, 2000 to:

i. Bring in suitable amendments in the existing laws in India to facilitate e-commerce.

ii. Provide legal recognition of all electronic records and digital signatures.

iii. Enable the conclusion of contracts and the creation of rights and obligations through the electronic medium.

iv. Provide for a regulatory for a regulatory regime to supervise the Certifying Authority issuing Digital Signature Certificates.

v. Prevent the possible misuse arising out of transactions and other dealings concluded over the electronic medium.

vi. Create civil and criminal liabilities for contravention of the provisions of the Act.

vii. Facilitate Electronic-Governance by creating provision for the use and acceptance of electronic records and digital signatures in the government offices and its agencies, which will make the citizen's interacting with the government offices hassle free.

In brief, the Act aims at providing legal recognition for transactions carried out by the means of electronic data interchange and other means of electronic communication (i.e. e-commerce), which involved the use of alternatives to paper-based methods of communication and storage of information, to facilitate electronic filling of documents with the Government agencies and further to amend the Indian Penal Code 1860, the Indian Evidence Act 1872. The Bankers' Book Evidence Act 1891 and the Reserve Bank of India Act, 1934 and for matters connected therewith or incidental thereto.

This Act comprises of 93 sections divided into 13 *chapters*. It includes 4 *schedules* which lay down the relative amendments made to the Indian Penal Code 1860, the Indian Evidence Act 1872. The Banker's Book Evidence Act 1891 and the Reserve Bank of India Act 1934. The 13 chapters respectively deal with preliminary matters, digital signature, electronic governance, attribution, acknowledgement and dispatch of electronic records, secure electronic records and secure digital signatures, regulation of certifying authorities, Digital Signature Certificates, obligation of subscribers, penalties and adjudication, the Cyber Regulation Appellate Tribunal, offences, network service providers not to be liable in certain cases and miscellaneous provisions.

This Act *aims at to curb* computer crimes, and provides for penalties, punishment and compensation for hacking, unauthorized access to computer network, databases, spread of computer viruses, disruption of services, copying of software, tampering with source documents and electronics forgery.

Apart from the enactment of this Act, the Central Government, in order to implement the various provisions of the Act has framed:

i. The Information Technology (Certifying Authority) Rules, 2000.
ii. The Cyber Regulation Appellate Tribunal (Procedure) Rules, 2000.
iii. List of Chairman and Members of the Cyber Regulation Advisory Committee, *Chapter XI deals with the following offences:*

1. Sec. 65– tampering with computer source documents.
2. Sec. 66–hacking with a computer system.
3. Sec. 67–publishing of information which is obscene in electronic form.
4. Sec. 68– power of Controller to give directions.
5. Sec. 69–directions of Controller to a subscriber to extend facilities to decrypt information.
6. Sec. 70–protected system.
7. Sec. 71–penalty for misrepresentation.
8. Sec. 72–penalty for breach of confidentiality and privacy.
9. Sec. 73–penalty for publishing Digital Signature Certificate false in certain particulars.

10. Sec. 74–publication for fraudulent purpose.
11. Sec 75–Act to apply for offence or contravention committed outside India.
12. Sec. 76–confiscation.
13. Sec. 77–penalties and confiscation not interfere with other punishments.
14. Sec. 78–power to investigate offences.

Chapter XII deals with network service providers not to liable in certain cases under Sec. 79.

Chapter XIII deals with miscellaneous provision of the Act.

Sec. 80–power of police officer and other officers to enter, search, etc.

Sec. 81–Act to have overriding effect.

Sec. 82–Controller, Deputy Controller and Assistant Controllers to be public servants.

Sec. 83–power to give directions.

Sec. 84–protection of action taken in good faith.

Sec. 85–offences by companies.

Sec. 86– removal of difficulties.

Sec. 87– power of central government to make rules.

Sec. 88–constitution of advisory committee i.e. the Cyber Regulations.

Advisory Committee.

Sec. 89– power of controller to make regulations.

Sec. 91–provision for the amendment of the Indian Penal Code, Act 45 of 1860 i.e. offences relating to documents. A new definition section containing "electronic record", is inserted in Sec. 29-A. Similarly, Sections 167, 172, 173, 175, 192, 204, 463, 466, 468, 469, 470, 476, and 477-A, are amended to include "electronic recorded". Section 464 is amended to provide punishment for making a false document or false electronic records.

Sec. 92–Act 1 of 1872 is amended to provide the meanings for expressions "Certifying Authority", "Digital Signature", "Digital Signature Certificate", "Electronic Form", "Electronic Records",

"Information" and "Subscriber", as assigned to them tin the Information Technology Act, 2000.

Sec. 93– Act 18 of 1891 i.e. the Bankers Books Evidence Act 1891 amended.

Sec. 94– Act 2 of 1934 amended with reference to the regulation of the fund transfer through electronic means.

SCHEDULES

The First Schedule

Amendments to the Indian Penal Code (45 of 1860):

Amendments are made to the Sections 29, 167, 172, 192, 463, 464 and the like. The key amendment relates to the widening of the term ***document***, to include electronic records, Sec. 464 now recognizes the concept of ***digital signature***.

The Second Schedule

Amendments to the Indian Evidence Act (1 of 1872).

Sec. 65 B recognizes admissibility of computer outputs in the media, paper, optical or magnetic form. There are detailed provisions relating to admissibility of computer output as evidence. New Sec. 73A prescribes procedure for verification of digital signatures. New Sections 85A and 85B creates presumption as regards electronic contracts, electronic records and digital signature, digital signature certificates and electronics messages.

The Third Schedule

Amendments to the Bankers' Books Evidence Act (18 of 1891).

The amendment is made to include printouts of data stored in a floppy, disc, tape or any other form of electromagnetic data storage device in the 'Bankers' Books'.

The Fourth Schedule

Amendment to the Reserve Bank of India Act (2 of 1934).

A clause is inserted in Sec. 58, sub section 2 of the RBI Act of 1934, about the regulation of fund transfer through electronic means between the banks/financial institutions.

The Fifth Schedule

Glossary of thermos used in IT Law 2000. [*Law Publishers (India) Pvt. Ltd. 2001*].

The *Information Technology (Amendment) Bill 2006* makes amendments to a number of provisions in the Information Technology Act 2000. 'Digital Signature' is substituted by 'Electronic Signature'. There are 50 clauses which have amended the different sections of the Act 2000. There have also been amendments to the Indian Penal Code (45 of 1860) and the Indian Evidence Act (01 of 1872).

[*The Information Technology Amendment Bill, 2006*].

VI

INTELLECTUAL PROPERTY RIGHTS–THE INDIAN SCENARIO

The tradition of scholarship and intellectual creativity in India goes back to a few millennia. Yet the concept of Intellectual Property Rights in the modern sense is rather new and would appear to have no cultural moorings or sanction in our country. The history of intellectual property rights in India backed by enforceable legal provisions scarcely goes back to 150 years.

Brief History and the Present Scenario of IP Legislation in India

The first Indian statute on ***patents*** was passed 1856 granting some exclusive rights to inventors for 14 years. It was re-enacted with some modification as the Act of 1859. It granted to inventors of 'new manufacture" exclusive rights to make, sell and use the invention in India, or to authorize someone to do so. Its cope was expanded to include designs underrate "new manufacture' in the Patents and Designs Protection Act, 1872. Then the Inventions and Designs Act of 1888 came, and later the Indian Patents and Designs Act of 1911 (modeled on the British Patents and Designs Act 1907).

After independence, the government felt the need for a more effective patent legislation. The then existing situation with regard to patents was reviewed by two expert committees: one, headed by Justice Rajagopal lyengar and another headed by Bakshi Tek Chand. It was revealed that the MNCs, who owned 90% of all the patents in India had misused patents largely to ensure a protected market in India for their products, denying availability of many essential goods to people at competitive prices. The Patents Bill following the reports of these Committees was debated for a decade when finally the Indian Patent Act of 1970 was enacted. It was highly acclaimed by UNCTAD as a most progressive patent law and inspired similar legislations in many developing countries.

Indian becoming a member of WTO has to follow obligations under TRIPs agreement. Hence, the Indian Patents Act of 1970 was amended by Patents Act, 1999 and Patents Act, 2002, which came into force on May 2, 2003.

No specific legislation existed on ***trademark*** before 1940. However, remedies were available under the IPC 1860 and Specific Relief Act 1877. The Trademarks Act 1940 was replaced by the Trade and Merchandise Mark Act 1958, which has now been repealed and replaced by the Trademarks Act 1999.

Designs continued to be governed by the provisions of the Indian Patents and Designs Act 1911, until the Designs Act 2000 was passed.

In matter of ***copyright***, the English Copyright Act 1842 was deemed applicable to India. The application of the Copyright Act 1911 of England was extended to India as a British Dominion. The Indian Copyright Act 1914 introduced criminal sanctions for infringement and continued till the Copyright Act 1957, came into force in 1958. This was necessitated as much by the changed status of India as an independent nation as by the advancement of technology of reproduction and communication. The Act had several original features: registration of copyright was voluntary, administrative machinery for the registration of copyright was establishment, the government was empowered to protect copyright of citizens form other countries. It has been amended since then in 1983, 1992, 1994 and 1999– the last one after India ratified the TRIPs Agreement as a member of the WTO.

Besides these four principal fields for intellectual property protection namely, patents, trademarks, industrial designs and copyright. India has enacted the IP Laws for geographical indications of goods, protection of plant varieties and farmers' rights, semi-conductor IC layout design, information technology and bio-diversity. These are:

1. The Patents Act, 1970 as amended by the Patents (Amendment) Act, 1999, and the Patents (Amendment) Act, 2002.
2. The Copyright Act, 1957 as amended in 1999.
3. The Trademarks Act, 1999.
4. The Designs Act, 2000.

5. The Geographical Indications of Goods (Registration and Protection) Act, 1999.
6. Integrated Circuit Layout Designs Act, 2000.
7. The Biological Diversity Act, 2002.

[IGNOU and WIPO Study Material, MIP 001, General Overview of Intellectual Property, 2004].

VII

IT LAW CASES IN INDIA AND ABROAD

Four Cases in the European Court of Justice (ECJ), November 2004

These cases are concerned with the interpretation of the EU Directive on Legal Protection of Databases. This interpretation of the judgments in these cases provide a "sui generic database right" (to be distinguished from copyright) to the maker of a database, if there has been a substantial investment in either the obtaining, verification or presentation of the contents of the database. The cases relate to similar circumstances and concerned databases of sporting information (horse racing information and football fixture lists). Certain pieces of information from these databases were used by third parties for commercial gambling operations. In proceedings before the relevant national courts, the claimants alleged that these uses by the gambling operators were an infringement of the claimant's sui generic rights under the Directive. In each case, the national courts referred a set of questions to the ECJ.

In these cases, the ECJ, inter alia, now has clarified the definition of the term "database" as used in the Directive; determined the scope of protection (especially) with regard to the "substantial investment" requirement); and, specified infringement of the sui generic right through extraction or re-utilization.

Out of these four cases, let us take two cases for discussion:

Case 1

Free/Open Source Software Development

The open source movement, like digital technologies generally, presents both opportunities and challenges within the intellectual property contexts. Over the past decade or so, a large globe community of software developers has turned itself into a major economic and political force by developing new software on a collaborative model known variously as "open source", "liber" and "free" software. While open source technologies have not yet become a major player in the desktop computing space, the majority of the web pages are served using open sources technologies. Chief Information Officers of corporations, government agencies and other large institutions around the world routinely run flavours of LINUX, a major open source platform as either the predominant or at least a substantial part of their IT systems. International technology firms, most prominently IBM and Sun Microsystems, have championed the use of open sourer technologies. Even Microsoft, ordinarily perceived as the world's proprietary software leader, has begun to offer major segments of its software to users under its growing "shared source" program.

Open source presents opportunities to countries that are growing their ICT infrastructure because it is often a low cost software choice (and free, at least in its simple form), more secure than proprietary technology choices and can foster a local technology development community rather than sending license streams to large technology companies in other countries, frequently the United States. Countries and municipalities frequently consider policy to favour open source technologies over proprietary choices. In 2003, the city of Munich decided to procure open source solutions instead of Microsoft products.

The intellectual property rights regime related to open source is not altogether clear. Most opens source technologies are, into first instance, protected by copyright, and then distributed by their authors to others subject to one of about 50 open source or free software licenses, such technologies to do certain things, such as re-restrictions. Doubts have cropped about the legality of such licenses, which have only rarely been tested in court. Likewise, some purported rights-holders in the chain of title to important open source code have challenged uses of the technologies on intellectual property grounds, most prominently in the case ***SCO v IBM***, pending in the United States' court system and which could have implications for open source software projects around the world.

Activists and policy makers are presented with a series of problems related to open source. These are: Is promotion of open source technologies, rather than proprietary choices, sound public policy? Does the intellectual property regime, whether in individual countries or in a global sense, need to be adjusted to support open sourer technology development? What do local software developers have to gain from a legal and policy regime supportive of open source technologies?

Case 2

Dmitry Sklyarov and the International Reach of Intellectual Property Laws

One of the most pressing issues related to the development of intellectual property law and the interest is the management of conflicting legal regimes over international borders. On the one hand, harmonization and co-operation across national borders would no doubt help the flow of commerce, as the supporters of the TRIPs and WIPO regimes argue; on the other, such harmonization and enforcement would likely to export and reinforce the existing US-based view of the intellectual property law, which is a relatively strong strand of protection for copyright holders and those how make copy-protective technologies. The DS case presents a variant of this problem : how the US law and technologies, itself can affect the actions of these based in the Eurasia region.

With annual revenues of more than $ 1 billion, Adobe is the second largest PC Software Company in the US. In an effort to lead the market for software that enables the digital distribution of books, Adobe developed the Adobe Acrobat e-Book Reader (now integrated into Adobe Acrobat Reader). Development of the market for digital books distribution software also requires adoption of the technology by book publishers. *Adobe's e-Book Reader* is designed as a 'trusted system', offering publishers a spectrum of copyright protection options when encoding their content.

Founded in 1990 and headquartered in Moscow. ElcomSoft, is a software company that "specializes in producing Windows productivity and utility applications for business and individuals". Among the many software products developed by ElcomSoft is the 'Advanced e-Book Processor (AEBPR), which used to be available for download from their site (but seems to have been removed). The program enables users to: (i) disable the copyright protection controls deployed by book publishers using Adobe's software and to repackage their digital books I variety of common formats without copyright controls.

DS is a young programmer and cryptographer formerly employed by ElcomScft has been researching crypt analysis in furtherance of a PhD, he hopes to earn from a Moscow university. He is allegedly responsible for much of ElcomSoft' AEBPER, most notably, the decryption algorithms it employs to circumvent Adobe's copyright protection controls.

In its first criminal prosecution under the Digital Millennium Copyright Act (DMCA), the US Department of Justice ('D.O.J.') indicated both ElomSoft and Sklyarov for violations stemming from the development and marketing of ElcomSoft's AEBPR. (Abode officers brought ElcomSoft's AEBPR to the attention of the FBI on June 26, 2001). Sklyarov was most likely targeted largely because of his plans to enter the US for a conference in Las Vegas (making it easier for the DOJ to persuade a US Court to exert jurisdiction over him). After his presentation, Dmitry was arrested as he was leaving to return to Russia. On August 28, 2001, the DOJ announced that the ElcomSoft Company Ltd. and Dmitry Skyarov were indicated on five counts of copyright violations. They were indicated on one count of conspiracy to traffic in technology, primarily designed to circumvent and marketed for use in circumventing technology that protects a right of copyright owner, in violation of Title 18, US Code, Sec. 371, two counts of trafficking in technology marketed for use in circumventing technology that protects a right of a copy owner in violation of Title 17, US Code, Section 1201 (b) (1)(C).

Sklyarov's arrest promoted outcries of outrage from software developers, civil libertarians and all who generally oppose the DMCA. He faced a maximum Fine of $2.25 million and up to 25 years of imprisonment. Not surprisingly. The D.J.O. promptly reached an agreement with Sklyarwov, under the terms of thwich they have agreed not to prosecute him personally if he assists in their (criminal) prosecution of ElcomSoft.

In Dec. 2002, a federal jury acquitted ElcomSoft of criminal charges against it and Sklyrarov was released subject of a plea agreement. This case is highly fact-specific and unlikely to be repeated. But it demonstrates the power and reach of copy right-related laws-such as the US's DMCA-outside the geographic boundaries of a given jurisdiction. It also raises issues that a country debating adoption of similar anti-circumvention provisions might be well advised to bear in mind.

Cases in India

There are a good number of cases in India regarding the use of domain names. The Indian Legal framework, there is no specific Law or Act which deals with the protection of domain names. However, such cases are to be studied in the light and principles of the Trade Mark Act, 1999.

The Civil and Criminal remedies available under the Trade Mark Act. 1999, for infringement and/or passing off of the trademark are also applicable to the domain name disputes.

Infringement and passing off are to be studied in the light of 'likelihood of confusion' principles. However, the principles applicable to trademarks cannot in their entirety be applicable to domain names.

We consider here in detail the case of Indya.com Portal Pvt. Ltd. V. Akram Ali, V.M. Hardware and 13 other cases in brief.

Case 1

This case is presented as viewed by Maninder Singh, the Sole Panelist, appointed by the WIPO Arbitration and Mediation Center, dated January 01, 2001.

WIPO Arbitration and Mediation Center

ADMINISTRATIVE PANEL DECISION

Indya.com Portal Pvt. Ltd. v. Akram Ali, V.M. Hardware

The Parties

Indya.Com Portal Pvt. Ltd, Registered Office at No. 58, Microland House, L.V. Complex, Koramangala 7th Block, Bangalore–560 095, India (Complainant).

Mr. Akram Ali, V.M. Hardware, No: 494, Jumma Masjid Road, OPH Road, Bangalore, Karnataka 560 008, India (Respondent).

The Domain Names and Registrar

The Respondent is the registrant of the following domain names: *<indyanews.com>, <indyanews.net> and <indyanews.org>.*

Dotster, Inc (a wholly owned subsidiary of Columbia Analytical Services Inc), 1338, Commerce Avenue, Longview, WA 98632, USA is the Registrar of the said domain names.

Procedural History

The Complaint in this case was filled by e-mail on October 31, 2000 and in hardcopy con November 13, 2000 with the WIPO Arbitration and Mediation Center (the "Center").

The Center has found that the Complaint satisfied the formal requirements of the Uniform Domain Name Disputer Resolution Policy, the Rules for Uniform Domain Name Disputer Resolution Policy and the Supplemental Rules for Uniform Domain Name Dispute Resolution Policy.

On November 10, 2000 the Center transmitted a request to Dotster, Inc, to verify the following facts:

- To confirm that a copy of the Complaint was sent to Doster, Inc.
- To confirm that *<indyanews.com>*, *<indyanews.net>* and *<indyanews.org> are registered with Dotster, Inc.*
- To confirm that the entity identified in the present case as the Respondent is the current registrant of the domain name:
- To provide full contact details that are available in Dotster, Inc database for the registrant, technical contract, administrative contract and billing contact, for the said domain name:
- To confirm that the Uniform Domain Name Dispute Resolution Policy applies to the registered domain name:
- To indicate the current status of the domain name:

  Vide communication dated 10.11.2000 Dotster, Inc informed the Center as under.
- That Dotster, Inc is the Registrar of the domain name registration.

- That Mr. Akram Ali, V.M. Hardware is the current registrant of the *<indyanews.com>*, *<indyanews.net>* and *<indyanews.org>* domain name registrations.
- That the UDRP applies to these domain names.
- To current status of the domain names is ACTIVE.

On November 13, 2000 the Respondent was notified of the Complaint filled by the Complainant and opportunity was granted as per the Rules for filling of a Response. This notification of Complaint was done by e-mail and normal post/courier. The Administrative Panel finds that the Center has satisfied its notification obligations under Rule 4 (a).

The Center on December 2, 2000 received Responses from the Respondent.

On December 22, 2000, the Center appointed an Administrative Panel consisting of a single member viz., Maninder Singh and this was notified to the Complainant and the Respondent.

The language of the administrate proceeding is English.

Factual Background

The Complainant in this administrative proceeding is Indya.Com Portal Pvt. Ltd. Registered Office at No. 58. Microland House, L.V. Complex, Koramangala 7th Block, Bangalroe-560095, India. The Compliment is the proprietor of trade mark "indya.com" and has been using this mark since its incorporation. As per the records, the Complainant is using its website *http://www.indya.com* a horizontal portal of interest to the general public with India relevant contents since September, 1999.

The dispute arises out of the grievance of the Complainant that the Complainant has a website, viz., *<indya.com>* for which the Complainant is known. The Respondent has got registered as domain names, viz., *<indyanews.com>*, *<indyanes.net>*, *<indyanews.org>* for which the Respondent is not entitled.

Parties' Contentions

The Complainant's Contentions in Brief are as Under:

The Complainant is the proprietor of and is entitled to the use of the trademark "indya.com". This mark has been in use sine the incorporation of the Complainant and has been used on its website *http://www.indya.com* a horizontal portal of interest to the general public with content related to India. The mark has been extensively advertised in both print and electronic media.

The Complainant has also applied for the registration of the trade mark "indya.com" under the Indian Trade and Merchandise Marks Act 1958. Which has been taken on record by the Registrar of Trade Marks, Madras, India, vide application number 914331 dated March 30, 2000, under class 16 (dealing with printed matters, newspapers and periodicals, computer printoutism, jackets for programme discs and tapes, operating systems and programme manuals, spread shets, plotters) which application is pending before the Registrar of Trade Marks.

The word "Indya" is a unique word coined by the Complainant and uniquely identifies (a) the Complainant and (b) the Complainant's website /portal/.web property at the URL *http: / / www.indya.com* and at no other location.

The Complainant has also registered the domain names indya.net and indya.org with Network Solutions, Inc.

Further the mark is also part of the Corporate and trade name of the Complainant. Judgments of High Courts in India have held that holder of a domain name is entitled to the same protection as in the case of a trade mark. (*See Yahoo!Inc v Akash Arora & Another* IPLR 1999 April 196 (Delhi High Court; and *Rediff Communication Ltd. v. Cybarbooth & Another* 1999 (3) ALL MR 164 [Bombay High Court].

The Complainant in the Complaint further states that by using the domain names, the Respondent is intentionally attempting to attract for financial gain, interest users to the registrant's web site, by creating a likelihood of confusion with the Complainant's mark as to the source, sponsorship, affiliation, or endorsement of the registrant's web site or service on the registrant's web site. There is no possibility whatever of avoiding the confusion: the mark and common word "news" it implies or indicates a news section of the "Indya" website.

It has been contended by the Complainant that the offending domain registrations are deceptively and confusingly similar to the Complaint's domain and mark. This ha been done deliberately to traffic in the enormous goodwill and reputation developed by the Complainant. It has been further submitted by the Complainant that it undertook a massive media campaign to promote the site and it has, today, over 300,000 subscribers and enjoys traffic in excess of 14 million page-views per month.

One of the other submissions made by the Complainant in the Complaint is that there is no evidence at any stage, of the Respondent's use of, or demonstrable preparations to use, the domain names or a name corresponding to the domain names in connection with a bona fide offering of goods or services.

It has also been contended by the Complainant that the Respondent is not and cannot be commonly known by the domain names. The question of the Respondent acquiring any rights (trademark, service mark or other) does not arise.

The Complainant had issued a legal notice dated June 12, 2000 to the Respondent. The notice was received by the Respondent but has not been replied to or complied with.

Respondent's Contentions

In its Response, the Respondent has contended that the Respondent's domain names are *<indyanews.com>*, *<indyanews.net>* and *<indyanews.org>*. According to the Respondent, these domain names are distinct from the Complainant's domain name *<India.com>* and there is no likelihood of confusion. The Respondent's site *<indyanews.com>* is a vertical portal exclusively dedicated to news and provides a one stop news site for its consumer s and quite distinct from the Complainant's portal which is a horizontal portal.

The Respondent further states that the Complainant's registration of the "trademark" "indya.com" under the Indian Trade and Merchandise Mark Act 1958 is still pending before the Registrar of Trade Marks, India. The Registrar of Trade Marks, India is required to call for objections to the proposed trade mark, a procedure that has not yet been commenced by the Registrar. Only after all objections are considered by the Registrar of Trade Marks, can it take a decision on the proposed trade mark and.

It has also been contented by the Respondent in his Response that the word "Indya" is a homonym of India-it is pronounced exactly the same way as 'India' is and the consumer identifies "Indya" to the geographical entity 'India', which by no stretch of imagination can be called unique and does not exclusively identify itself with (a) the Complainant and (b) the Complainant's website/portal/web portal.

In reply to the reliance placed by the Complainant on certain judicial pronouncements in the Complainant, the Respondent submits that the decisions cited in favour of the Complainant being *Yahoo!Inc. v. Akash Arora & Anr.* IPLR 1999 April 196 (Delhi HC) and *Rediff Communication Ltd. V. Cyberbooth & Another* 1999 (3) All MR 164 (Bom HC) and *Rediff*

Communication Ltd. V. Cyberbooth & Another 1999 (3) All MR 164 (Bom HC) are not relevant to the dispute in question. Both the above cited cases dealt with domain names that were unique and where they were already established web sites. The Complainant had launched its website only in the four the week of April, 2000, much late to the date the Respondent registered its domain name which was on March 20th, 2000, with its intention to launch an exclusive news portal dedicated to make it a one stop for news for Non Resident Indians as well as Resident Indians. The idea is unique to the Respondent and there is no similarity to the Complainant's websites which is a horizontal portal.

It is further the case of Respondent that his domain names and website encapsule a unique concept-a one stop news shop for its consumers from all the leading news agencies around India and the globe. According to him, his concept is unique and in no way causes any confusion with the consumer's website. The word "indya" per se is not unique and is a homonym of India. There is no possibility of confusion between indya and Indy news which are entirely different concepts.

The Respondent, in his Response, has denied the contention of the Complainant that his domain names are deceptively similar and confusingly similar to the Complainant's domain and mark. The Respondent denies that this has been done deliberately to traffic in the goodwill and reputation developed by the Complainant. The Respondent highlights his contention that his domain names were registered on March 20, 2000 before the Complainant even launched its website and hence the argument relating to goodwill and reputation is specious and untenable .The Respondent's registration of its domain names were bonafide and done in good faith without any prior knowledge of the Complainant launching its web site four weeks later.

It has been further stated by the Respondent that he has been in discussions with venture capital funds and private investors nasd has launched its website indyanews.com. The website is a dedicated one stop news shop from leading news agencies all over India and the globe.

The legal notice that the Complainant issued dated June 12, 2000 has been replied to by the Respondent denying all the allegations within. The Complainant has not acknowledged the reply to the notice of the Respondent.

FINDINGS AND DISCUSSION

Paragraph 4(a) of the policy directs that the Complainant must prove each of the following:

(1) That the domain names registered by the Respondents are identical or confusingly similar to a service mark or trade mark in which the Complainant has rights; and

(2) That the Respondent has no rights or legitimate interests in respect often domain names, and

(3) That the domain names have been registered and used in bad faith.

Identical and Confusing Similarity

It is clear from the record that the Complainant is the proprietor of trade mark "India.com" and has been using this mark since it incorporation. It is clear from the record that the Complainant is the proprietor of trade mark "indya.com" and has been using this mark since it incorporation. It is also clear that the impugned domain names are deceptively similar to the name of the Complainant i.e. *<indya.com>*.

There is no doubt that the name *<indya.com>* of the Complainant and the impugned domain name i.e. *<indianews.com>*, *<indyanees.net>* and *<indyanews.org>* by the Respondent are identical and confusingly, similar.

Legitimate Interest

I have no hesitation in accepting the contention of he Complainant that the word "indya" has been confined by its and as such, the contention of the Respondent that this word is homonym of India and is pronounced exactly in the same way as "India", therefore, there would be possibility of confusion, deserves to be rejected. The Complainant as stated in the legal notice dated 12.06.2000, had registered the domain name *<indya.com>* in September, 1999. The Respondent, in his response stated that he had replied to the legal notice but had not appended the copy of the reply along with his Response. In any case, the contention of the Complainant that it registered the domain name *<indya.com>* in September, 1999 stands admitted. In view of this position, the contention of the Respondent that the Complainant had launched the website after the registration of the above-mentioned three disputed domain names by the Respondent on March 20, 2000, is of no consequence to the Complainant.

The Complainant has placed on record the copy of its application for registration of trade mark "*indya.com*" which the Registrar of Trade Marks, Madras (India). It is also relevant to note that this application was filed by the Complainant with the office of the Registrar of Trade Marks on March 7, 2000, which was numbered by that office on March 30, 2000. Even though it may not be of any consequence but it is relevant to notice that the filing of the application for registration of trade mark, by the Complainant is also prior to the registration of the impugned domain names on March 30, 2000 by the Respondent.

I am also not impressed by the contention of the Respondent that since he has added a suffix of 'news' with the world "indya", the case of the Complainant may be rejected. I am clearly of the view that since the website "*indya.com*" has contents related with India, there would certainly be confusion in the mind of a common user in relating the domain names of the Respondent "indyanews.com", "*indyanews.net*" and "indyanews.org" with the domain name of the Complainant. Further, I clearly find that the Judgements relied upon the Complainant in the cases of (a) Yahoo.Inc vs. Akash Arora & Anr. And (b) Rediff Communication Lt. vs. Cyberbooth & Anr., copies whereof have been placed before me: squarely support the contentions of the Complainant including the contention that addition of the suffix 'news' will into rule out the possibility of confusion. I reiterate the proposition that in certain cases, the addition of words to an established website/domain name may even add to the confusion rather than reducing confusing. It would be easy for any user to believe that indyanews is an extension of indya.com rather than a separate new portal.

In view of the above, I have not doubt that the Complainant has rights and legitimate interest in the trademark "indya.com" and the Respondent, in these facts and circumstances of the case, does not have any right or legitimate interest in the word "indyanews".

Bad Faith

It stands established that the Complainant has invented the word "indya" and which is quite unique. The Complainant has registered the domain name "indya.com" in September, 1999. The registration of the impugned domain names by the Respondent is only on 20.03.2000. There is no evidence produced by the Respondent of any use or demonstrable preparation to use, the domain names or a name corresponding to the domain names in connection with a bonafide offering of goods or services. The Respondent has only made a bald statement that he has been in discussions with the venture capital funds and private investors and has launched its website. Whereas, the Complainant has placed on record documentary evidence in abundance, the Respondent has place none. I, therefore, hold that the registration and use of the domain names "indyanews.com", "indyanews.net" and "indyanews.org" by the respondent is in bad faith within the meaning of the Policy, paragraph 4(a)(iii).

Decision

The Panel decides that the Respondent's domain names *<indianews.com>*, *<indianews.net>* and *<indianews.org>* should be transferred to the Complainant.

[*www.wipo.int–WIPO Domain Name Decision: D2000-1489*]

OTHER CASES IN BRIEF

Case 2

Zee Telefilms Ltd. and Ors. Vs. Zee Kathmandu and Ors. 2006 (32) PTC 470

The Respondents were permanently restrained from using the word "ZEE" as a part of any domain name, as the plaintiff was continuous user of the trademark ZEE, and it was held that adoption of the word ZEE by the respondent was malafide and with the intention to mislead internet users and take advantage of the plaintiff's goodwill.

Case 3

Yahoo! Inc. vs. Akash Arora and Another, 1999 (19) PTC201

The Plaintiff *www.yahoo.com* alleged that by using a similar domain name, i.e. *www.yahooindia.com*, the defendants were indulging in deceit and "passing off". Thus, by applying the doctrine of passing off, the court granted an interim injunction restraining the defendants from dealing in services or goods on the Internet or under the trademark domain name *<yahoindia.com>*. It was held that a domain name is entitled to equal principle that the use of domain names which was identical or deceptively similar to trademarks makes a prima facie case of passing off.

Case 4

Rediff Communication Ltd. vs. Cyber Booth and Another, 2000 (20) PTC 209.

In the above case plaintiff domain name was REDIFF. Defendant adopted RADIFF as a part of their domain name. The Court cannot the conclusion that the defendant's adoption of the domain name "RADIFF" was illegal and unlawful and the sole object of he defendants was to trade upon the reputation of the plaintiff. Considering the facts and applying the principles of passing off, the defendants were injected from using any domain name comprising the word "rediff".

Case 5

Dr. Reddy's Laboratories Ltd. vs. Manu Kosuri, 2001 (21) PTC 859

The plaintiff had registered the domain name *www. drreddys.com*. The Defendant adopted the domain name drreddyslab.com. The Court held that the defendant's acts of adoption of similar domain name were dishonest and malafide, and as such the defendant was liable for an action of passing off, since the domain name serves the same function as a trade mark.

Case 6

Acqua Minerals Ltd. vs. Pramod Borse, 2001 (21) PTC 619

The plaintiff was registered proprietor of the famous trade mark BISLERI for water. It was held that domain names are entitled to equal protection for an action of infringement is such a name is registered with the Registering Authority under the Trade Marks Act. Injunction was granted in respect of domain name <*bisleri.com*>.

Case 7

Info Edge India Pvt. Ltd. & Anr. Vs. Shailesh Gupta & Anr. 2002 (24) PTC 355

Plaintiffs domain names "*NAUKRI.COM*", was deceitfully adopted by the defendants as "*NAUKRI.COM*". Held, that the plaintiff was entitled for the injunction as both the domains were considered to be same, and defendant's adoption was considered as malafide by the court.

CASE 8

Sony Ericsson Mobile Communication AB VS. Chen Shenglu 206 (33) PTC 597 (NIXI), IN REGISTRY, NATIONAL EXCHANGE OF INDIA (NIXI)

Complaint was made w.r.t. the registration of Domain Name *www.sonyericsson.co.in* by the respondent in bad faith and being identical to the complainant's website/domain *www.sonyericcson.com* The complainant is proprietor of the trademark and domain name *sonyericsson.com* China where the respondent is based. The complainant, Sony Ericcson, also registered its domain name in more than 100 countries. The allegations of likelihood of confusion and deception were made. It was held that domain name of the respondent was identical to the trademark and domain name of the Complainant. The registration of country level domain in India by the Respondent based in China found to be in bad faith to cause confusion to the Internet users and to make such users to falsely believe that the disputed website is sponsored, endorsed or authorized by the complainant.

Respondent failed to show any right or legitimate interest in registering the disputed domain name. It was directed that the complainant is entitled to the transfer of the disputed domain name *www.sonyericsson.co.in.*

Case 9

CITICORP & Anr. Vs. Todi Investors Anr. 2006 (33) PTC 631 (Del)

In the above mentioned case, the dispute was w.r.t. the domain name "citi.in". The issue before the court was, whether Domain Name Dispute Resolution Policy providing mechanism for resolving such disputes, oust the jurisdiction of courts. It was held by court that the alternate dispute resolution policy in domain name matters does to take away the jurisdiction of the courts to adjudicate upon and decide domain name cases.

Case 10

Mawana Sugars Ltd. vs. Panalink Infotech Ltd. 2006 (32) PTC 537

The complainant company has been in the sugar producing and marketing business under the trademarks MAWANA and MAWANA SUGARS for the past 55 years. The complainant registered its domain names through the respondent, who illegally transferred the same to some third party during the tendency of he proceedings .It was held that it was a typical case of "***Cyberflying***", which means a phenomenon where a registrant of a domain name, when named as a respondent in a domain name dispute case, systematically transfers the domain name to a different registrant to disrupt the Policy. Held that respondent failed to show any legitimate right in the domain names and transfer of the domain name without the consent of the complainant was an action in bad faith. It was held that the respondent was involved in "CYBERFLYING".

Case 11

Tata Sons Ltd v The Advanced Information Technology Association Case No. D2000-0049 of WIPO

The dispute was regarding the registration of the domain name "*tata.org*" by the respondent .The complainant contended that they were the exclusive owners of the mark TATA. The dispute was regarding registration of the domain name "*tata.org*" by the respondents for illegal benefits. The complainants were the registered proprietors of the trademark TATA in India and the same was also registered in Bangladesh, Brunei, Kuwait, Malaysia, Nepal, Sabah, Singapore and Pakistan in favour of the complainants. It was held that the registration of the domain name was in bad faith, and consequently the said domain name was ordered to be transferred to the complainant.

Case 12

Bennett Coleman & Co. Ltd. v. Long Distance Telephone Company (Cases No. D2000-0014 and 2000-0015 of WIPO)

The complainant was the publisher of the famous Indian newspaper "The Times of India". The dispute was regarding the domain name "*thetimesofindia.com*" which had been registered by the respondent and the complainant held the domain name "*timesofindia.com*". It was held that respondent's registration and use of the domain name "thetimesofindia.com" was in bad faith. Hence, the said domain name was transferred to the complainant.

Case 13

Satyam Computer Service Limited vs. Vasudeva Varma Gokharaju: (Case No. D2000-0835 of WIPO)

The complainant is the flagship company of the Indian information technology giant, Satyam Group of companies. The complainant's trademark SATYAM in relation to software services was for the first time adopted and used in the year 1987, and its application for registration for the trademark/word SATYAM and corporate logo was pending in India. The respondent had registered the domain names "*satyam.net*" and "*satyam.org*" in 1999 and 1989 respectively. Held, that the said domain names were identical to the complainant's trademark SATYAM and that the respondent has no rights or legitimate interest in respect of the domain names and the same were transferred to the complainant.

VIII

CONCLUSION

There are many grey areas in countering the cyber crimes. The first and the most difficult problem concerning the combating of the cyber crime are to identify the culprits. As the Net can be accessed from any part of the globe, the field is wide open for hackers. Even if the identity of the hacker is established after following the electronic trail, it would be highly problematic to decide under which country's law the culprit can be prosecuted. The legal framework for initiating the persecution of a culprit of a foreign nationality is still not certain, especially in the absence of the extradition treaty and the necessity of the equivalent law in the culprit's native country.

In developing countries like India, the problem is still more complicated because of the lack of training of the police on subjects like computer forensics to investigate into cyber crimes. Unless the police are able to retrieve data from a computer, they would not be able to deal with the cyber crimes in the right earnest.

The Indian Information Technology Act prescribes low penalty for hackers. The maximum penalty for hackers is only Rs 3 lakh, which his very low, compared to the damages they cause, ideally, the penalty should be over and above the damages caused.

The Indian Act also does not have any specific mention of frauds related to misuse of credit card numbers. Since the computer crime has international dimensions, the international co-operation is a pre-requisite to prevent computer crimes.

There is also an absence of bilateral treaties/international legislatures to deal with cross-border cyber crimes which leaves organizations vulnerable to threats of attacks from other countries. In fact, an international agreement on dealing with cyber crimes is urgently needed to address the problem in a holistic manner. [*Atul Kumar, 2004*]

Since, cyber crime is altogether a different form of crime, the law enforcing agencies are finding it difficult to deal with. The public awareness is very low. Hence, combating cyber crimes needs a well panned strategy and a multi pronged attack with the co-operation from different agencies like national governments, business organizations, software industry, law enforcement agencies and international investigating agencies.

In this background, we would like to make the following suggestions:

Creating Public Awareness

It is essential to create public awareness about the extent to which computer crime can affect their lives, finances, business and family. A strong public education is essential. There is a need for making learning about computer crime a part of the curriculum in schools and colleges.

Enacting Stringent Laws

The present legal framework to deal with cyber crime is very weak. Only 20-30 countries have enacted laws to deal with cyber crime committed across the boundaries of the countries. India is one the countries which have enacted the IT Law. India enacted the Information Technology Law in 2000 and in 2006 many amendments have been made further to make it stronger.

Training of Law Enforcement Agencies

The law enforcing agencies requires special training to investigate cyber crimes. High levels of computer technology skills are essential for investigating cyber crimes.

Specialized Task Force

It is essential to establish specialized investigation units/ organizations to speed up the process to effectively deal with cyber crimes.

Reporting of Crimes

Different studies have shown that only 30% of cyber crimes are reported to law enforcing agencies. The reason is that many organizations are scared of loss of reputation and public trust, which in turn can affect their business. They are also scared that the reporting may lead to copycat violations in future. However, individuals and organizations must realize that reporting will help in controlling the crime.

Strict Security Measures

Organizations should follow strict policies for cyber security. Use of encryption, firewall and other technologies and conducting regular checks to monitor cyber attacks can reduce the chances of cyber crimes.

Training to Personnel of Organizations

Studies have revealed that the senior mangers have not realized the importance of computer crimes. Hence, training of managers, employees on cyber crime related aspects and conducting awareness programmes will definitely improve the overall security of the organization.

Government–Industry Co-operation

The co-operation between the law enforcement agencies and the hi-tech industry is very essential. The private industry can help the investigating agencies by joining investigating teams, providing hi-technology tools and assistance.

REFERENCES

Atul Kumar (2004), *"Cyber Crime and Indian Information Technology Act, 2000"*, in Cyber Crime–Combat Strategies, Ed. Col. R.S. Prasad, the ICFAI University Press, pp. 192-200.

Intellectual Property and Information Technology News Bulletin, Vol. 1, Issue 2, 1st December, 2006. Vaish Associates Advocates, New Delhi.

www.wipp.int–WIPO Domain Name Decision: D2000-1489.

cyber.law.harvard.edu / ilaw / Eurasia_2004.

IGNOU and WIPO Study Material, MIP 001, General Overview of Intellectual Property, 2004, IGNOU, New Delhi.

The Information Technology Amendment Bill 2006.

"The Information Technology Act, 2000", 2001.

Law Publishers (India) Pvt. Ltd. Allahabad.

Col. R.S. Prasad (2004), *"Cyber Crime: An Introduction",* the ICFAI University Press, pp. 03-14.

N. Vidyashankar (2006), *"Infotech Laws–A Presentation".* Secretary. IIIT Law, Bangalore.

Implementation of Intellectual Property Rights in Current Political System

*Ujjwal Kacker**

> *"The views on some of the controversial matters relating to Intellectual Property Rights can not be same all over the world. They depend upon the degree of the industrialization of the country concerned. The National laws have to be constant with the national aspirations and the good of the community."*
>
> ***Hon'ble Justice E.S. Venkataramiah***

INTRODUCTION

Intellectual property rights are legal rights governing the use of creations of the human mind .The recognition and protection of these rights is recent origin. Patents, designs and trade marks are considered as industrial property. As per international convention for the protection of Industrial property (Paris convention) the protection of industrial property has as its object, patent, utility models, industrial designs, trade marks, service trade names, indications of sources or appellations or origin, and the repression of unfair competition (Art. 1(2) of Paris convention, 1967) when Copyrights, Geographical Indications, layout designs and confidential information were included to industrial property, they all become intellectual property. The mundane object of Intellectual property rights, generally, is to exclude third parties from exploiting protected subject matter without explicit authorization of the right holder for a certain duration of time. Intellectual property rights help creative and inventive activity of orderly marketing of proprietary goods and services.

Intellectual property rights relates to items of information or knowledge, which can be incorporated in tangible objects at the same time in an unlimited number of copies of different locations anywhere

* Gujarat National Law University, Old NIFT Building, E-4, GIDC, Electronics Estate, Gandhinagar-382028, *E-mail: ujjwalkacker@gmail.com*

in the world. The property is not in those copies but in the information or knowledge reflected in them .It's importance was first recognized in the '*Paris convention for the protection of industrial property*'[1], in 1833 and the *Berne convention* for the protection of literary and artistic works in 1886. Both the treaties are administered by World Intellectual Property Rights Organization. For the enactment of any legislations or the signing of any treaty requires a scientific rationale of '*cause and affect*'. And this rationale must be emphasized, otherwise the intention with which the observations should be made will be tainted. Thus countries mainly have laws to protect Intellectual property rights for two main reasons:

1. One is to give statutory expressions to the moral and economic rights of creators in their creations.
2. To the rights of the public in accessing those creations.

IMPACT OF WTO LEGAL REGIME ON INDIAN SOVEREIGNTY:

TRIPS agreement has put substantial impact on Indian traditional knowledge, occupation and pharmaceuticals health remedies in three ways–

1. Drugs are becoming expensive and beyond the reach of the common man due to heavy royalties being charged by the patent holder of such drugs raising drug prices.
2. In the agricultural sectors the farmers would be loaded with the burden of paying royalties to the suppliers of improved variety of seeds who would be the patent owners of such seeds.
3. The traditional knowledge of yogic, ayurvedic and yunani health remedies have become vulnerable to patentability by foreign multinationals. Leaves, fruits and roots which are medicinal in nature are known to the people since ages and biopiracy by the multinational companies is in clear violation to the *Preamble of the TRIPS*. Unani and ayurvedic systems of treatment are exposed to the system of product patent. These medicinal products have existed in our country without any one exercising a monopoly right over them. In the post trips scenario if a foreigner gets a patent for such a product, he would be entitled to get the exclusive rights in the product[2].This implies that we Indians have to pay the price fixed by the patentee as he would have the monopoly right to determine the price and supply of such product. That clearly says that if we go by the spirit of the

above mentioned provision then we have to loose what has been ours for centuries.

This refreshes the bitter memories of legal battles of Trichopus Zeylanicus, turmeric and basmati rice. It would be inappropriate to skip these as they reflect the struggle of rights, struggle for conservation of values and lastly it reflects the spirit of Indian patriotism:

Case Study 1: Trichopus Zeylanicus[3]

The basic intention behind referring this case study is to facilitate *equitable sharing of benefits with indigenous people[4]*.

- The TBGRI, Thiruvananthapuram, Kerala State, India developed an innovative procedure for the equitable sharing of benefits with the tribal families who discovered the anti-fatigue properties of the plant Trichopus Zeylanicus.
- Members of the Kani tribe living in the Western Ghats Region of the State of Kerala drew the attention of the All India Coordinated Research Project on Ethnobiology team (AICRPE) to the energy and strength giving properties of the fruits of this plant.
- Scientists from the Regional Research Laboratory Jammu (India), and TBGRI verified the tribal claims by chemically analysing the fruits and developing an anti-fatigue drug named *Jeevani*.
- The invention has been patented by TBGRI and licensed for manufacture to an ayurvedic pharmaceutical company.
- The agreement between TBGRI and the company contains the following benefit sharing provisions. 50% of the license fee and 2% royalty at ex-factory sales price to be paid to Kani tribal families.
- Additionally TBGRI arranged for the cultivation of the plant by 50 tribal families on the basis of a buy back arrangement with the company and receive a steady annual income by domesticating the plant for commercial use.

Case Study 2: Revocation of Turmeric Patent

This case reflects the erroneous granting of patents by the World Intellectual Property Rights Organization[5].

The case of the revocation of the turmeric patent [US Patent 5401504] in a proceeding initiated by the Council of Scientific and

Industrial Research (CSIR, India) at the USPTO illustrates the significance of proper documentation of traditional knowledge. Non-availability of an authentic database of traditional knowledge and practices can often lead to erroneous granting of patents in such areas by patent offices around the world. The title of the patent granted by the US patent Office was "Use *of Turmeric in Wound Healing*" assigned to University of Mississippi Medical Centre, Jackson, Mississippi, USA. The chronology of events for US There was no comprehensive database in which to search to directly identify the relevant prior art. Thirty two references were cited in the revocation proceedings by CSIR at the USPTO. A few typical ones are given below:

- The Effect of Indigenous Remedies on Wounds, J.Ind. Med. Asso (1953).
- Ayurvedic Healing (1989).
- The Wealth of India (1950).
- Indian Materia Medica (1976).
- Economic and Medical Plant Research (1990).
- Home Remedies (1958).
- The Ayurvedic Pharmacopea of India (1986).
- Selected Medicinal Plants of India (1992).
- Bustanul Mufredat (1867).
- Khazanatul Adviy Vol. 3 (1920).
- Chakhambha Orientalia (1979).
- Kyaa Khya aur Kyoon? by G.N. Chauhan.

Based on these references the USPTO took a decision in favour of the opposition and revoked the granted patent. The basis was that the invention claimed in the patent lacked novelty with respect to the prior art. The turmeric opposition has exposed several issues *vis-à-vis* traditional knowledge systems and IPR such as[6]:

- The strength of the US patent system which is transparent to enable fair proceedings.
- Significance of following patent information especially linked to gazette notification of the patents filed, issued etc. Familiarity with patent office practices or a rigorous follow-up is necessary to meet statutory deadlines for filing of oppositions, submission of documents to the statutory offices, etc.

- Problems of establishing relevant prior-art due to non-existence of any comprehensive, reliable and authenticated database on information related to traditional and ethno-medicinal practices. In the present case a nationwide hunt to identify relevant literature had to be made. In several cases one will have to conduct a global search. A global program is necessary to construct a good database. While constructing a database one will have to structure the information so that it is easily indexed for user-friendly retrieval. Several fields will have to address the topic, such as approximate date of creation of that knowledge, geographical area of its origin, the community involved in the activity, the details of the process or product, the applications with data if possible, broad indications etc.
- Appreciation of the techno-legal issues involved while tackling soft information.
- Training of Science and Technology (S&T) personnel to critically read and interpret patent claims to assist in any techno-legal proceedings.
- These proceedings will alert patent offices to look for appropriate prior art before granting patent in fields related to claimed inventions derived from traditional practices.

Case 3: Basmati Rice[7]

There was a clear case of bio-piracy and theft with regard to the way Basmati patent was obtained in 1997 by the Texas based Rice-Tec Inc. The Texas Company was already trading in basmati rice with such brand names as temati, jusmati, and kasmati. The American Patent Office declared: "The invention relates to novel rice lines and to plant and grains of these lines and to a method for breeding these lines. The invention also relates to a novel means for determining and starch properties of rice grains and its use in identifying desirable rice lines."

The Texas company claimed a patent on basmati variety of rice on the ground that it was derived from Indian Basmati crossed with semi dwarf varieties, including *indica* varieties. The patent is for a variety essentially derived from a farmer's variety–a simple case of cross-breeding. It had to be treated as a false claim for an invention. The Indian research foundation pointed out that *"basmati covers about 15 per cent of the area under rice cultivation and that the country exported large quantities of Basmati Rice earning foreign exchange of Rs.1100 crores in 1996-97 .it is unique to Punjab in the same way that champagne is unique to certain areas in France*". The patent represented a theft of collective intellectual biodiversity heritage of Indian farmers- an act of stealing markets for Indian aromatic rice varieties and a theft of the name basmati itself. The patent was cancelled.

Substantial number of village and town people round the country even to this day are using twigs from the neem trees to brush their teeth every morning and using locally made preparations from the neem tree to keep away pests. We have savored the aroma of basmati rice worked in our homes for centuries. Similarly yoga is the 5000 year old Indian tradition. Turmeric has been the effective wound healing potion. How would someone even think of patenting such commonly used ingredients and practices that form part of the rich traditional folklore of India?

Realizing how adversely such bio-piracy could hit us, India challenged the offending references and arming themselves with sufficient evidence of traditional use. Following the contention and verifying the truth, the patents granted to neem and turmeric were revoked after the patents offices ascertained that there was no novelty involved and that the so called 'innovations' as it has been used in India for centuries. In fact, the fight for revoking the turmeric patent in the US Patent Office has even been dubbed the *'second' battle of 'Haldighati'*.

Not only this, on March 8 2005, the European patent office revoked the neem patent .But challenging the patents has not been easy by any standards. It has been a time consuming and extremely costly affair. And there are still a host of patents that need to be battled, such as those on Amla, Anar, Gulmendhi, Karela, Rangoon-ki-bel, and hundreds of others. Contesting patents given on traditional knowledge would always mean a long drawn battle with the high, mighty and moneyed powers of the global pharma industry.

Contemporary Position of Intellectual Property Rights in Indian Political System

For understanding the present position of intellectual property rights in Indian Political System, it is expedient and mandatory to consider the *'Mashelkar Report on Patent Law Issues'* which had two questions before it:

1. Whether it would be TRIPS compatible to limit the grant of patent for pharmaceutical substance to new chemical entity or to new medical entity involving one or more inventive steps?
2. Whether it would be TRIPS compatible to exclude micro-organisms from patenting?

In response to the question 1 it was said in the report that if the patents would be granted to new chemical entities and to new medical entities then the very fundamentals of the *Article 27 of the TRIPS agreement* would be violated whose clause (1) when read along with clause (2) manifests it which runs through as[8]:

Clause (1)

'Patents shall be available for any inventions, whether products or processes, in all fields of technology, provided that they are new, involve an inventive step and are capable of industrial application.'

Clause (2)

'Members may exclude from patentability inventions, the prevention within their territory of the commercial exploitation of which is necessary to protect *ordre public* or morality, including to protect human, animal or plant life or health or to avoid serious prejudice to the environment, provided that such exclusion is not made merely because the exploitation is prohibited by their law.'

Thus restricting patentability just to NCEs or NMEs could have both legal and scientific ramifications. There is a perception that even the current provisions in the Patents Act could be held to be TRIPS non-compliant. Drug discovery research is still finding its feet in India. Though many companies are investing, it will at least be a decade before a critical mass is in place and results start accruing. Thus, restricting patentability to just NCEs would mean that most of the pharmaceutical product patents would be owned by MNCs.[9]

Thus in response to the above question the report mentions:

'In the light of the above discussion, it would not be TRIPS compliant to limit granting of patents for pharmaceutical substance to New Chemical Entities only. However, every effort must be made to provide drugs at affordable prices to the people of India. Further, every effort should be made to prevent the grant of frivolous patents and 'ever-greening'. Detailed Guidelines should be formulated and rigorously used by the Indian Patent Office for examining the patent applications in the pharmaceutical sector so that the remotest possibility of granting frivolous patents is eliminated.'[10]

With reference to second question before the committee it was held on the basis of substantial provisions and guidelines that microorganisms should not be excluded from patenting but regarding to it strict

O

regulations and rules should be made which must be implemented stringently:

1. Position of Micro-organisms in the Indian Patents Act, 1970 as amended up to 2005 is as follows:

Section 3 of the Patents Act specifies inventions which are not patentable. The relevant provisions of that Section are as below[11]:

3(c): *"the mere discovery of a scientific principle or the formulation of an abstract theory or discovery of any living thing or non-living substances occurring in nature."*

3(j)[12]**;** *"plants and animals in whole or any part thereof* ***other than micro-organisms*** *but including seeds, varieties and species and essentially biological processes for production or propagation of plants and animals."*

As it has been explicitly mentioned that the legislation itself provides it an exception and the same has been upheld by the *Hon'ble High Court of Kolkata* in 2002:

2. In the *Dimminaco AG vs. Controller of Patents,* Court held that a patent on a micro-organism is valid. The court ruled on the basis of the above provisions that, Act did not preclude a living end product from being patented.

In concurrence with the above view of the courts, the provisions of the Indian Patent Amendment Act 2005[13] the current position of the country was also analyzed and it was observed that Biotech industry is one of the fastest growing industries in the world, including in India. India being one of the bio-diversity rich countries, it would, thus, be prudent for us to protect biotechnological inventions as that would help Indian biotechnology research compete globally attracting collaborations, FDI, contract R&D, etc. to the best advantage of the Indian R&D and biotech industry. India needs to reap the due benefits from its rich bio-resources with an enabling provision for protection of intellectual property in bio-technological innovations and inventions.

Case 4: Novartis A.G.V Assistant Controller of Patents and Design, Chennai

This case[14] reflects the current position of patents in the country and the mindset of courts regarding it applicability and feasibility. In this case Pharmaceutical major Novartis A.G. has moved the Madras High Court challenging the rejection of its patent application for beta crystal line form of *imatinib mesylate*, as well as the provisions of the patents (Amendment) Act 2005 under which it was rejected .

- According to the writ petition filed by the Switzerland based Novartis A.G. represented by its power of attorney holder Ranjana Mehta Dutt, the company had filed an application to patent beta crystalline form of imatinib mesylate, sold under the brand name Gleevec/Glivec. But the assistant controller of patents and design in Chennai rejected the application after the pregnant objection from other companies and on the basis of Section 3(d) of the Patents Act 1970 as amended by Patents (Amendment) Act 2005.
- Assailing the rejection order dated January 25,2006 as well as the amended provision of the act, the petitioner said the latter was unconstitutional as it was against the agreement on trade related aspects of intellectual property rights of the world trade organization, to which India was signatory.
- Section 3(d) of the act was a conscious breach of India's obligation under trips, she said, adding that while amending the section the legislature completely ignored the rationale underlying in Article 253 and 51(a) of the constitution which mandate the government of court to mould original law in harmony with international treatises.
- She said the assistant controller had passed the erroneous order folding that the subject compound did not differ significantly in properties with regard to efficacy as compared to the known compound despite recording that there was a 30 per cent increase in bioavailability of the subject compound over the known substance. The official had concluded that the subject compound had been already disclosed in public documents, thereby destroying the novelty of the invention.

Maintaining that the company had procured patents for the compound in 35 countries, the petitioner said the impugned order had no legal or factual basis of justification.

'The Assistant controller has arrived at conclusions[15] without citing the material relied upon or the reasoning adopted', she said. *The Novartis claiming patents on Gleevec, an anti leukaemia drug, is being seen as an assault on the Indian Patents Act.* The Central Government is being asked to vigorously defend the Act in the Indian courts and on the international platform in the interests of those suffering from life threatening disease. The challenge by the Swiss multinational pharmaceutical company in the Madras High court was seen as a precursor to more challenge. There is a growing demand that Government should mobilize public opinion against the 'greed for profits' of such companies.

India was forced to adopt in 2005 to make the Act TRIPS compliant. These safeguards were now being targeted by the pharmaceutical companies.

Gllevac was a test case for the Indian Patents (Amendment) Act 2005. If the Patent was accepted, then it would cost Rs. 1,20,000 for a month's medicine against the indigenous cost of only Rs. 8000.[16]

Novartis had filed a patent application for a slightly modified version of a drug that it had patented in 1993. Section 3(d) of the Patents (Amendment) Act, which prevents frivolous patents based on small tinkering on existing molecules, was being challenged. A number of second line AIDS drugs ere also known before 1995 and therefore could not be granted patents in India. However, drug MNCs were trying to patent them by offering two drugs as a mixture of claiming new use or in a new form, some of the common tricks in 'ever greening' old patents. If section 3(d) was removed or diluted as the drugs majors are demanding, these tactics might work as a major public health protection in India would then be breached.

This will result in the deterioration of the prices of the AIDS drugs as more and more patients would succumb to second line AIDS drugs. As India is the major source of AIDS medicine today, this would have a worldwide impact. The drug majors were also trying to confuse the existing Section 3(d) provisions of the Act with the Mashelkar Chemical Entities. The left parties has asked that in addition to 3(d), patents for pharmaceuticals should be restricted to only new chemical or pharmaceutical entities. While the CPI (M) disagreed with the Mashelkar Committee's recommendation, and says that in no manner whatsoever it resembles Section 3(d) of Indian Patent (Amendment) Act.

For this purpose it is mandatory to go through the bare provisions of Section 3(d) of Indian Patents (Amendment) Act 2005 which runs through as:

> *"the mere discovery of nay new property or more new use for a known substance or of the more use of a known process, machine or apparatus unless such known process results in a new product or employs at least one new reactant"*

PATENT PRACTICES IN OTHER COUNTRIES

Examination Guidelines for Patent Applications Relating to Biotechnological Inventions at the UK Patent Office[17]

These Guidelines set out the practice within the UK Patent Office as it relates to patent applications for biotechnological inventions. The 2000 Regulations came into force on 28 July 2000 and implemented the provisions of Articles 1 to 11 of the European Directive 98/44/EC on the legal protection of biotechnological inventions.

In the UK, the Patents Regulations 2000 confirmed and clarified that inventions concerning biological material, including gene sequences, may be legitimately the subject of patent applications. In other words, these Regulations have established beyond doubt the legitimacy of biotechnology patents in the UK.

> *"An invention shall not be considered unpatentable solely on the grounds that it concerns (a) a product consisting of or containing biological material; or (b) a process by which biological material is produced, processed or used."*
>
> *[Paragraph 1, Schedule A2 to the Patents Act 1977]*

Universally, it is an established practice that a natural substance which has been isolated for the first time and which had no previously recognized existence, does not lack novelty because it has always been present in nature.

It is generally agreed, and it is particularly relevant in the field of biotechnology, that a patent should not be granted merely because the applicant had been involved in laborious and costly effort. If the goal is known and sufficient of the theory and practice is known for the applicant to predict where he is going, without there being an original step, then an obviousness objection would be well founded.

Following the sequencing of various genomes, there is unlikely to be an inventive step in identifying from within a sequenced genome any new gene, even those without known homologues. It is obvious to trawl the genome for previously unidentified genes, and any skilled worker would have some expectation of success. In *Genentech,* an idea was considered obvious if "the materials in question were lying in the road and ready for a research worker to use", even if the skilled man faced a number of obstacles in proceeding to his goal. However, if overcoming these obstacles required "a spark of imagination....beyond the imagination properly attributable to him as a man skilled in the art" then there may be some element of inventive step. The use of bioinformatics tools would not seem to pose obstacles requiring a spark of imagination to overcome.[18]

Paragraph 2 of Schedule A2 to the British Patents Act, 1977[19]: Permits biological material which is isolated from its natural environment or produced by means of a technical process to be the subject of an invention even if it previously occurred in nature. Claims to micro-organisms *per se* have been allowed on the grounds that they are products of microbiological processes. This applies even when they are merely isolated from their natural surroundings, their isolation, culture, characterization and the finding of a utility turning what would be a discovery into an invention.

Claims for micro-organisms *per se* which have been isolated or obtained by artificially induced random mutation, are allowed but generalizations from such specific micro-organisms to novel species would not normally be permitted. On the other hand, claims to genetically modified micro-organisms derived from readily available known micro-organisms where the invention resides in the gene introduced, may be claimed more generally. Also claims to mutants and variants of a specified deposited micro-organism are allowed provided they possess the same inventive property as the deposited micro-organism.

Patenting of Micro-organisms in China

Claims for micro-organisms *per se* are allowed in China. DNA sequences are considered to be large chemical compounds, and may be patented as compositions of matter.[20] Although patent claims to naturally occurring DNA sequences might be expected to trigger the 'products of nature' rule, courts have upheld patent claims covering 'purified and isolated' DNA sequences as new compositions of matter resulting from human intervention. An excised gene is eligible for a patent as a composition of matter or as an article of manufacture because that DNA molecule does not occur in that isolated form in nature; or synthetic DNA preparations are eligible for patents because their purified state is different from the naturally occurring compound.[21]

Article 25 of the Chinese Patent Law states that:

For any of the following, no patent right shall be granted:

1. Scientific discoveries;
2. Rules and methods for mental activities;
3. Methods for the diagnosis or for the treatment of diseases;

4. Animal and plant varieties;
5. Substances obtained by means of nuclear transformations.

For processes used in producing products referred to in items (4) of the proceeding paragraph, patent right may be granted in accordance with the provisions of the Law.

Patenting of Micro-organisms in Europe

The European Union has defined ""biological material" instead of "micro-organism", as under [Article 2.1 (a)].

"Biological material means any material containing genetic information and capable of reproducing itself or being reproduced in a biological system"

In Plant Genetic Systems application (T356/93) European Board of Appeal was seized with the question as to what is meant by the term 'micro-organism' The Board held that a micro-organism would include bacteria, yeast, fungi, algae, protozoa, plasmids and viruses, but also animal or plant cells and generally all unicellular entities with dimensions beneath the limits of human vision.[22]

Article 53(b) of the European Patent Convention (EPC) provides that European patents shall not be granted in respect of 'plant or animal varieties or essentially biological processes for the production of plants or animals; this provision does not apply to microbiological processes or the products thereof'.

In its decision of 16 June 1999[23] the Administrative Council inserted a new Chapter VI entitled 'Biotechnological inventions' in Part II of the EPC Implementing Regulations. The new provisions entered into force on 1 September 1999 and implemented the requirements of the EU Biotechnology Directive in European patent law. The EPO has introduced four new rules, Rules 23b to 23e. Rule 23b sets out general matters and defines the meaning of biotechnological inventions, biological material, plant variety, and microbiological process. Rule 23c states patentable biotechnological inventions, including:

- Biological material isolated from their environment, even if known in nature. This particularly applies to genes that are isolated from their natural environment by means of technical processes and made available for industrial production.
- Plants or animals if the invention is not confined to a single variety.

The provision clarifies the scope of Article 53(b) of EPC. It indicates that a plant grouping characterized only by a particular gene, but not by its whole genome, is not covered by the protection of new varieties and therefore is in principle patentable. This also applies if such plant grouping comprises plant varieties.

Rule 23d sets out what is not patentable. This includes processes for cloning human beings, processes for modifying the genetic identity of human beings, using human embryos for commercial purposes and modifying the genetic identity of animals such as may cause them suffering without substantial medical benefit. The list is to be seen as giving concrete form to the concepts of 'ordre public' and 'morality'.

Rule 23e indicates what is and is not patentable with respect to the human body. The human body and its elements cannot be patented. However, elements of the body, when isolated from the body, may be patented.

Patenting of Micro-organisms in Japan[24]

In 1997, the Japanese Patent Office (JPO) published its 'Implementing Guidelines for Inventions in Specific Fields'. Inventions in the biotechnology field in the Guidelines are divided into four types: genetic engineering, micro-organisms, plants and animals. Inventions relating to genetic engineering include those of a gene, a vector, a recombinant vector, a transformant, a fused cell, a recombinant protein, and a monoclonal antibody. Inventions relating to micro-organisms include micro-organisms *per se* as well as those relating to the use of micro-organisms.

In Japan, micro-organism means yeast, molds, mushrooms, bacteria, actinomycetes, unicellular algae, viruses, protozoa, etc. and further includes undifferentiated animal or plant cells as well as animal or plant tissue cultures.

"Japan already possesses some of the best patents and other IP in the world. Iwill set as one of our national goals that the results of research activities and creative endeavors are translated into IP rights that are strategically protected and utilized so that we can enhance the international competitiveness of Japanese industries."[25]

Patenting of New Chemical Entity in US

According to the United States (US) Food and Drug Administration (FDA), a new molecular entity (NME) or new chemical entity (NCE) means a drug that contains no active moiety that has been approved by FDA in any other application submitted under section 505(b) of the Federal Food, Drug, and Cosmetic Act.

Patenting of Micro-organisms in USA

Art. 35 USC Sec. 101 of the US patent law states: whoever invents or discovers any new and useful process, machine, manufactures, or composition of matter, or any new and useful improvement thereof, may obtain a patent thereof..."

In USA[26], utility requirement in respect of biotech inventions are very strict. A discovery that is not a creation does not meet the requirement of utility. A newly discovered micro-organism existing in nature, newly discovered plants per se are discoveries because they do not involve creativity. Inventions that are incapable of industrial application do not meet the requirement of utility. Inventions of a gene, a vector, a recombinant vector, a transformant, a fused cell, a recombinant protein and a monoclonal antibody whose utility is not described in a specification or cannot be inferred, do not meet the requirement of utility. An invention of a micro-organism *per se*, a plant *per se* or an animal *per se* whose utility is not described or cannot be inferred does not meet the requirement of utility.

According to the new 'Utility Examination Guidelines' of the USPTO, if an isolated DNA fragment has a specific, substantial, and credible utility, the DNA fragment invention satisfies the requirement of utility and a patent can be granted for the DNA fragment. Where a new use is discovered for the patented DNA fragment, that new use may qualify for its own process patent. Of course, the later patent is a dependent patent of the DNA fragment patent.

Patenting of Micro-organisms in Australia

The Australian patent law defines invention as "any new manner of manufacture."

The question of patents for living organisms was considered at length in Ranks Hovis McDougall Ltd.'s Application [1976 A OJP 3915] and the Court held that:

- No objection can be taken to a claim to a new organism on the ground that it is something living;
- Any new variants claimed must have improved or altered useful properties and not merely have changed morphological

characteristics which have no effect on the working of the organism; and

- Naturally occurring micro-organisms *per se* are not patentable as they represent a discovery and not an invention, but a claim to a pure culture in the presence of some specified ingredients would satisfy the requirement of a technical intervention.

The guidelines for a micro-organism in Australian Patent Law states, "what is discovered in nature without any practical application, is a mere chemical curiosity"' and is not patentable [Part 8.2.5.3 Australian Manual of Patent Practice]. However, isolated micro-organisms are considered patentable.

Patenting Practices of Micro-organism in Brazil

Article 10 states that the following shall not be considered inventions or utility models:[27]

"all or part of natural living beings and biological materials found in nature or isolated there from, including the genome or the germ plasm of any natural living being and any natural biological process."

Article 18 states that the following should not be patentable:

"Living beings, in whole or in part, except for transgenic micro-organisms meeting the three requirements of patentability-novelty, inventive step and industrial application-in accordance with Article 8 and which are not mere discoveries."

For the purposes of this law, transgenic micro-organisms mean organisms, except for plants or animals in whole or in part, that due to direct human intervention in their genetic composition express a characteristic that cannot normally be achieved by the species under natural conditions.

CONCLUSION

The Patent laws in India are yet in transitional phase and thus the courts are lacking expertise to resolve the domestic disputes relating to it. But despite of all that it must be remembered that every monopoly is liable to be abused and patent monopoly is no exception. Therefore, sufficient safeguards are required in law to ensure that patent inventions are properly worked in the country to protect the public interest.[28]

RECOMMENDATIONS

1. The inclusion of the plants and plant products in the list of non patrntable items is a praiseworthy one but simultaneously the recommendation given by the Mashelkar committee report[29] should be heeded and 'new medical entity 'though literally fails to fulfill the general criteria of involving an 'inventive step' but is still it is in accordance with the Article 27 of TRIPS and Section 3(d) of Indian Patents (Amendment)Act in it's spirit. Thus even though if any new product fails to involve 'an inventive step' it should not be rejected merely on the individual criteria but a **'dual test'** of 'utility' must also be seen in accordance with it.

2. A comprehensive legislations in respect of geographical indications is must for the protection of rich bio-diversity in India.

3. India carries a huge potential of becoming the centre for the world with respect to Research and Development Department in Intellectual Property Rights. Thus at this transitional phase each and every policy has to be scrutinized stringently before implementing it.

4. It is also recommended to fix the price of the medicines.

5. As the common law maxim says:

   'Power corrupts and absolute power corrupts absolutely'.

U.S. and U.K. are not always right and the recent changes at the cosmopolitan scenario are the best era to manifest this change. Hence India will have to be bold enough to disagree with these dominant members, if that agreement adversely affects the interest of the Indian Public.

Current Position under WTO system states that:

A single minute delay in filing the patent may cost and damage us substantially. While the rich countries like U.S.A., Australia, Canada and Europe are over flooding the applications before the Patent Authorities. While India is far lagging behind and we are acting only defensively to defend our patentable products from patenting.

NOTES

1. Mysore Sudha, "Adoption and Implementation of Intellectual Property Rights: Experience of selected countries", *Journal of Intellectual Property Rights*, Vol. 7, January 2002, pp 36

2. Article 3 of the TRIPS agreement stipulates that each member shall accord to the nationals of other member's treatment no less favorable than it accords to its own nationals. This provision shall keep the patent holders on strong footing in a position to exploit the Indian vulnerable social & economic conditions.
3. Mira T. Sundra Rajan, "Moral rights in developing countries: The example of India Part I", *Journal of Intellectual Property Rights*, Vol. 8, September 2003, pp. 364-366.
4. A conceptual framework for promoting benefits in the area of conservation and use of plant genetic resources. A report prepared by the M.S. Swaminathan research foundation Chennai for UNEP (December 1988, 1989).
5. This case was more extensively analysed by R.K. Gupta and L.Balasubrahmanayam. This case has also been highlighted by Mr. Prabuddha Ganguly in his article named: *Mothering Innovation to Markets.*
6. Sabuj Kumar Chaudhari, "Medical Bio-Piracy in India: How to fight back?", *Journal of Intellectual Property Rights,* Vol. 8, September 2003, pp. 390-394.
7. Cecila Oh, "*IPR and Biological Resources: Implications for developing countries*", *Journal of Intellectual Property Rights*, Vol. 8, September 2003, pp. 408-411.
8. WTO. 1995. "Trade Related Aspects of Intellectual Property Rights (TRIPS) Agreement". Geneva: WTO.
9. Assafa Endeshaw-'*Do Asian Nations take Intellectual Property Rights Seriously.*'
10. Mashelkar Report Dated 29 December 2006.
11. Government of India. 1970. "Patents Act", Ministry of Industry. New Delhi: Government of India.
12. Supra.
13. V.J. Taraporevala-"Law of Intellectual Property", p. 87.
14. '*People's Democracy*'-Weekly Organ of the Communist Party of India (Marxist), Vol XXXI, Issue No. 36, 9 September 2007.
15. *http://timesofindia.indiatimes.com/articleshow/1647455.cms*, '*Novartis case raises fresh controversy*', 21 February 2007.
16. *http://infochangeindia.org/TD_article14.jsp*, '*The struggle for affordable medicines*'-Chan Park.
17. Rodney D. Ryder, "Intellectual Property Law: Concept to Commercialization", Macmillan Publications, P. 101.
18. Genetic Resources: Intellectual Property Rights and Rights of indigenous communities.
19. *Ibid.*
20. J.P. Mishra, "An Introduction to Intellectual Property Rights", Central Law Publications, p. 49.

21. *http: / / www.biodiv-ip.gov.cn, 'The Patent Protection for Biological Inventions in China'.*
22. *'Patenting of Biotechnological Inventions'*-Malathi Lakshmikumaran and Prashant Phillips.
23. Zorina Khan-'IP Rights and Economic Development', *WIPO* Magazine, June 2007, No. 3.
24. Hisamitsu Arai-"IP Revolution: How Japan Formulated a National IP Strategy", *WIPO* Magazine, June 2007, No. 3.
25. Former Prime Minister Koizumi.
26. Vandana Shiva-'Patents 'Myths and Reality', Penguin Books, p. 49.
27. *http: / / www.biotech-monitor.nl / 2710.htm.*
28. P. Narayanan-"Intellectual Property Law", Eastern Law House, 3rd edition.
29. *http: / / www.indianembassy.org / policy / ipr / ipr_2000.htm, 'Intellectual Property Rights in India'.*

REFERENCES

'Law of Intellectual Property'- V.J. Taraporwala.

'Intellectual Property Law: Concept to Commercialization'–Rodney D Ryder, Macmillan Publications.

'An Introduction to Intellectual Property Rights'-J.P Mishra, Central Law Publications.

'Intellectual Property Law'-P.Narayanan, Eastern Law House.

Patents 'Myths and Reality'-Vandana Shiva, Penguin Books.

Journal of Intellectual Property Rights, Vol.7, January 2002.

Journal of Intellectual Property Rights, Vol. 8, September 2003.

M.S. Swaminathan, Research Foundation, Chennai for UNEP (December 1988, 1989).

Mashelkar Report, Dated 29 December 2006.

WIPO, Magazine, Geneva, June 2007, No. 3.

'People's Democracy'-Weekly Organ of Communist Party of India (Marxist), Vol. XXXI, Issue No. 36, 9 September 2007.

WTO 1995, *"TRIPS Agreement"*, Geneva: WTO (World Trade Organization).

Patents Act 1970, Government of India, New Delhi.

http: / / www.timesofindia.indiatimes.com / articleshow / 1647455.cms

http: / / www.infochangeindia.org

http: / / www.biodiv-ip.gov.cn

http: / / www.biotech-monitor.nl / 2710.htm

http: / / www.indianembassy.org

http: / / wikipedia.com

Nutraceuticals; Need for Patenting in India

B. N. Nimbur & D. S. Naik***

INTRODUCTION

During the early 1960s itself, the WHO, (World Health Organization) reported that every fourth man in India suffers from one or the other type of nutritional deficiencies.[1] This is an indicator to the unhealthy human development in the country. Indeed, this should be taken as a serious issue as the country is, in terms of numbers the second biggest populated nation in the world.

In India, reduction in mortality has doubled life expectancy at birth in the last 50 years and almost tribled it in the last 100 years but this has come with a greater incidence of sickness (morbidity) an epidemiological transition seems to suggest a shift from communicable to non-communicable diseases.[2]

With increasing life expectancy the epidemiological transition points towards greater incidence of non-communicable or life style diseases. This goes hand in hand with continuing serious problems of communicable diseases. However an increase in longevity is, unfortunately associated with greater incidence of sickness. It assumes serious dimension in India which is burdened by both communicable and preventable as well as life style disease.[3] This has serious implication the qualify human developed. International consensus to fight against communicable and preventable diseases finds mention in the Millennium Development Goals (MDGs)[4] and also in India's new National Health Policy (NHP) 2002.[5]

Similarly a recent survey in the NCR (National Capital Territory) has brought out the finding that in every hundred children (in the age group of 5 to 15 years) there are as many as 15 per cent who are abnormally bodily fat. This is a matter of great concern in the context of the health of the human capital.[6]

* Professor, Department of Economics, Gulbarga University, Gulbarga.

** Senior Lecturer, Department of Economics, Gulbarga University, Gulbarga.

However, in recent days, it has become very difficult to quantify the ageing population in India. Specially, due to the growing unemployment, increased higher educational opportunities, desire to earn or make fast money have put heavy mental strain on the people.[7] Further, the work culture, less leisure, non-availability of parks, morning walk space and changed habits (long sitting before the T V sets, sitting before the computers etc.) along with adaptation to the junk foods have brought many health hazards.[8] On the top of these a recent report of the scientists of CSIR (Conical for Scientific and Industrial Research) has explicitly noted that the entire Indian race (though multi-racial) does not possesses the genetic capability to withstand the disease AIDS.[9] Therefore, under these circumstances the nutraceuticals have a very important role to play. As India is one of the largest manufacturer of pharmaceuticals, the nutraceuticls should be accorded patenting rights to the surgeons, physicians and doctors who develops them.

The present paper is an analytical approach to study the nutraceuticals, which has been divided into the six sections. Section (1);deals with the meaning of nutraceuticals, section, (2) narrates the patenting in india. Section (3) deals with the advantages nutraceuticals in the recent social health scenario, section (4), presents briefly the development of nutraceuticals by the expert doctors and surgeons, section (5) deals with the need for patenting of nutraceuticals in the present era of globalization and section (6) contains a brief conclusion.

I

NUTRACEUTICALS

With the advent of time new developments and discoveries have to be given new conceptual identification which are not hitherto in use , either in discussion or in the literature The nutraceuticals are thus a new medicinal arrivals on the seen which are given new identification It is; perhaps, very important to know or understand what are the nutraceuticals. First of all, the nutraceuticals are not any plants or herbs from which these are made. Similarly, they are not the drugs which are commonly used for controlling deadly diseases. The nutraceuticals act as preventive and curatives in most of the problems of human health.[10] The nutraceuticals are most useful substance or compounds [developed with great efforts by surgeons, doctors and physicians] for treating and curing many problems of human health. These are the combinations of many readily available pharmaceutical products. The experts working in the field, out of their work experience found that some combination of available medicines are suitable in curing some diseases rather than one or two medicine available in the existing form. The medicine available in the market may not be so effective in treating certain diseases. The experts prepare a new compound by using combination of few drugs.[11] That new product is an intellectual creation of an expert who is working as doctor or surgeon. These intellectual progenies are identified as nutraceuticals.

The nutraceuticals are very useful substances, especially, in reducing the growing obesity among the young people who are afflicted by the habit of consuming junk foods, more and more fat contents, addiction to the soft drinks, lesser amount of physical work, more dependent on automobiles for moving form one place to another. As result of this, his/her body will not get any sort of physical stress or strain as a result of this they are prone to obesity. The junk foods are prepared not with good quality oil or vegetables and are prepared in most unhygienic conditions. And also stored for longer days when they remain unsold in the markets with some arbitrary storage machines. For instance, storage of junk food in refrigerator for week, even some times more than a week.[12] Make it unworthy consumption.

The nutraceuticals are particular pharmaceutical elements prepared by doctor and injected into the body of a man in that place in which he is developing diseases. Similarly, diabetic's patients are given nutraceuticals in a particular proportion so that, either it can be prevented or can be reduced.

They are the exact nutritional compounds to fill the nutritional deficiencies existing in the human body and which in term either causing or aggravating nutritional deficiency diseases. In particular, the nutraceuticals in the present era may be considered as tailor made device for curing many diseases.[13] Thus, in short, in the allopathic or homeopathic of pharmaceuticals and herbics the nutraceuticals have emerged as an Eldorado or elixir. As noted above, they are not conventional drugs at all.

II

PATENTING IN INDIA

India established its patent act in 1970 after detailed study and forethought to the role of patents in the overall development agenda. The history of patenting in India dates back to 1856, but the policy makers turned their attention seriously towards patents only immediately after independence. Two expert committees were established in India to study the patent and provide suggestions on the type of patent system that India should implement. The patent Enquiry Committee (1948-50) and the Ayyangar Committee (1957-59) suggested that a patent system that focused on access to resources at lower prices would be beneficial to India.[14] This was in tune with the science and technology mission of developing indigenous technology and fostering Research and Development activities in area of national significance. The patent act of 1970, the current legislation on patents in India, was based on the recommendation of these committees. The main aim in India was to ensure that patent should not lead to monopoly by foreign companies. India sought to ensure this in its patent act by granting only process and not product patent in pharmaceutical,[15] restricting the term of patent and formulating an elaborate system of licenses to ensure that patents are worked in India. In tune with this policy, India refused to join the main international treaty on patents known as Paris Convention, as it stipulated higher standards of patent protection.[16]

The statement by Indira Gandhi at the World Health Assembly in 1982 that 'the idea of a better-ordered world is one in which medical discoveries will be free of patents and there will be no profiteering from life and death[17] symbolized India's stance on patents. In India, patents were seen more as a tool for economic development. Industrialized nations conceive patents as a fundamental right comparable to the right of physical property, whereas developing nations view it fundamentally as an economic policy question. From the perspective of developed countries, intellectual property is a private right that should be protected as any other tangible property, but for developing nations, intellectual property is a public good that should be used to promote economic development.[18]

India's philosophy on patents underwent a revision with the Patent Amendment Act of 1999 and 2002. India also joined the Paris Convention and the Patent Cooperation Treaty in 1998. The amendment led to the revisions in India's policy on granting only process and not product patents in the pharmaceuticals field, increasing the term of patents to 20 years as demanded by TRIPs, and restricting the system of licences found in India's Patent Act. Provision was also included to protect the Indian system of medicine and to protect public health.[19] The amendments essentially pave the way for full product patents in pharmaceuticals, which must be granted according to TRIPs from 2005.

III

THE MERITS

Before liberalization and emergence of WTO India was greatly handicapped internationally in the pharmaceutical products. But it to be noted that a country which has not only huge population, great demand for new and newer pharmaceutical products was compelled to import its requirement from other countries. In fact, it is a shad historical past that even the life saving and life supporting drugs and products were to be obtained from abroad.[20] As a developing country it was side tracked in terms of the development of pharmaceutical industry because of having only and only the process patenting. However, from 2005 onwards India became party to both product and process patenting in the field of pharmaceuticals in the international arena. Due to the prominent attention given to chemical industry in India during the plan periods India has emerged as one of the pharmaceutical giant in the world. It has capabilities to supply a minimum of one-third of pharmaceutical product to the world.[21]

Even after 60 years of independence the health indicators status is a matter of great concern. The following Table 1 reflects clearly some selected health indicators for India. The crude birth rate [per 1000 population] in 1981 was 33.9. Similarly for the year 1991 it was 29 .5 and 23.5 in 2006. Likewise the crude death rate in the year 1981 was 12.5 and 9.8 for the year 1991. Similarly in the year 2006 it was 7.5. Therefore, the net growth of population is higher in India.

Table 1
Selected Health Indicators in India

Parameters	*9181*	*1991*	*2006*
Crude Birth Rate [CBR] [per 1000 population]	33.9	29.5	23.5
Crude Death Rate [CRD] [per 1000 population]	12.5	9.8	7.5
Total Fertility Rate [TFR] [per women]	4.5	3.6	2.9
Maternal Mortality Rate [MMR] [per 100000 live births]	–	450	301
Infant Mortality Rate [IMR] [per 1000 live births]	110	80	57
Child [0-4 years] Mortality Rate per 1000 children	41.2	26.5	17.3
Life expectancy at birth			
Male	55.4	59.0	62.3
Female	55.7	59.8	63.9

Source: Economic Survey 2007.

Besides the crude birth rate and death rates, the other important indicators like, total fertility rate, maternal mortality rate, infant mortality rate, and child mortality rates are also very high in India therefore, the nutrceuticals have very important role to play in country like India.

The incidence of infectious and parasitic diseases is very high in India. For example, the HIV infected persons in India as per an estimate for 2002 were in the range of 3.82-4.58 million, but only 68,809 cases were reported to National Aids Control Organization (NACO) until March 2004. The proportion of women among reported cases are increasing. In case of TB in 1998 almost 7.6 million disability adjusted life years (DALYs) and 0.42 million lives were lost this puts India with little more than one-fourth of the world TB deaths. TB is a major killer of adults and greater prevalence among the poor and malnourished. Similarly, Polio cases were estimated to 268 in 2000, but there has been resurgence to 1600 cases in India in 2002. This accounts for 83 per cent of cases in the world. Efforts to control/ eradicate have been on from the early 1950s. But the incidence is still prevalent. However One-third of the deaths from parasitic and infectious disease in India in 2000 were from diarrhoeal diseases which mostly affect children below five years of age.[22] Therefore, the nutraceuticals have very important role to play in the Indian health sector.

Similarly, the incidence of life style diseases is growing in recent days. The life style diseases are those which are due to the no control over DATES [diet, alcohol, tobacco, exercise, and stress]. According to an estimation cardiovascular disease account for nearly two-thirds of the deaths due to non-communicable diseases, which account for half of the overall deaths? Mortality from non-communicable diseases is likely to increase further. Life style diseases need not afflict the rich alone. To have an idea of the risk factor for non-communicable diseases across socio economic groups. A study by Parikh (2003) study based on three major States of rural north India calculates risk factor for four respiratory diseases [bronchitis, asthma, chest infection, and TB. The first two being non-communicable diseases. And eye irritation [can also be non-communicable]. It show greater health risk for illiterates over literate, for those who have higher lifetime exposure to cooking [mostly females], for the poor, for those who use biofuel as against clean fuel. It suggest that 'polycyclic aromatic hydrocarbons', a hazardous carcinogenic leading to non-communicable diseases, emitted from auto- exhaust and fuel biomass puts the economically underprivileged at greater risk. Therefore, the nutraceuticals have important role to play in the modern time.

With the strong hold in the pharmaceutical industry, India has the advantage of developing and supplying (to other countries, if need be) the nutraceuticals. Further advantages or merits of nutraceuticals developed in India may be ascribed to its pricing in other words, the nutraceuticals are not only useful to people of this country but also to the people of other nations.

IV

TRAIL AND ERROR

As such the nutraceuticals are by definition not the new chemicals or not complete pharmaceutical product, further as noted above they are not the traditional drugs or pain killer substances one may presume. The nutraceuticals are number of composite variety of compounds prepared by surgeons in the course of their treatment process of patient. It is the common place experience of doctors to use any one or two chemicals which are already manufactured in the pharmaceutical industry; the surgeons use a microelement to treat a particular organ of the suffering patient in a particular quantity so as to prevent the growth of virus from aggravating the dieses. There are many dreaded diseases afflicted by large number of patient. In premier medical centers and organization many doctors and surgeons have developed these nutraceuticals through the trail and error method. A great success has been achieved in reducing obesity, heart disease, aging, cancer and other. These nutraceuticals are clearly and truly the creations of individual doctors and surgeons.

Therefore, as India has large health sector the development of nutraceuticals as against general pharmaceuticals is the need of the hour. It is because of nutraceuticals only; together the finger tipped doctors and surgeons, the health care has became very cheap in India. In recent years the health tourism has been growing and growing as most favored destination. Besides, Pakistan, Nepal, Bangladesh, patients from European and Latina American countries has found India as a paradise for their health care and health cure. If sufficient attention is not given to nutraceuticals, gradually, there will be not only brain drain but also the problems of outsourcing of health services.

V

NEED FOR PATENTING

Although, patenting of pharmaceuticals has been provided to the manufacturer as early as in the early 1960s. In particular, the product patenting has been provided to the pharmaceutical industry under the

TRIPS.[23] However, as noted above, with the down of new era of liberalization, the Indian industries could obtain the product and process patenting from 2005. Thus, this marked the new era and vista for the entire pharmaceutical sector of the economy. With the beginning of the process of liberalization, greater support given to research and development activities, in this sector, most of the pharmaceutical products became almost easily available to all section in the country. As a result there are many doctors' surgeons and research in the abetment, cure and prevention of most commonly found diseases in the country. There are many national level medical centers and institutions in which tens and hundreds of doctors are constantly working in specialized manner. The result of this is, the development of nutraceuticals. These are the intellectual progenies of these specialists. If these doctors retire or give up the profession for varies reasons these nutraceuticals also disappear along with them. Therefore, in addition to the general, sectoral, and industry wise product and process patenting is need for providing these too to the doctors who develop the specialized nutraceuticals, the individual patenting is need of hour.

The nutraceuticals are micro nutrients which help to cure many numbers of diseases at go-away-cost. Therefore, the patenting of nutraceuticals to individual doctors would thus enhance the value of pharmaceutical industry, especially in the Indian context, it is better to do as early as possible through a legislative enactment at central and the stat level. Besides, the enactment also ensures free mobility of nutraceuticals from one medical practitioner to another, from one institution to another institution, one country to another country.

VI

CONCLUSION

In the hundred and plus cores of population fifteen per cent of children are subjected to obesity. This is a matter of grave concern, because this is against the dictum that a sound mind in a sound body. The lesser interest for learning, getting tired very soon, more and more hours of sleep, unable to participate in any sporting activities or the major problems of nearly 15 years of young children of the Indian society.

The adaptation to table work not undertaking any physical exercise, very easy going style of life, such as getting up late in the morning ,tuning the music, sitting before computers, doing other activities with easy modern technical instruments and not doing any manual work throughout the day [including walking] is one aspect. While fully adaptation and dependence on fast and junk foods has made the people of 30 to 50 as a aging population. Therefore, the development of a country will be hampered very significantly. Therefore, for providing accurate nutritional quantity for prevention of ills and curing of ailment through a cell technology, the nutraceuticals are a kind of elixirs having no side effects. Therefore, there is need for development, protection and patenting of nutraceuticals for the social health of a country.

NOTES AND REFERENCES

1. World Health Report, WHO, 1954.
2. Kirit, Parikh and R, Radhakrishna (2005), 'India Development Report 2004-05.' Indira Gandhi Institute of Development Reasearch Bombay. Oxford University Press, New Delhi p. 54-63.
3. Central Bureau of Health Intelligence (CBHI) 2002, p. 60.
4. National Sample Survey Organization (NSSO) 1998, p. 19
5. NSSO (1998), Morbidity and Treatment of Ailments; NSS 52nd Round July 1996 June 1996. No 441 Government of India New Delhi p. 2.
6. The World Health Report 2002; Reducing Risks, Promoting Healthy Life WHO, p. 62.
7. Visraia, L. (2004), 'Mortality Trends and Health Transition in India [Ed] Twenty India Population, Economy, and Human Development. Oxford University Press, Oxford, p. 36.
8. Baru, R. (1998), Private Health Care in India; Social Characteristics and Trends, Sage, New Delhi.
9. Black R. E., S.S. Morris and J. Bryce (2003), Where and Why are 10 million Children Dying Every Year Lancet, Vol. 361, No. 9376, p. 2233.
10. Group of Scientists, Council for Scientific and Industrial Research Report, 1998.
11. Chakravarti A. (2001), Single Nucleotide Polymorphism; To a Future Genetic Medicine; Nature Vol. 409, No. 6822, p. 832.
12. Chanda R. (2001), Trade in Health Services'Working paper No. 70, Indian Council for Research on International Economic Relation, New Delhi.
13. Das Gupta, M. P. Khaleghain and R. Sarwal (2003), Governance of Communicable Disease Control Services: A Case Study and Lesson from India; World Bank Policy Reasearch Working paper 3100, The World Bank, Washington D.C.
14. Lanjow, Jean (1997), 'The Introduction of Pharmaceutical Product Patents in India: Heartless Exploitation of the poor and Suffering? Economic Growth Centre, Yale University, August.
15. Chaudhuri, Sudip (2002) TRIPs Agreement and Amendment of Patent Act

in India, *Economic and Political Weekly*, 10 August, pp. 3354-60

16. Alam, Ghayar (1996), Impact of the Proposed Changes in IPR on India's Pharmaceutical Industry, Centre for Technology Studies, New Delhi, December.
17. Gadbow, Michael and Timothy Richards (1988), 'Intellectual Property Rights'. Global Consensus, Global Conflicts?, Westview Press, Colorado. Sci. in ed.
18. CBHI (2002), Health Information of India. Government of India, New Delhi.
19. Census of India Provisional Population Total (2003).
20. Lalitha, N. (2002), Drug Policy 2002: Prescriptions for Symptoms; *Economic and Political Weekly*, Vol. 37, No. 30, p. 3102-4.
21. Parikh, J. and V. Laxmi (2000), 'Biofuels, Pollution and Health Linkages: A Survey of Rural Tamil Nadu', *Economic and Political Weekly*, Vol. 35, No. 47, p. 4125-37.
22. Pai, M. (2000), 'Unnecessary Medical Intervention: Caesarean Section as a Case Study, *Economic and Political Weekly*, Vol. 35, No. 31, p. 2755-61.
23. Kirit, Parikh and R. Radhakrishna (2005), 'India Development Report 2004-05'. Indira Gandhi Institute of Development Reasearch Bombay. Oxford University Press New Delhi.
24. *Economic Survey*, 2007-08. Finance Ministry, Government of India.

Patent Law in India: A Perspective

Preethi Venkataramu & Sreenivasulu N. S.***

INTRODUCTION

Although the concept of intellectual property[1] is very old, there appeared the need to harmonize laws to facilitate international trade and the free flow of technology. This became necessary because it was difficult to obtain sufficient protection in other countries of the world, in view of the disparity in the laws in each country. As per the World Intellectual Property Organization (WIPO) definition, intellectual property refers to creations of the mind, inventions, literary and artistic works, symbols, names, images and designs used in commerce.[2] Broadly, intellectual property is divided into two categories. The first category covers industrial property, which includes patents, industrial designs and trademarks, all of which have industrial applications. The other refers[3] to copyright laws, which are applied to such things as literary, dramatic and artistic works; rights relating to performing artists, the production of phonograms and rights of broadcasters in their radio and television programs. Patented inventions have, in fact, pervaded every aspect of human life, from electric lighting (patents held by Edison and Swan) and plastic (patents held by Baekeland), to ballpoint pens (patents held by Biro) and microprocessors (patents held by Intel, for example). All patent owners are obliged, in return for patent protection, to publicly disclose information on their invention in order to enrich the total body of technical knowledge in the world. Such an ever-increasing body of public knowledge promotes further creativity and innovation in others. In this way, patents provide not only protection for the owner but valuable information and inspiration for future generations of researchers and inventors.

* B.A.L.LL.B, Legal Executive, SDD Global Solutions, SDD Law Firms, New York, New Jersey, London and Mysore-570006, Karnataka, India.

** Associate Professor of Law & Head, School of Economic and Business Laws, National University of Juridical Sciences, (NUJS) Kolkata, India.

PATENTS AND PATENTING

A patent is an exclusive right granted on an invention, which may be either a product or a process that provides, in general, a new way of doing something, or offers a new technical solution to a problem. Patents provide incentives to individuals by offering them recognition for their creativity and material reward for their marketable inventions in exchange of full disclosure of the invention. These incentives encourage innovation, which assures that the quality of human life is continuously enhanced. Patent grants an exclusive right to the inventor for limited period over his invention[4] in exclusion of others, for making, using, selling, and importing the patented product or process producing that product for those purposes. The purpose of this system is to encourage inventions by promoting their protection and utilization so as to contribute to the development of industries, which in turn, contributes to the promotion of technological innovation and to the transfer and dissemination of technology. Patents ensure property rights (legal title) for the invention for which an exclusive right has been granted, which may be extremely valuable to an individual or a Company. One should make the fullest possible use of the Patent System and the benefits it provides[5]. After the monopoly period[6] expires, everyone else is free to practice the invention on the basis of the disclosure made by the inventor at the time of obtaining the patent.

HISTORY OF THE INDIAN PATENT SYSTEM

The history of the development of international patent reforms makes fascinating reading.[7] Based on the British Patent Law of 1852, certain exclusive privileges were granted to inventors of new manufacturers for a period of 14 yrs by the Act of 1857 on Protection of Inventions. However, less well known is the fact that the Government of India has offered citizens of the country the opportunity to protect their intellectual property for exactly 150 years: the first IPR legislation was enacted in British India in 1856. Even if the Government of India is being reticent about celebrating the achievement of this extraordinary milestone, DePenning and DePenning, a Chennai-based firm of IPR Attorneys whose history runs a close parallel with that of the IPR industry in the country and whose founder was granted the first ever patent in the country. Patent system is not new to India. The first patent law was enacted in 1858. A comprehensive law was, however enacted by the British rulers in 1911. This act was designed to serve the foreign interests and for control over markets for finished goods by multi-national corporations. In so far as pharmaceutical products were concerned over a period almost 85 per cent of medicines were supplied by the multi-national corporations. Kefauver Committee of USA that deliberated extensively on the availability of medicines worldwide and the role of the multi-nationals pointed out in their report that the prices of antibiotics and other medicines in India were the highest in the world. The Patent and Designs Act of 1911 was followed by 1970 Act.[8]

INDIAN PATENT ACT, 1970

Immediately after the Independence in 1947 our leaders were seriously concerned about the enactment of a national patents system relevant to the stage of our development. The objectives were that there should be faster industrialization of the country and law should be designed to serve the public interest in a balanced manner. Two important committees headed by Justice Bakshi Tek Chand and Justice Rajagopal Iyenger dealt with the patent law issues relevant for our country in their reports. Based upon the recommendations in these reports a comprehensive Patents Bill was framed and debated extensively in parliamentary committees and both Houses of Parliament. Finally the National Patents Act was enacted in 1970. With the passage of the Act, having received enough support for their inventions, Indian companies in particular pharmaceutical sector grew at a fast pace and their share of market in the availability of medicines went up to about 85 per cent. As regards the prices of medicines due to competitive environment and because of the new patent system the prices of medicines became the lowest in the world. The industry has also developed enough surplus capacity to meet export demands from the developed and developing countries.The main features of the Patents Act 1970 were as follows:

1. There was no product patent for pharmaceuticals, food and chemical based products. These industrial sectors were covered by process patent only.
2. The term of the patent was 7 years from the date of application or 5 years from the date of sealing of patent whichever period was lower.
3. In order to ensure pronounced role of the domestic enterprises in the patents field a system of 'licensing of right' was also provided.
4. There were no constraints on exports.

5. The patent holder was under obligation to use the patent. There was also provision for revocation of patent for non-use.
6. For licenses of right the royalty ceiling was stipulated at 4 per cent.

However with the coming into being of the TRIPS agreement which mandated certain drastic changes in the patent systems through out the world including the grant of product patent the Government of India amended the patent Act.[9] With the enactment of Patents (Amendment) Act 2005[10] the amending process of Indian Patents Act 1970 to bring it in line with the TRIPS[11] agreement has been completed. The earlier two amendments were enacted by Parliament during 1999 and 2002. In the amending process some safeguard provisions have been incorporated. However, still some more possibilities in this direction within the framework of the TRIPS Agreement have been ignored. In addition there are a few others stipulations, which need to be rectified to avoid legal disputes.

The original Patents Act 1970 was a balanced Act, which helped the growth of industry and also adequately covered the public interest angle. The pharmaceutical industry produces high quality products of almost all therapeutic groups and exports the generic produce to the developing and developed countries at most competitive prices. The developing countries are now apprehending difficulties in importing pharmaceuticals from India because of the tight provisions in regard to the compulsory licenses for effective role of the domestic enterprises in the patented products.

THE TRIPS AGREEMENT AND THE UNIFORM PATENTS SYSTEM

The TRIPS Patents System is based upon a joint statement (paper) presented by the multinational associations of USA, Europe and Japan to the GATT Secretariat in June 1988 during the Uruguay Round Negotiations. The main features of the TRIPS patent system are as follows: The TRIPS agreement provides for patent protection for any inventions whether products or processes in all fields of technology provided that they are new, involve an inventive step and are capable of industrial application. The foreign patent holders have been absolved from working of their patents and imports by them are to enjoy the same patent rights without discrimination as to the place of invention, field of technology and whether the products are imported or locally produced. The term of all patents shall not end before the expiration of 20 years from the date of application. There is no 'licensing of right' provision. The compulsory license provisions are having strict conditions with constraints for exports. There is no royalty ceiling for compulsory licenses. The royalty payment is based on the economic value of the license. The above features of the TRIPS agreement have been implemented in the Indian Patents Act 1970 by bringing following changes.

1. Term of patent is for a period of 20yrs from the date of filing.
2. Time for restoration of a ceased Patent has increased from 12 months to 18 months.
3. Publication of the application after 18 months has been introduced;
4. A request for examination system has been introduced.
5. Provision for filing request for examination by any other interested person (other than applicant) also has been introduced.
6. Provision for the withdrawal of application by applicant any time before grant has been introduced.
7. Fees required to be paid on documents can now be paid within 1 month from its date of filing.

Patentable Inventions

An invention means any new and useful art, process, method or manner of manufacture; machine, apparatus or other article; or substance produced by manufacture, and includes any new and useful improvement of any of them, and an alleged invention.[12] An invention must, in general, fulfill the required conditions to obtain patent. That is it must be of practical use; it must show an element of novelty, that is, some new characteristic that is not known in the body of existing knowledge in its technical field and it must be capable of described in written form or with the help of the actual deposit of the invention. This body of existing knowledge is called "prior art". The invention must involve an inventive step, which could not be deduced by a person with average knowledge of the technical field. Finally, its subject matter must be accepted as "patentable" under law. In many countries, scientific theories, mathematical methods, plant or animal varieties, discoveries of natural substances, commercial methods, or methods for medical treatment (as opposed to medical products) are generally not patentable. However following inventions are not patentable; as per the present patent Law of the country.

(a) An invention which is frivolous or which claims anything obviously contrary to well-established rules of natural law;

(b) An invention the primary or intended use or commercial exploitation of which could be contrary to public order;

(c) The mere discovery of a scientific principle;

(d) The mere discovery of any new property or new use for a known substance or the mere uses of a known process, unless such known process results in a new product or employs at least one new reactant;

(e) A substance obtained by a mere admixture;

(f) The mere arrangement or re-arrangement of known devices;

(g) A method of agriculture or horticulture;

(h) Any process for the medicinal, surgical, curative, prophylactic (diagnostic therapeutic);

(i) Plants and animals in whole, biological processes for production or propagation of plants and animals;

(j) A mathematical or business method or a computer programme per se or algorithms;

(k) A literary, dramatic, musical or artistic work;

(l) A mere scheme or rule or method of performing mental act or method of playing game;

(m) A presentation of information;

(n) Topography of integrated circuits;

(o) An invention, which in effect, is traditional knowledge;

(p) Inventions relating to atomic energy and prejudicial to the defense of India;

ESSENTIAL REQUIREMENTS FOR GRANTING PATENT

Inventions could be patented only on the fulfillment of certain requirements. In general inventions should satisfy the following requirements, which are universally recognized.[13] The requirements are as follows:

1. **Novelty**: The invention must be new and hitherto not in existence. The inventor shall demonstrate that his invention is novel, which is not in the public domain or in the public

knowledge. Inventions cannot be granted patent if are in the public domain

2. **Inventive Step or Non-obviousness**: The invention should involve certain inventive step, which takes it further from the existing knowledge in the society. Inventions must involve certain creativity and innovation, which adds to the knowledge of the society. An invention which does not demonstrate inventive step remains obvious and does not quality for patent grant
3. **Industrial Application or Utility**: Invention should be capable of industrial application or the invention should be commercially viable. Inventions, which are of just theoretical, interest without any commercial application, are not encouraged in the patent system.
4. **Written Description or Deposit of the Invention**: Finally invention should be capable of being described in written form. The inventor needs to disclose and describe the invention in written form while applying for patent in order to see that public can use the invention on the basis of the disclosure once the invention falls into public domain after the patent monopoly granted to the inventor/owner expires. However in case of living invention where written description is not possible the same can be compensated by depositing the invention.

WHO CAN APPLY FOR A PATENT?

An Indian resident can file application[14] for patent at the appropriate Patent Office under whose jurisdiction he resides or has his principal place of business. For non-residents, the address for service in India or principal place of business of his agent determines the appropriate patent office where applications for patent can be filed.[15] We have four patent offices, at Delhi, Calcutta, Mumbai and Chennai, Calcutta being the Head office. Patent applications could be filed from any of the four offices. (a) An application for an ordinary Patent[16] for an invention may be made by any person, whether a Citizen of India, or not, claiming to be the true and first inventor of the invention or his assignee. The first importer of an invention into India or the first communicator of an invention from outside India cannot be considered as the 'true and first inventor'. The term 'person' includes the government. (b) An application for a Patent of Addition may be made only by the applicant for the original patent to which it is an addition, if the application for the main patent is pending; or by the patentee of such main patent, if it has been granted.[17]

(c) A convention application[18] may be made by any person who has made an application for a patent in respect of that invention in a convention country or by his assignee or his legal representative.

PROCEDURE FOR OBTAINING A PATENT

The first step in securing a patent is the filing of a patent application. The patent application generally contains the title of the invention, as well as an indication of its technical field; it must include the background and a description of the invention, in clear language and enough detail enabling an individual with an average understanding of the field could to use or reproduce the invention. Visual materials such as drawings, plans, or diagrams to better describe the invention usually accompany such descriptions. The application also contains various "claims", that is, information which determines the extent of protection granted by the patent. The Patent Office in India allows only Patent Agents to file Applications on behalf of the clients. While filing the application the following documents needs to be enclosed:

(1) Provisional or complete specification[19] in duplicate. If the provisional specification is filed, it must be followed by the complete specification within 12 months/15 months with extension (Form 2).

(2) Drawing in duplicate (if necessary).

(3) Abstract of the invention in duplicate.

(4) Information & undertaking listing the number, filing date & current status of each foreign patent application in duplicate (Form).

(5) Priority document (if priority date is claimed) in convention application.

(6) Declaration of inventor-ship where provisional specification is followed by complete specification or in case of convention application (Form 5).

(7) Power of attorney[20] (if filed through Patent Agent).

(8) Fees (to be paid in cash/by cheques/by demand draft).

Patent Laws differ from country to country and there is no "World patent" or "International Patent'. However, there is an international filing system that is accessible in accordance with patent cooperation treaty (PCT). When a PCT application is filed in one of the member-states of the PCT, this is legally in effect equivalent to filing in all PCT member states, which have been designated in the application. Only the particular member country grants patent right after entering the national phase in that country on receipt of applicant (Corresponding to the International applicant). The first to file system is employed, in which, among persons having claimed the same invention, first one to file the application is granted a patent. Therefore, a completed invention should be filed promptly. There is no objection to the secret working of the invention by way of reasonable trial or experiment, or to the disclosure of the invention to other confidentially. The inventors frequently wait until their inventions are fully developed for commercial working, before applying for patents. It is, therefore, advisable to apply for a patent as soon as the inventor's idea of the nature of the invention has taken a definite shape. It is permissible to file an application for a patent accompanied by a "Provisional Specification" describing the invention. The following are the successive stages of the procedure for obtaining a Patent.[21]

1. Filing an application for a patent accompanied by either a provisional specification or a complete specification.
2. Filing complete specification if a provisional specification accompanied the original application.
3. Examination of the application by the patent office.
4. Acceptance of the applications and advertisement of such acceptance in the official gazette.
5. Overcoming opposition, if any, to the grant of a patent.[22]
6. Sealing of the patent.[23]

PUBLICATION & EXAMINATION OF PATENT APPLICATIONS

Publication of all the applications for patents is done except the applications prejudicial to the defense of India or abandoned due to non-filing of complete specification within the prescribed time limit.[24] The publication will include the particulars of the date of the application, application number, name and address of the applicant along with the abstract. After the date of publication[25] of the application, as stated above, the complete specification along with provisional and drawing, if any, and abstract may be inspected at the appropriate office by making a written request to the Controller in the prescribed manner. No application for patent will be examined if no request is made by the applicant or by any other interested person in Form-19 with prescribed fee of Rs. 1,000/- and Rs. 3,000/- for individual and for legal entity respectively, within a period of 48 months from the date of filing of the application for patent. However, in case of applications for patents filed before 20th May, 2003, the request is required to be made by the applicant or any other interested person within a period of 12 months from 20th May, 2003 or within 48 months form the date of application whichever is later. Where no request against the application for patent has been filed within the prescribed period, the aforesaid application will be treated as withdrawn.[26] Applications for patent, where requests have been made by the applicants or by any other interested persons, the applications will be taken up for examination strictly according to the serial number of the requests received in Form 19.

A First Examination Report (FER) stating the objections/requirements is communicated to the applicant or his agent according to the address for service. An applicant shall submit his first reply to the FER within a period of 4 months from the date of FER. Application or complete specification is required to be amended in order to meet the objections/requirements within a period of 12 months[27] from the date of First Examination Report (FER). If all the objections are not complied with within the period of 12 months, the applications will be deemed to have been abandoned. When the applications are in order for acceptance, it is notified in the Gazette of India.

PROVISIONAL SPECIFICATION AND COMPLETE SPECIFICATION

Application for patent may be accompanied by the provisional specification. It should contain the description of invention with drawing, if required.[28] However, the complete specification should be fairly based on the matter disclosed in the provisional specification and should be filed within 12 months (extendable by 3 months) from the date of filing of provisional specification. If the complete specification is not filed within 12 months or within the extended period, the application will be deemed to have been abandoned. The complete specification is an essential document in the procedure of patent application with drawing required to be attached according to the necessity. Complete specification shall fully describe the invention with drawing, if required, disclosing the best method known to the applicant and end with Claim/Claims defining the scope of protection sought.[29] The protection under the Patents Act depends upon the detailed disclosure of the invention. The specification[30] must be written in such a manner that person of ordinary skill in the relevant field, to which the invention pertains, can understand the invention. The specification must start with a title and describe the general nature of invention. The title should not contain anyone's name, a fancy name and trade name or personal name or any abbreviation etc.

Normally, it should contain the following matter–

(1) Title of invention.

(2) Field of invention.

(3) Background of invention with regard to the drawbacks associated with known art.

(4) Object of invention.

(5) Statement of invention.

(6) A summary of invention.

(7) A brief description of the accompanying drawing.[31]

(8) Detailed description of the invention with reference to drawing/ examples.

(9) Claim(s).

(10) Abstract of the inventions.[32]

WITHDRAWAL, OPPOSITION, GRANT OR SEALING OF PATENT

The application for patent can be withdrawn at least 3 months before the first publication which will be 18 months from the date of filing or date of priority whichever is earlier. The application can also be withdrawn at any time before the grant of the patent. The application can also be withdrawn after the date of publication, cannot be refilled as it is already laid open for public inspection. However, applications withdrawn before the publication can be refilled provided it is not opened otherwise. Notice of opposition must be filed within 4 months of notification in the Official Gazette, Extension of one month is available, but must be applied for before expiry of initial four month period in Form-4 with prescribed fee. A patent is granted by a national patent office or by a regional office that does the work for a number of countries, such as the European Patent Office and the African Regional Intellectual Property Organization. Under such regional systems, an applicant requests protection for the invention in one or more countries, and each country decides as to whether to offer patent protection within its borders.

The WIPO-administered Patent Cooperation Treaty (PCT) provides for the filing of a single international patent application, which has the same effect as national applications filed in the designated countries. An applicant seeking protection may file one application and request protection in as many signatory states as needed. If the application is not opposed or the opposition is decided in favor of the applicant or is not refused, the patent is granted or sealed on making a request in Form 9 along with sealing fee within 6 months from the date of notification of acceptance of the complete specification in the Gazette of India at the appropriate office where the application was filed. However, it is extendable by three months. If the sealing fee is not paid within the prescribed period, it will be treated as "NO PATENT".[33] Application for restoration of a patent that lapses due to non-payment of renewal fees must be made within 18 months of lapse. The application is to be filed to the appropriate office according to the jurisdiction. The term of every patent will be 20 years from the date of filing of patent application, irrespective of whether it is filed with provisional or complete specification. Date of patent is the date on which the application for patent is filed, irrespective of whether it is accompanied with provisional or complete specification.

RIGHTS CONFERRED ON THE GRANT OF PATENT

Where a patent covers a product, the grant of patent gives the patentee the exclusive right to prevent others from performing, without authorization, the act of making, using, offering for sale, selling or importing that product for the above purpose. Where a patent covers a process, the patentee has the exclusive right to exclude others from performing, without his authorization, the act of using that process, using and offering the sale, selling or importing for those purposes, the product obtained directly by the process in India, wherein product for which no patent is granted is excluded. These rights created by statute are circumscribed by various conditions and limitations as provided in the Patents Act, 1970 as amended by The Patents (amendment) Act, 2002. A patent owner has the right to decide who may-or may not-use the patented invention for the period in which the invention is protected. The patent owner may give permission to, or license, other parties to use the invention on mutually agreed terms. The owner may also sell the right to the invention to someone else, who will then become the new owner of the patent. Once a patent expires, the protection ends, and an invention enters the public domain, that is, the owner no longer holds exclusive rights to the invention, which becomes available to commercial exploitation by others.

MAINTENANCE OF THE PATENT

To keep the patent in force, Renewal fee is to be paid every year. The first renewal fee is payable for third year of the patent's life and must be paid before the patent's second anniversary. If the patent has not been issued within the period, renewal fees may be accumulated and paid immediately after the patent is sealed, or within three months of its recording in the Register of Patents or within extended period of six months up to 9 months from the date of recordal.[34] However, provision to restore the patent is possible provided application is made within eighteen months from the date of cessation. A Register of Patents will be kept in the Patent Office and its branch offices.[35] Register of Patent can be inspected or extract from it can be obtained on payment of prescribed fee. Register of Patent contains the names and addresses of the patentee, notification of assignment etc., particulars in respect of validity or proprietorship of patent and payment of renewal fee.

CONCLUSION

Patent system provides the stimulation for inventions and research, which are rewarded through the grant of exclusive rights. Patent is a reward for ones labor in inventing either a process or a product. However products were not patentable in India earlier to the amendment made to the Patent Act in 2005. The patent Act has been amended to give effect to the mandates of the TRIPS agreement and product patenting being one among those mandates which has been recognized through out the world today. Though there are certain opposition against the implementation of the TRIPS mandates on patents the agreement has uniformed the laws across the world. Further the Patent Co-operation Treaty made it possible to obtain international patents through local patent office, which has drastically changed the patent granting procedure across the globe. Practically speaking patent system encourages research and development in any given field, which ultimately benefits the society. Considering the benefit of the community at large patent system may be appreciated though it confers monopoly rights to individual over inventions in exclusion of the entire society.

NOTES

1. Intellectual Property: A Power Tool for Economic Growth.
2. See WIPO Publication for a Broad Introduction of Intellectual Property.
3. Classification According to TRIPS Agreement.

4. A patent is a temporary government-granted monopoly right of something made by the inventor.
5. Patent is a much stronger right than copyright.
6. Monopoly right is usually for 20 years.
7. See International Patent Classification (IPC)
8. Indian Patent Act 1970.
9. India is member country to the TRIPS agreement and the WTO.
10. Sec: 1(1) & (2) for Patents (Amendments) Act, 2005.
11. TRIPS is one of the most contentious agreement of the WTO.
12. Conditions to be satisfied by an invention to be patentable.
13. Article: 37, The TRIPS agreement.
14. The application for registration of a design can be filed at the Patent Office at Kolkata and its Branch Offices at New Delhi, Mumbai and Chennai.
15. See Territorial Jurisdiction of Appropriate Office for the Applicants.
16. Alternatives to an ordinary patent– (1) The utility model (2) The short-term patent (3) The "petty patent".
17. Patent of addition may be made as independent patent when the original patent is revoked.
18. The Convention Application has to be made within one year from the date of the first application.
19. Contents of provisional and complete specification have been specified under the Act and the Rules.
20. Power of Attorney can be filed any time within 90 days of filing of patent application.
21. Extracted from the 'General Information for applicants for patents in India' published by the patent office, Calcutta.
22. Overcoming by applicant for Patent.
23. To be done by Head Office at Calcutta.
24. Provisional or withdrawal of the application will be published in the official Gazette after 18 months from the date of filing of the application or the date of priority whichever is earlier.
25. No application for patent shall be opened for public inspection before publication.
26. Application treated withdrawn cannot be revived.
27. No extension of time is available for amendments.
28. Not necessary to include Claim.
29. The complete specification must have at least one Claim.

30. The specification must be written in good and clear English or Hindi.
31. Drawing should be filed on standard A4 size sheet in duplicate.
32. Abstract is the concise summary of the invention preferably within 150 words.
33. There is no provision in the Act to revive the said Patent.
34. If the renewal is not paid within the prescribed time, the patent will cease to have effect.
35. The Patent Office and its branches have Technical Library Services which are available to the public.

WTO and Agricultual Issues

Lakshya Pal Singh Shekhawat & Prashant Kumar**

INTRODUCTION

The WTO is the lead organization when it comes to regulation policy decisions for the developing countries. Guidelines pertaining to subsidies, liberalization of the policies for the upliftment of the least countries forms a part and parcel of its agenda. The Uruguay conference brought about drastic transformation in the entire set up. The quota restrictions and other restrictive practices were done away with. It was realized that it's high time that there should be integration of the domestic market with that of the global market. Import substitution and export promotion techniques were adopted to address the needs of the least developed Countries.

The AoA targeted to reduce the distortion present in global agricultural trade by attempting to discipline three key areas of agricultural trade, viz. (a) market access (b) domestic subsidies and (c) export subsides. The Uruguay Round AoA marked a significant departure from this trend. AoA prohibited the use of Non Tariff Barriers (NTBs) like quotas and import restrictions for agricultural products6 and introduced 'Tariffication'. Tariffication required that all NTBs on the import of an agricultural product would have to be replaced by a single 'bound' tariff rate so that the resulting protection would be equivalent to the nominal protection in the base period.

Support measures, which are exempt from reduction commitments, are categorized as Blue Box and Green Box subsidies. Production and trade distorting subsidies are classified as Amber Box subsidies and are subject to reduction commitments.

* Law Student, Gujarat National Law University, E-4, GIDC, Old NIFT Building, Electronic Estate, Sector 2, 26, Gandhinagar, Gujarat.
Email: rajputana.rifels@gmail.com, lakshya.gnlu@gmail.com.

Till the 1980s, all the South Asian countries were following import-substituting industrialization strategies and were among the least globally integrated economy in the world. However, since the mid-1980s, most of these countries, with the possible exception of Nepal, moved away from inward looking economic policies and adopted a strategy of development based on export-orientation, liberalization and privatization. To make their economies more globally integrated, these countries initiated trade liberalization, started moving away from a regime of quantitative restrictions to tariff based regime and started reducing their average level of protection.

WTO AND AGRICULTURE AGREEMENT

Prior to the Uruguay Round (UR), trade in agriculture was highly distorted. Market access for agricultural products was limited as most markets were restricted by physical import barriers. The presence of massive domestic subsidies led to the overproduction of temperate crops in developed countries. Coupled with stagnating demand for temperate crops in these countries, this led to an excess supply. Export subsidies were used to dump the surplus agricultural output in the international markets. This resulted in depressed market prices, and in spite of being low cost producers of agricultural items; agricultural exporters from developing countries could not compete with the subsidized exports from developed countries. Only a handful of players were active in the global market and the thinness of the global farm trade resulted in high price fluctuations of agricultural commodities.

Market Access

Nominal protection was measured by calculating the difference between domestic prices and international prices of the reference period, 1986-90.[1] 'Bound' rate implied that the base period tariff rates were to act as ceiling rates. No countries were allowed to increase tariff rates beyond the bound rate. AoA then stipulated that the average 'bound' tariff rate of agricultural products would have to be reduced over a period of time with a minimum cut on the tariff rate of each product. Developing countries were given the additional flexibility of offering bound rates for agricultural products[2]. This implied that for fixation of tariff for agricultural items, developing countries did not necessarily have to compute of the tariff equivalents but they could propose a tariff rate they thought appropriate for the concerned product. Tariffication led to the concern that it could result in high bound tariffs, which, if applied, could be prohibitive for any trade to take place. This gave rise to the concept of "minimum market access". In minimum market access WTO Members were required to maintain current import access opportunities at a certain minimum level. This was achieved through 'Tariff Rate Quota' (TRQ). Tariff Quota is a two-leveled tariff where the tariff rate charged depends on the volume of imports. A lower tariff is charged on imports to ensure minimum market access or the quota volume. A higher tariff is charged on imports in excess of the quota volume.

Domestic Subsidies

During the UR negotiations it was explicitly recognized that domestic support distorts trade and it is necessary to impose restriction on them. Domestic support encourages over-production which in turn increases supplies on world markets (by reducing import demand or increasing export supply) and depresses world prices[3]. AoA distinguishes between support programmes that stimulate production and trade directly, and those that are considered to have no direct effect. The AoA does not impose restrictions on the later category. AoA allows developed countries to have amber box subsidies up to 5 per cent of the value of agricultural production. This is called the 'de minimis' level. Amber Box subsidies above the de minimis level come under reduction commitments.

Export Subsidies

The high level of domestic subsidies apart, the widespread use of export subsidies is perhaps the most disruptive element in the global agricultural markets. Agriculture in unique in this respect as, apart from agriculture, export subsidies are prohibited in WTO[4]. Export subsidies led to inefficiencies and high costs to both consumers and taxpayers in the subsidizing country. Countries, which do no subsidize their exports, get affected in several direct and indirect ways. In general, export subsidies increase the share of the exporter in the world market at the cost of others, tend to depress world market prices and may make them more unstable because decisions on export subsidy levels can be changed unpredictably, thereby causing random changes in the volume and prices of the exported commodity. AoA required that both the amount of export subsidies and quantities that receive export subsidies should be reduced over the implementation period. Though most of the WTO members have reduced export subsidies in the post Uruguay Round phase, its continued presence led to distortions in global markets[5]. Export credits, which have similar distortion effect as export subsidies, are not disciplined under the AoA. In Uruguay round AoA, Export credit programmes were not specifically listed as subsidies subject to reduction commitments.[6] Export credits were given a special status that exempted them from any reduction commitments. Although it was not explicitly mentioned in the Agreement, it was agreed that the talks on export credit would continue in OECD and an arrangement which would place limits on export credit conditions and terms and the length of credit extension would be negotiated. Though some progress has been made in OECD regarding disciplining export credits, till date no agreement on export credit has been signed in the OECD forum.

WTO AGREEMENT AND SOUTH ASIA

The biggest achievement of the AoA is that for most of the agricultural products non tariff barriers were abolished and were replaced by tariff bindings. However, it did not benefit the developing countries much because the current global agricultural trade scenario has brought a new set of problems for the South Asian countries. They are:

1. Prices of a number of agricultural commodities are on a steady decline since 1995-96. This decline in price of agricultural commodities is directly attributable to the huge amount of subsidies given to the agricultural sector in the developed countries. As a result of this steep decline in prices, producers of a large number of agricultural crops in the South Asian countries are becoming increasingly uncompetitive on an international level. Though imports of these cheap and subsidized food grains can be beneficial for the net buyers of agricultural commodities in the short run, in the medium run, it will threaten the livelihood of a very large number of small and medium farmers of this region. After the abolition of quantitative restrictions (QRs), the only instrument of protection available to the domestic governments is the tariff rate. If the price decline continues, then it is possible that the tariff adjusted prices of these imports can make the local production uncompetitive even at a domestic level. This is likely to lead to an erosion of domestic production base and will have serious consequences on the food security and rural employment of this region. Here it is noteworthy that none of the countries in South Asia has the right to impose the Special Safeguard (SSG) mechanism allowed in the AoA[7]. It is also to be remembered that because of the protection granted by the "Due Restraint Clause" or "Peace Clause", it is difficult to impose countervailing duties on subsidized imports of agricultural commodities.

2. It can be argued that in a free trade regime, producers of uncompetitive commodities should shift to the commodities where the country is internationally competitive. Under the current set of circumstances, this basically suggests that farmers of South Asia should diversify towards the cultivation of cash crops. However, this argument does not take into account the fact that for small and medium farmers of poor developing countries, it is not easy to shift from one crop to another. Low capital, inadequate rural credit which results from increased withdrawal of state and lack of information about the international commodity market conditions make it difficult for the farmers to make this transition[8]. Also it is important to recognize that diversification is crucially dependent on food security. Unless a basic cushion of food security is assured, it will be extremely risky for small and medium farmers to diversify into non-food grain crops.

3. Furthermore, as export competitiveness of agricultural commodities is a derivative of complex interaction of domestic supply parameters, policy regime and external market conditions, it is subject to frequent changes. Coupled with this, the volatility of commodity prices in the international market can shift the export competitiveness of a product in a very unpredictable manner. Given less than perfect transmission of information to farmers in a developing country, this makes it extremely difficult for a farmer to plan their output both for the domestic as well as the international markets.

4. Comparative study of price movements in the pre and post Uruguay Round period shows that for a number of crops price volatility has actually increased in the post-UR period. Bhattacharyya and Pal (2000) show that for rice and wheat, international prices are much more volatile than domestic prices in India. Shekhar (2003) also concludes that for a large number of commodities, inter-year variability is higher in the international markets than in the domestic market in India. In a tariff only regime, instability of international commodity prices will be transmitted directly to the domestic market. High volatility of agricultural commodities will alter the risk perception and will introduce a speculative element in agricultural prices. This is likely to have serious implications for food security and livelihood issues in South Asia.

5. Most of the pre UR projections estimated large gains for developing countries from the agricultural trade liberalization because they assumed that market access in developed countries for agricultural goods would increase substantially in the post-UR period. However, data show that in reality, agricultural trade is still highly protected. A study by Gibson *et al*[9] (2001) reports that the world average of agricultural tariff is as high as 62 per cent. Also there are problems of tariff peaks and tariff escalations. As a result, in the post Uruguay Round period, agricultural exports from developing countries showed only sluggish growth rate.[10] In fact, a WTO secretariat paper published in 2000, shows that the average annual growth of the value of agricultural exports of Developing Asia has declined from 8.2 per cent during 1990-94 to 0.5 per cent for the period 1994-98. Lack of market access for agricultural goods in developed countries is said to be the reason behind this poor performance.
6. Also, taking advantage of the WTO agreement on Sanitary and Phytosanitary Measures (SPS), developed countries are often imposing irrationally high food standards. There have also been instances where the SPS standards are made stricter without giving proper scientific reasoning.[11] These are acting as Non Tariff Barriers for exporters from developing countries as they are finding it increasingly difficult to match the high SPS standards adopted by the developed countries. Marine products, fishery products, peanuts and tea exporters of South Asia have faced considerable market access barriers in developed countries. Recently, a number of firms exporting marine and fish products from India have closed down because they could not meet the SPS standards imposed by the EU. This has resulted in significant job loss in those industries16. India also notes that in the context especially of the WTO's SPS Agreement, import restrictions are being imposed in the food sector due to health and safety concerns. To address these concerns, food items are being brought under mandatory export certification. In addition to fish and fish products, egg and milk products, it has been proposed to subject honey, live fish, fresh poultry and poultry products, rice, and dried fish and fish maws to compulsory export certification. As the official export inspection and certification body, the EIC is working to develop equivalence agreements, as envisaged under the SPS Agreement, with the official import control bodies of its trading partners[12]. In this context the EIC's export certification is recognized by the European Union for fish

and fish products and Basmati rice and by the U.S. Food and Drugs Administration for black pepper.

7. Basmati rice is one of the biggest agricultural exports for both India and Pakistan. In the areas adjacent to the Himalayas, a large number of farmers in both these countries are engaged in Basmati cultivation. A serious threat to their livelihood and employment can come from inadequate WTO intellectual property protection for this product[13]. Article 22.1 of the TRIPS Agreement defines geographical indications which are protected by the TRIPS Agreement as "indications which identify a good as originating in the territory of a Member, or a region or locality in that territory, where a given quality, reputation or other characteristic of the good is essentially attributable to its geographical origin"[14]. Although, there is one identical definition for all geographical indications, the WTO TRIPS Agreement provides for two different levels of protection for geographical indications. Article 22, which is applicable to all products and covers products like Basmati Rice and Darjeeling tea, limits the protection of geographical indications to cases where the public is misled by the use of a geographical indication as to the true geographical origin of the product, or where such use constitutes an act of unfair competition ('misleading test'). On the other hand, Article 23 is exclusively applicable to wines and spirits and provides additional legal protection for these commodities. Under Article 23, there is no need to prove that the public is misled or that there is unfair competition by using a certain geographical indication.

The use of accompanying expressions such as "style", "type", "kind", "imitation" or the like are prohibited and protection is also provided when the indication is used in translated form. The burden of proof does not rest with the plaintiff of the geographical indication. Under Article 23, competitors not producing within the geographical area are simply prevented from using the corresponding denomination, and they may not use trademarks containing or consisting of geographical indications used to identify wines or spirits. Taking advantage of lax WTO rules on products other than wine and spirits, an American company called Rice Tec Inc, obtained a patent from the US patent office to call the aromatic rice grown outside India 'Basmati'. Rice Tec Inc had been trying to enter the international Basmati market with brands like 'Kasmati' and 'Texmati' described as Basmati-type rice. However, with the Basmati patent rights, Rice Tec was allowed not only to call its aromatic rice

Basmati within the US, but also to label it Basmati for its exports[15]. This posed a great danger for Indian and Pakistani exporters as it had the potential to completely wipe out their market-share in USA. However, after a legal battle with the Indian government, Rice Tec dropped most of the patent claims and the US Patent Examiner has officially changed the title of Rice Tec's patent from the original `Basmati lines and grains' to `Rice lines Bas867, RT1117 and RT1121'[16]. This will prevent Rice Tec from using the 'Basmati' name for their variety of rice. But Article 21 of TRIPS, unlike Article 23, does not provide protection from misleading names like Kasmati and Texmati. So, without Article 23 type protection, the potential for misuse of geographical Indicators like Basmati rice and Darjeeling tea will always be there.

WTO AND INDIAN AGRICULTURE: IMPLICATIONS FOR POLICY AND R&D

Agriculture will continue to remain at the centre stage of socio-economic development in India. Notwithstanding its outstanding performance in making the country self-sufficient in food grains, deceleration of its performance beginning with mid-nineties is of serious national concern.

It is also a fact that WTO agreements are now a reality and these agreements can only be modified. The global scenario in future is going to become more competitive and the pressure for liberalization of domestic market would also grow. In this context, India needs to follow two pronged strategy. One, based on the post WTO experience of last 10 years India should continue taking active part in negotiating agreement to its advantage with sound arguments.[17] This would require objective understanding of the implications of the changed trade regime, promoted and planned under the auspices of WTO. Such an understanding is of critical importance to play an effective role in future negotiations as well as to plan adequately for designing our policies and economic activities including agricultural R&D programmes which are basic to accelerated sustainable agricultural development. Two, in order to effectively operate in the WTO driven environment, the member countries need to devise appropriate domestic policies and strategies. The crux of these policies should be to identify weaknesses and strengths of domestic produce vis-à-vis major competing players, and to improve competitive attributes of our produce, involving production, processing, marketing, trading practices and other processes from the farm to the final destination[18]. Upgradation of competitive strength requires improvement in policies, infrastructure, institutions and technology. Out of these, the major role lies in technology and its favorable interplay with institutions and policies. India's agricultural research system has stood several tests successfully in the past and has helped the country to tide over formidable food crises and other challenges. An analysis of the global trends after WTO indicates unprecedented decline in the global prices of agricultural commodities, severely hitting earnings from agricultural exports of the countries. India too could not gain much from WTO and global liberalization, though India generally performs better than the other countries when the international price situation is favorable. As the exports are becoming increasingly competitive, it is not possible to promote exports without improving produce quality, efficiency and cost reduction. From the analysis of the trade scene and suggested future strategy by commodities, it is evident that: India is facing challenges in traditional export items; the challenge is not from the developed countries, but from the developing countries; major import of vegetable oils are from the developing countries (Malaysia and Indonesia); and India has done well in export of high value products to the developed countries. Export of raw products like cotton, wheat, sugar, coffee and tea is likely to become very competitive and India would be required to relook into the benefit of promoting export of these commodities. Export prospects are brighter with soybeans, oilseeds, oil meal and cake, fruits and vegetables, and fruit preparations. Thus, high export prospects are seen with high value products, horticultural products, processed products, marine products etc. India has to learn lessons from these trends and other experiences.

The Agreement on Agriculture created an environment of trade reforms and initiated trade liberalization in agriculture. The other lessons include: (i) WTO seeks to remove the barriers of "our own market" and "their own markets", (ii) India need not be extremely defensive and inward looking, as our agriculture has demonstrated strength which needs to be appropriately used to compete in the global market, otherwise it will become a case of missed opportunity, (iii) as a net exporting country, India stands to gain from increase in international prices, which is possible only if we relentlessly fight for reduction of domestic subsidies and support and export subsidies in the developed countries (once this is done, the possibility of import threat for our key export products like dairy, wheat, cotton, sugar, etc. will disappear), (iv) import threat can be surmounted by general provision of raising tariff to bound level and of asking for special treatments /packages like S&D treatment, sensitive product, etc. and (v) to comply with quality standards to effectively compete in the global market, we must demand as a first step that all countries should notify their quality requirements.

POLICY RECOMMENDATIONS

WTO is receiving the deepest indulgence of everyone, as it is affecting the major sectors of Indian economy and agriculture in particular now and more intensively in the coming years. A major concern growing with the increasing impact of WTO is, as to how the small and marginal farmers' who dominate the Indian agriculture, depend heavily on agriculture for their livelihood, have small marketable surplus and operate under heavy constraints to be competitive in a subsidized agriculture production and trade regime, could benefit from WTO. The concern more often swings to the other side that the spreading tentacle of WTO with reduced tariff regime and increased access to Indian market for the products from subsidized agriculture could severally damage the agriculture based livelihood of majority of Indian farmers. The challenge to policy makers is how to protect Indian agriculture from the impending WTO threat, enhance the competitiveness of Indian farming and make farming a viable and self sustaining enterprise to improve and ensure livelihood security of the farmers. A strategy to address this challenge shall necessarily involve re-orientation and injection of market linked dynamism in Indian agricultural R&D, strengthening of supportive institutions to serve the resource poor farmers, and steering fast the change with appropriate policies and trained human ware. The deliberations of the workshop suggested the following policy initiatives and action points:

- India needs to devise appropriate domestic policies (extensive domestic market reforms, heavy investment in building and maintaining infrastructure, etc.) to improve efficiency and competitiveness of domestic produce.
- It should continue to play leadership role in negotiating agreements with sound analytical basis and support of other developing countries with similar interest. A dedicated group of about 100 experts, on full time basis, should work on the WTO issues to provide analytical basis for negotiations and to help in planning appropriate strategies to strengthen Indian agriculture to face increasing trade liberalization and globalization.
- Export of high value products, horticulture products, processed products, marine products and rice should be promoted.
- India has to counter the challenges in the export of traditional items from the developing countries. In this regard, prioritization, enhancing production and processing efficiency, marketing and transport infrastructure, maintaining quality, stable supply etc. need immediate attention.

- There is a need to go whole hog in reforming domestic market as has been done by China. The constraints of multiplicity of laws in agricultural marketing, processing, storage, transport should be immediately addressed to impart simplicity, reduce transaction costs and attract private investments in post harvest management. Further, enforcement of Model APMC Act which encourages direct marketing and contract farming should be implemented in true spirit.
- There should be continuous insistence for reduction in domestic and export subsidies in the developed countries. Developing countries should put up a unified approach to ensure substantive reduction in subsides by the developed countries?
- All countries should notify their quality requirements of agricultural produce clearly on the WTO website.
- There is a need to assess the priorities of our national projects including the R&D programmes, and to develop and maintain the quality of infrastructure at the highest level. There should be strict monitoring of the national projects to ensure expected output as per the time schedule.
- Since IPR is becoming an important issue, a clear-cut policy on IPR, its protection, maintenance, evaluation, handling of IPR infringements, etc. should receive priority attention at the Central, State and institutional levels.
- There is necessity to establish Export Processing Zones and Commodity Boards for targeted commodities.
- Agriculture needs to be brought under the Concurrent list of the Constitution.
- There should be a merger of several related departments like irrigation, fertilizer, food, agriculture, etc. for better coordination and synergy.
- Public investment in agriculture has to be raised, particularly in R&D including extension.
- The system related efforts towards re-orientation of R&D system will include general moratorium on establishment of new institutions, development of first rate human resource through quality agricultural education, need-based training in India and abroad, coordination and convergence of all development departmental efforts, harnessing ICT for rural development,

adequate funding of research programmes, project based funding/budgeting, rigorous monitoring and impact assessment, strengthening social science skills, promoting public-private sector partnership, building leadership skills, reforms in financial and procurement management with full decentralization, strengthening policy analysis and vision-oriented market-led intelligence analysis skills, strengthening agri-business development and IPR management, and campaigning for better awareness and compliance in respect of produce quality by the farmers, traders, exporters, importers and the general public.

- The programme related efforts towards re-orientation of the R&D system will include priority attention to targeted export commodities particularly high value processed products, strengthening basic strategic and anticipatory research at ICAR and downstream research at SAUs where 4/5 of the scientists of NARS work, agro-ecological targets and functioning rather than national targets and functioning by the R&D system, profitability besides productivity as indicator of success, linking production with processing, marketing and consumption with focus on small and marginal farmers and farm workers, establishment of quality testing/referral labs, research on minimal non-renewable natural resource use, developing high yielding varieties which must combine high yields, high protein content and other characteristics demanded by the importing countries such as freedom from aflatoxins.

Understanding the direction and magnitude of the effects of WTO agreements on Indian agriculture is a very difficult proposition. Some attempts have been made in the past to quantify the effects of WTO agreement and trade liberalization on Indian agriculture. While the direction of the gains to Indian agriculture may be correct, one may not agree with the assumptions of their models, and the magnitudes and distribution of these gains. In the presence of imperfectly competitive export market structures, the increase in terms-of-trade for Indian agriculture may not be as high as predicted by the computable general equilibrium studies that implicitly assume perfectly competitive markets. Whatever little improvement may occur in the terms-of-trade, it will have negative or at best very little effect on farmers' welfare, as supply response to term-of-trade improvement is ambiguous. On this ground, developing countries may ask for further and sharp reductions in the export subsidies and domestic support given by the developed world.

Our agriculture will stand to gain if we bring about improvement in irrigation, transport, agricultural extension services and research. Expenditures on such items are exempt from domestic support reduction commitments under the green-box policies.

Given the complexities and escape routes available to the western world in the implementation of the agreements, one could question the methodologies followed in the reduction commitment norms. Market access commitments have been tampered with dirty tariffication, and, only the already low rates of tariffs have been reduced rather than reducing high tariff rates. Therefore, the Swiss Formula may be suggested to reduce higher tariffs by steeper cuts. On the other hand, some of India's low tariff bindings may be re-negotiated. Calculation of price support within the product-specific AMS is not clearly defined in the text. Therefore, it would be a good idea to bring a consensus among the member countries on this issue. Developing countries which have net-taxed their agriculture, may ask for credit of some sorts for having negative AMS. Further, Blue-Box policies may be suggested to be eliminated altogether or moved out of the exemptions for the calculation of current AMS. Moreover, along with export subsidies, export credits and guarantees may also be suggested to be brought under reduction commitments. The SPS and TBT agreements do affect agricultural markets. Modernizing our agricultural processing will not only enhance our export market potential but aid in reforming the domestic food quality as well.

REGIONAL TRADING ARRANGEMENTS &THEIR GROWING POPULARITY

The vast majority of WTO members are party to one or more regional trade agreements. The rush of RTAs (Regional Trading Agreement) has continued unabated since the early 1990s. Some 250 RTAs have been notified to the GATT/WTO up to December 2002, of which 130 were notified after January 1995. Over 170 RTAs are currently in force; an additional 70 are estimated to be operational although not yet notified. In most FTAs concluded in Asia, parties go well beyond their WTO commitments in terms of tariff concessions. However, while negotiators within the WTO have been increasingly shifting their agendas towards issues other than tariffs, such as environmental protection, intellectual property rights, labour standards and competition policies, with the exception of the recent bilateral agreements such as the US–Singapore agreement, FTAs in Asia have essentially concentrated on issues related to trade liberalization per se.

Regional trading arrangements and FTAs have increasing become the preferred mode of trade liberalization amongst the countries of a region even though they may be members of WTO. The reason for this can be traced to freedom that such arrangements provide for addressing the trade issues peculiar to a region or the member countries of an FTA.

In a nutshell FTAs/RTAs can be used as a tool for–

- Cheaper imports–domestic prices in control.
- Better quality products at competitive price.
- Better market access.
- Investments flow-JVs.
- Coverage of Services.
- Mutual recognition of standards & laboratories.
- Trade facilitation, Harmonization of Customs procedures etc.

The coverage and depth of preferential treatment varies from one FTA/RTA to another. Modern FTAs/RTAs, and not exclusively those linking the most developed economies, tend to go far beyond tariff-cutting exercises. They provide for increasingly complex regulations governing intra-trade (e.g. with respect to standards, safeguard provisions, customs administration, etc.) and they often also provide for a preferential regulatory framework for mutual services trade. The most sophisticated FTAs/RTAs go beyond traditional trade policy mechanisms, to include regional rules on investment, competition, environment and labour.

There exists an intricate relationship between WTO and FTA and when a WTO member enters into a regional integration arrangement through which it grants more favorable conditions to its trade with other parties to that arrangement than to other WTO members' trade, it departs from the guiding principle of non-discrimination embodied in the various WTO agreements. However, even though they seem to be contradictory, but often regional trade agreements can actually support the WTO's multilateral trading system. Regional agreements have allowed groups of countries to negotiate rules and commitments that go beyond what was possible at the time multilaterally. In turn, some of these rules have paved the way for agreement in the WTO. Services, intellectual property, environmental standards, investment and competition policies are all issues that were raised in regional negotiations and later developed into agreements or topics of discussion in the WTO. Normally, setting up a customs union or free trade area would violate the WTO's principle of equal treatment for all trading partners ("most-favored-nation"). But GATT's Article 24 allows regional trading arrangements to be set up as a special exception, provided certain strict criteria are met.

Article 24 says if a free trade area or customs union is created, duties and other trade barriers should be reduced or removed on substantially all sectors of trade in the group. Non-members should not find trade with the group any more restrictive than before the group was set up. Similarly, Article 5 of the General Agreement on Trade in Services provides for economic integration agreements in services. Other provisions in the WTO agreements allow developing countries to enter into regional or global agreements that include the reduction or elimination of tariffs and non-tariff barriers on trade among themselves. A key rule of the multilateral trade system is that reductions in trade barriers should be applied, on a most-favored nation basis, to all WTO members. This means that no WTO member should be discriminated against by another member's trade regime. However, an important exception to this rule is allowed for regional trade agreements (RTAs), under which reductions in trade barriers only apply to the countries that form the arrangement. This exception is contained in Article XXIV of the General Agreement on Tariffs and Trade (GATT) for trade in goods and in Article V of the General Agreement on Trade in Services (GATS) for Trade in Services.

CONCLUSION

Therefore, to sum up, it can be said that the initial expectation that AoA would induce higher production of agricultural goods in developing countries and thereby, would promote rural development and employment, has not materialized in practice. High subsidies given by developed countries to their agricultural sector continue to distort global agricultural trade. Existence of high tariff and non-tariff barriers in agricultural sectors of most developed countries have not allowed the developing countries to reap the full benefit of agricultural trade liberalization. On the other hand, a shift to a tariff only regime and opening up of the agricultural sector has made the small and medium farmers of South Asian countries vulnerable to external shocks. Given this scenario, it is unrealistic to expect that agricultural employment will benefit much from AoA. Moreover, creation of rural infrastructure can be extremely labour intensive in nature. WTO imposes no ceilings on expenditures incurred by governments towards building or improving rural infrastructure as these comes under the 'Green Box' category of subsidies in AoA. Increased public and private expenditure on rural infrastructure can not only boost rural employment in the short run, but it also contributes to make the agricultural sector more internationally competitive in the medium to long run.

Here it should also be mentioned that WTO reduction commitments on domestic subsidies (the reduction commitments on Aggregate Measure of Support or AMS) are not likely to impose any significant burden on the governments of the member countries of South Asia in near future. As a least developed country, Bangladesh does not have any reduction commitment in AMS. The level of AMS in India, Pakistan and Sri Lanka are well below the permissible *de minimis* level. Subsidization of agriculture in South Asian countries will be constrained more by fiscal compulsions rather than any WTO rules.

NOTES

1. Malhotra Kamal, Making Global Trade Work for People, Earthscan Publications 2003, p. xxv
2. Laird, Sam (2002): "Market Access Issues and the WTO: An Overview" in Development, Trade and WTO: A Handbook, edited by Hoekman, Mattoo and English, The World Bank.
3. Moore. Mike (2002): "How Trade Liberalisation Impacts Employment", Speech to the International Labour Organization (ILO), Geneva, 18th March 2002.
4. World Bank (2003): World Development Indicators 2003 CDROM.
5. The EC's proposal for modalities in the WTO Agriculture Negotiations, 29.01.2003.
6. WTO (2001), "Market Access: Unfinished Business: Post-Uruguay Round Inventory and Issues"-Special Study 2001.
7. P. Gibson, J.Wainio, D. Whitley, and M Bohman (2001). Profiles of Tariffs in Global Agricultural Markets. Market and Trade Economics Division, Economic Research Service, USDA Report No. 796.
8. The EC's proposal for modalities in the WTO Agriculture Negotiations, 29.01.2003.
9. P. Gibson, J.Wainio, D. Whitley, and M Bohman (2001). Profiles of Tariffs in Global Agricultural Markets. Market and Trade Economics Division, Economic Research Service, USDA Report No. 796.
10. WTO (2003): WTO Annual Report 2003, Geneva.
11. Sekhar, CSC (2003): "Volatility of Agricultural Prices–An Analysis of Major international and Domestic Markets" Working Paper number 103, ICRIER, New Delhi.
12. See Global Economic Governance Programmer Available at *www.globaleconomicgovernance.org* accessed on 5th Jan, 2008.

13. Satish Mihir, WTO: Abolish or Reform?, John Bunzl–Director, 2005.
14. Meléndez-Ortiz Ricardo and Dehlavi Ali, Sustainable Development and Environmental Policy Objectives: A Case for Updating Special and Differential Treatment in the WTO.
15. *Current Science*, Vol. 80, No. 12, 25 June 2001.
16. Global Economic Governance Programme, Breaking the Deadlock in Agricultural Trade Reform and development.
17. Deohar Satish, WTO Agreements and Indian Agriculture: Retrospection and Prospects, IIMA Working Paper # 99-11-06.
18. Trade facilitation in the WTO: Implication for INDIA, Taneja Nisha, April 2004, Working Paper No. 128.

REFERENCES

Krugman, Paul and Robert Lawrence (1994), "Trade, Jobs, and Wages," Scientific American, April.

Laird, Sam (2002), "Market Access Issues and the WTO: An Overview" in *Development, Trade and WTO: A Handbook*, edited by Hoekman, Mattoo and English, The World Bank,

Moore Mike (2002), "How Trade Liberalisation Impacts Employment", Speech to the International Labour Organization (ILO), Geneva, 18th March 2002.

Pal, Parthapratim (2002): "Implementation Issues of the Agreement on Agriculture and its Implications for Developing Countries" available at *www.networkideas.org* and *www.kisanwatch.org*.

Patnaik, Utsa (2003), "Employment and Poverty among India's Neighbours", Macroscan website, Jun 10th 2003, available at *www.macroscan.net*.

Rodrik, Dani (1997), "Has Globalization Gone Too Far?" Washington, DC: Institute for International Economics, 1997.

Rodrik, Dani (1999), *The New Global Economy and Developing Countries: Making Openness Work*, (Overseas Development Council, Washington, D.C. 1999).

Rodrik, Dani (2000), "Institutions for High Quality Growth: What They Are and How to Acquire Them". NEBR Working Paper 7540. National Bureau of Economic Research, Cambridge, Mass.

Sekhar, CSC (2003), "Volatility of Agricultural Prices–An Analysis of Major International and Domestic Markets" Working Paper number 103, ICRIER, New Delhi.

Srinivasan, T. N. (2002), "Developing Countries and the Multilateral Trading System After Doha" available at http://*www.publicpolicies.org*/Research/*TN%C2%A0Srinivasan-pres.pdf*

UNCTAD (1999), "Preparing for Future Multilateral Trade Negotiations: Issues and Research Needs from a Development Perspective." UN sales no. E.99.II.D.17. Geneva.

Geographical Indications: Feasibility of Extending Protection Under the TRIPS Regime

*Shouvik Kumar Guha**

INTRODUCTION

Geographical indications of origin (since it hasn't been mentioned as geographical indications later, no need for this part), constituting an integral part of intellectual property rights, have always been the precipitating factor for raging debates within the international community. Such debates have sought to create two opposing factions entirely different in composition from the traditional North-South antagonism–the 'old world' and the 'new world', comprising vocal supporters of geographical indications like the European Community, along with India, Sri Lanka, Turkey, Egypt and Slovenia and other developing and transitional economies on the one hand, and nations like United States, Canada, Japan, Australia, New Zealand, Chile, Argentina and Mexico on the other. The crux of the debate seems to be the extent of protection that should be accorded to geographical indications, since they identify the unique qualities, characteristics and reputation of the products to which they are affixed and improper use of them can lead to potential catastrophe in the form of consumer confusion as to the origin of the said products. Such catastrophe can assume even greater proportions especially with respect to the Indian scenario, wherein geographical indications are numerous, possess tremendous resource-potential and are prone to exploitation. While the advocates of increasing geographical indications protection seek to centralize their argument around the aforementioned issue of consumer confusion, many 'new world' countries vociferously keep defending the right of their nationals to use foreign generic geographical indications in their respective nations. In particular, United States would always like to remind the rest of the world that most of the renowned geographical

* National University of Juridical Sciences, (NUJS) Kolkata.

indications are considered generic terms in U.S. and therefore, there can seldom be raised any related question of consumer confusion with regard to the origin of the products identified by such geographical indications.

The adoption of the Agreement on Trade-Related Aspects on Intellectual Property Rights (TRIPs) in 1994 represented considerable progress in the front of extending protection to geographical indications, with the Agreement having pioneered the requirement from all signatories of incorporating at least a degree of protection for geographical indications, with particular stress on those identifying wines and spirits, as well as requiring the signatories to agree to participate in future negotiations aimed at expanding the scope of such protection. Nevertheless, the lack of consensus that plagued the pre-TRIPs discussion on geographical indications have unfortunately continued to define even the post-TRIPs consultations, especially in relation to the modalities to implement the said enhanced protection promoted by TRIPs. Such a regrettable absence of meeting of minds on an international level have resulted into TRIPs having been proven a failure, albeit a partial one, in respect of enhancing the protection attributed to geographical indications, with diplomatic efforts to further global negotiations having reached a stalemate. In course of this article, the author would like to assume the position that extension of protection to geographical indications under Article 23 of TRIPs to a reasonable degree may prove to be beneficial to both the parties to the debate. The article begins with a brief overview of geographical indications, including the meaning and significance thereof, the traditional rationale for their protection and the extent to which such protection had indeed been offered before the adoption of TRIPs. The author would then like to discuss the prevailing status of the law under the TRIPs regime and the failure of the diplomatic agenda to expand the aforesaid protection, along with a careful analytical consideration of the arguments advanced both for and against such expansion. Finally, the article seeks to delve into the matter whether the advantages of extending the current protection could outweigh the resultant disadvantages. An optimal solution to the existing conundrum has also been searched for, with such search being accompanied by feasibility analysis of a number of probable solutions offering such optimality.

GEOGRAPHICAL INDICATIONS: CONCEPTUALIZATION AND SIGNIFICANCE

The concept of geographical indications owes its origin to the Paris Convention for the Protection of Industrial Property, held on March 20,

1983. Article 1(2) of the convention, although refraining from using the term 'geographical indications' itself, did mention expressions like 'appellation of origin' and 'indications of source'.[1] Article 22.1 of Section 3 of TRIPS defines geographical indications as "*indications which identify a good as originating in the territory of a Member, or a region or locality in that territory, where a given quality, reputation or other characteristic of the good is essentially attributable to its geographic origin.*" The wide scope of the term 'indications' seek to imply that geographical indications can be varied in nature, ranging from a geographic place name to a symbol, a color or anything else capable of identifying the source of a good or a service. The indication need not even be of a direct geographical name, even non-geographical indication, like the term 'basmati' for instance, would be eligible for protection. *Ceteris paribus*, each one of the qualifiers, viz. 'quality', 'reputation' or 'other characteristics' is on its own an adequate condition for the grant of protection. The use of the term 'goods' instead of 'products further' seek to suggest an exclusion of services from the purview of Section 3.[2] Much like trademarks, geographical indications act as a signaling device that helps producers to differentiate their products from competing products in the market, and enables them to build a reputation and goodwill around their products, which often fetch a premium price. Although geographical indications and trademarks perform somewhat similar functions of building reputation and goodwill, each of the two has distinguishing features of its own. Geographical indications bring into play both the region where the product is produced, where natural climatic and soil conditions contribute to its distinctive quality, as well as time–honored traditions of producing a product in a particular way. Thus, they may also include non-agricultural products such as Belgian chocolates, Sheffield sterling and Swiss watches. In general, geographical indications are used for what are referred to as 'search goods' and 'experience goods', i.e. goods where quality is known through either inspection and/or research goods or through use and experience, which then guides future consumer decisions. They also act as *source identifiers*, informing consumers about the origin of the goods that they identify i.e. they guarantee the qualities and characteristics of the products by informing the consumers that the products to which they are affixed "*come from an area where a given quality, reputation or other characteristic of the [products] is essentially attributable to their geographic origin.*" As a consequence of this, they serve the function of promoting the goods of a particular area, providing added value to producers.[3] In addition, geographical indications have features that respond to the needs of indigenous and local communities and small farmers–they are based on collective traditions and a collective decision-making process; they reward traditions while allowing for continued evolution, emphasize the relationship between human efforts, culture, land, resources and the environment and are not subject to free transfer from one owner to another. Irrespective of the divergences in opinion on geographical indications protection, most of the global community share a common appreciation of the economic value of such indications. A reference to a statement articulated by the government of Australia, a country opposed to geographical indications-extension, acknowledging the commercial value of 'distinctive signs' in its submission to the TRIPS Council, may prove to be really insightful in this context: "*...tea is more valuable than undifferentiated bulk tea in the market-place if it is sold as Darjeeling tea, more valuable still if it bears the distinctive certification mark 'Darjeeling–The Tea Board's Seal of Approval', and potentially yet more valuable again if it bears a distinctive trademark and is packed in distinctive packaging.*"[4]

PROTECTION ACCORDED TO GEOGRAPHICAL INDICATIONS IN THE PERIOD PRECEDING TRIPS

The tremendous commercial potential of geographical indications makes the necessity for legal protection for the same assume all the more significance. Without such protection, competitors not having legitimate right on a geographical indication may ride free on its reputation. Such unfair business practices result in loss of revenue for the genuine right-holder of the geographical indication and also mislead consumers, besides having the capacity to eventually hamper in the long-run the goodwill and reputation associated with the indication. It was in Europe that the use of geographical indications to identify products was pioneered, with France being the first nation to introduce legislation on protection of geographical indications in 1824 in response to a widespread wine-labeling fraud experienced in the 19th Century. Since then, geographical indications have emerged as an integral part of intellectual property in Europe. Such progress stands in sharp contrast with the scenario in U.S., which had historically never known any system apart from that of trademarks to protect geographical indications. Prior to the TRIPs Agreement, there were in existence three international agreements that sought to address geographical indications, viz. the Paris Convention for the Protection of Industrial Property, 1983 (hereinafter referred to as the Paris Convention), the Madrid Agreement for the Repression of False or Deceptive Indications of Source on Goods, 1891 (the Madrid Agreement) and the Lisbon Agreement for the Protection of Appellations of Origin and their International Registration, 1958 (the Lisbon

Agreement). The Paris Convention was the first international agreement to address the protection of geographical indications, albeit in a limited manner. Its 117 signatories agreed primarily to border measures for false indications and members were required to seize or prohibit imports with false indications of source, producer, manufacturer or merchant. In 1958, Article 10bis addressing unfair competition was brought into force to prohibit indications that were liable to mislead the public as to the nature, the manufacturing process, the characteristics, suitability for their purpose or the quantity of goods. The use of the word 'characteristics', which replaced the word 'origin'(at the insistence of the U.S., if one may add), restricted protection of geographical indications by prohibiting importations only of goods whose indications are false, as opposed to those that are misleading.

The Madrid Agreement professes a comparatively wider ambit than the Paris Convention, dealing with both border measures and prevention of 'genericisation' of geographical indications. One of its more controversial provisions is Article 4, which prevents members from treating geographical indications of wines as generic terms. Owing to the expansion of protection for geographical indications, the Agreement can boast of few signatories, the result being an unfortunate neutralization of its impact. Of the three aforementioned agreements, the Lisbon Agreement is perhaps the most serious attempt to achieve effective and enforceable protection for geographical indications through a system of international registration akin to that of trademark registration. As per the wordings of Article 1, once a geographical indication is registered in any member country, other member countries too have an obligation to extend protection to the same. According to Article 3, the members must prohibit imitations under their respective domestic laws, including the usage of terms like 'type' or 'style' along with the indication. Article 6 provides that no geographical indication can be considered generic in any other member country, so long as it is protected in the country of origin. The requirement of major upheavals in most of the legal regimes in the member countries as necessitated by such a strict level of protection has unfortunately rendered the Lisbon Agreement, like the Madrid Agreement, bereft of more than a handful of signatories.[5] The U.S. is not a signatory to either the Madrid Agreement or the Lisbon Agreement. On the other hand, several European Union members were signatories to all three agreements. The most significant drawback of these agreements lies in the fact that either the scope of protection was not clearly defined, so that implementation depended on the good will of countries, or that they called for uniformity in protection that was impossible to achieve. Nevertheless, these three agreements had collectively succeeded in paving the way for the current TRIPs framework; in fact, several anti-extension lobbyists suggest that Europe is attempting, through TRIPs, to achieve those wishes that had remained unfulfilled in the Lisbon Agreement.

THE TRIPS FRAMEWORK FOR PROTECTION OF GEOGRAPHICAL INDICATIONS

The true intention behind the negotiating storm that led to the TRIPs agreement of 1994 was to provide greater protection for intellectual property rights on a global scale. The U.S., a leader in the production of intellectual property such as trademarks, copyrights and patents spearheaded the development of TRIPs in order to defend its rights abroad, particularly in developing countries. Its position on greater protection was supported by the European Union (EU), Japan and Switzerland. However, when the discussion led to the protection of geographical indications, differences seemingly irreconcilable in nature came to the forefront. While the U.S., Canada, Japan and Australia were staunchly opposed to the inclusion of geographical indications protection, especially for wine, the EU was insistent on inclusion because it is in that area that European economic interest lay. A careful examination of the current framework for protection of geographical indications ought to reveal a victory on the part of the European negotiators.[6] In fact, the greater level of protection for wines and spirits under the said framework is often looked upon to have been granted solely for the political reason of persuading the European Community (EC) to join a consensus on the Uruguay Round package, overcoming strong objections from many other countries.

TRIPs provisions establishing geographical indications protection came into effect on January 1, 1996, in developed countries, on January 1, 2000, in developing countries, and on January 1, 2006, in least developed countries. The following is the scheme of protection for geographical indications under Articles 22 to 24 of TRIPs. Article 22.1 facilitates in providing a definition of the subject matter viz. geographical indications. Articles 22.2 -22.4 outlines the basic scope of protection for geographical indications for all goods other than wines and spirits, while Articles 23.1 and 23.2 lay down the additional protection available exclusively for wines and spirits. Articles 24.3 -24.9 provide schematics for exceptions to obligations for protecting geographical indications. Finally, Article 23.4 mentions the obligation to enter into negotiations for establishing a multilateral register for wine geographical indications and the scenario concludes with Articles 24.1 and 24.2 establishing provisions for further negotiations. Thus one can conclude that Articles 22, 23 and 24 of Section 3, Part II of the TRIPs Agreement collectively form the originating source for provisions aimed to extend protection to geographical indications. As per Article 22.1, to qualify for protection, an indication must (i) identify the good and its area of geographical origin, (ii) possess a given quality, reputation or other characteristics, which (iii) is essentially attributable to its area of geographical origin. Articles 22.2-22.4 establish the basic obligation for the protection of all geographical indications. Members must provide the "legal means for interested parties" to secure protection of their geographical indications. Three major elements can be distinguished within the protecting provisions under Article 22–protection against the use of indication in a manner that might mislead or deceive the public, protection against the use of indications in a manner that constitutes acts of unfair competition within the meaning of Article 10bis of the Paris Convention and provisions for refusal or invalidation of trademarks that contain or consist of indications, where such may mislead the public. In the absence of any specified legal means to achieve these objectives, Members are free to determine what can be construed as the most appropriate methodology. Such determination has traditionally culminated into, among others, laws relating to consumer protection, unfair competition, trademark law and a sui generis system. Article 23 contains additional obligations for providing the aforesaid legal means for the protection of indications of wines and spirits. Such additional protection begins with Article 23.1 that prohibits the use of geographical indications for wines and spirits *"even where the true origin of the good is indicated or the geographical indication is used in translation or accompanied by expressions such as 'kind', 'type', 'style', 'imitation' or the like."* Article 23.2 mandates invalidation or refusal of trademarks that 'contain or consist' of geographical indications identifying wines or spirits. In this context, the author would like to mention that unlike Article 22.3, the use of Geographical indications in a trademark does not have to be considered misleading for invocation of Article 23.2. Article 23.3 relates specifically to homonymous indications where there is an obligation to *"determine the practical conditions under which the homonymous indications in questions will be differentiated from each other"*, while ensuring equitable treatment of producers and that consumers are not misled.[7] Finally, Article 23.4 obliges Members to enter into negotiations "concerning the establishment of a multilateral system of notification and registration" of geographical indications for wines to "facilitate" their protection. Article 24 paves the way for certain significant exceptions that severely limit Articles 22 and 23. Under Article 24(4), ongoing use in a similar manner of a geographical indication by persons that had used it in the member state for ten years prior to the conclusion of TRIPs is permitted. Article 24(4) discusses parallel usage of geographical names for wines and spirits as in Article 23(3). As per its provisions, a Member is not required "*to prevent continued and similar use of a particular geographical indication of another member identifying wines or spirits in connection with goods or services,*" if that geographical indication was used "*in a continuous manner with regard to the same or related goods or services in the territory of that member either (a) for at least [ten] years preceding 15 April 1994 or (b) in good faith preceding that date.*"

Thus there exists a hierarchy in the kind of protection offered to wines and spirits and other goods. The first difference relates to the level of protection. Under Article 22, the holder of an infringed geographical indication can only have access to legal recourse if consumers have been misled by the allegedly infringing label or if its sale constituted an act of unfair competition, whereas Article 23 plainly prohibits any use of a geographical indication on wines or spirits that do not originate in the designated geographical region–irrespective of whether the true origin has been identified. The second distinguishing feature leads to the creation of a multilateral register for wines and spirits. The last section of Article 23, which has no analogue in Article 22, calls for negotiations to be undertaken in the Council for TRIPs concerning the establishment of a multilateral system of notification and registration for the geographical indications on eligible wines. Although the register does not give registered geographical indications any overt legal protections beyond those that they would otherwise enjoy, it does facilitate the protection of such geographical indications, albeit in an indirect manner.

It may be interesting to note that according to the present level of protection under Article 22, it is sufficient to simply indicate on a product, even in small print or on its back only, its true origin in order for such illegitimate use of geographical indications not to be misleading and therefore permissible. In contrast, labels like '*Chilean Tequila*' is outlawed as per Article 23 provisions, thereby resulting into a clear case of discrimination against producers of products such as rice, coffee, tea, cheese, watches, silk, cigars, ceramics, carpets etc. who are legitimately using the geographical indications of their products.[8]

The Debate Over Extension of Protection Under Article 23: *The Diplomatic Agenda: has it Really Failed?*

In spite of the obligations laid down in Articles 23 and 24, a concrete result is yet to be reached as far as the enhanced geographical indications protection advocated by TRIPs is concerned. A split runs down the TRIPs Membership in its entirety both as to the proposed modalities and the legal effect of the registration system for geographical indications and to the issue of extending protection for misleading uses of indications beyond wines and spirits. While European countries continue to promote stronger protection, nations like U.S., Canada and Australia do not appear to share such enthusiasm. A number of developing countries are to be found on both sides of the debate. The submissions that have been presented at the TRIPs Council as to the registration system to be implemented can be divided into two groups: a maximalist approach supported by the European Union, Switzerland, former Eastern Bloc countries, and several developing countries, and a minimalist approach supported by the United States, Australia, New Zealand, Japan, and many Latin American countries. The former approach envisages a compulsory system in which geographical indications would benefit from unconditional protection in the markets of all Members upon its inscription in the register. In contrast, the latter approach envisions a voluntary system that would not require protection for the registered geographical indications by other Members.[9]

Divergences in opinion can also be found in the proposals for the expansion of Article 23 beyond wines and spirits. In June 2002, the EU along with a few other countries put forth a proposal (European Proposal) that would significantly extend geographical indications protection. The European Proposal also included a "*claw-back*" clause that would allow countries to register as geographical indications terms that are currently generic or registered as trademarks in other countries, such as "feta" for cheese or "champagne" for sparkling wine.[10] Because of its impact on generic words and on existing registered trademarks, the European Proposal has been fiercely criticized by representatives of 'new world' countries who have argued that this proposal violates the parent provisions of Article 24, fails to provide adequate protection for non-misleading geographical trademarks, and adopts an overbroad definition of geographical indications that is per se inconsistent with Article 22.[11]

In October 2003, the 5th Ministerial Conference of the WTO was held in Cancun, Mexico, where the TRIPs Members convened to discuss the extension of geographical indications protection as provided by Articles 23 and 24. Unfortunately, owing to the deep divide on the issue that has plagued the international community pre-TRIPs, the Cancun negotiations collapsed before any viable solution could be reached at. In the absence of a consensus, the Conference closed with a six-paragraph Ministerial Statement, instructing Member governments' officials to continue work on outstanding issues with a renewed sense of urgency, taking fully into account the views expressed in the Cancun Ministerial Conference.[12] Following these instructions, the General Council (GC) of the WTO adopted a decision on August 1, 2004, in which it reaffirmed the mandates of the Doha Ministerial Declaration and renewed Members' determination to find appropriate solutions to outstanding implementation-related issues.[13] With regard to the issue of extending the level of protection accorded under Article 23 of the TRIPs Agreement to GIs for wines and spirits to *all* products, the GC requested the Director-General (DG) of the WTO to continue the consultative process he launched in 2003, with a decision that the General Council shall review progress and take appropriate action on the said extension no later than July 2005.

Pro-extension Arguments in their Collectivity

All in all, the issues involved in the raging debate regarding the discussion at hand can be roughly classified into 3 categories:

1. Legal issues concerning differences of general protection under Article 22 and additional protection for wines and spirits under Article 23 (including balance of rights and obligations between the Member States, the very rationale for intellectual properties like Geographical indications requiring the protection sought to be accorded to them and the desired scope of such protection).
2. Policy issues or economic issues such as impact of extended protection on producers and consumers (including potential impact on producers, rise in trading opportunities, especially with respect to developing countries, probable impact on third party's markets as well on consumers, who have to choose between greater clarity of the product's origin and higher prices arising from disruption to the existing marketing practices).
3. Practical issues concerning administrative cost and burdens of procedures associated with extended protection (including legislative amendments at various levels, dealing with increased number of applications both domestic and foreign in origin, effective enforcement requiring input from commercial interests concerned and governments and anticipation of increased litigation at national and international levels).[14]

Members demanding geographical indications extension argue that unlike any other provisions relating to intellectual property rights within TRIPS, Section 3 provides for a single definition of the protected subject matter in Article 22.1, but has two different levels of protection based on product categories. This discrimination between product categories is not based on any intrinsic characterization of the goods or the locality of or skills associated with the product's method of fabrication. In fact, it stands in sharp contrast with Article 27.1, which defines the precise requirements for patentable subject matter and simultaneously denies any possible discrimination on the grounds of place of invention, the field of technology and whether the products are imported or locally produced. Members opposing geographical indication-extension initially tended to circumvent this issue, instead suggesting that the existing imbalance should not be accentuated by extension of scope to all products. However, in a relatively recent drive, opposing Members have acknowledged that the hierarchy is scarcely anything more than a consequence of compromises made in the context of the Uruguay Round and as such, cannot be allowed to persist any further.[15]It is argued that the requirements under Article 22 of establishing 'unfair competition' or that the 'public has been misled' erect a relatively higher threshold in comparison to Article 23, thus making it relatively easier for other producers to use a reputable geographical indication and 'free-ride'. Moreover Article 22 does not prohibit the use of terms such as 'like', 'type', or 'style' accompanying the geographical indication, which arguably increases the risk of indications turning generic. This risk is considered by these Members as a 'key reason' for demanding geographical indications -extension. The argument does not seem to be devoid of merit altogether, especially when one begins to consider the range of erstwhile famous geographical indications that are now considered generic–Arabica coffee, India rubber, chinaware, Cheddar cheese and kiwifruit, to name a few.

Advocates of geographical indications extension also indicate the difficulties of ensuring geographical indications protection under Article 22. To begin with, the requirement of consumer confusion creates unnecessary legal uncertainty, since the use of public confusion as a prerequisite to an infringement action results in unpredictable and uncertain protection, dependent on several isolated factors like time and place. Apart from the inherent problems in using consumer confusion as a benchmark, the requirement also allows for wide judicial discretion in deciding what constitutes infringement. Moreover, the burden of proof promulgated in Article 22 creates excessive and unnecessary costs for plaintiffs. While protection under Article 23 requires the relatively simple test of establishing whether the product has originated from the place indicated by the geographical indications, leading to relatively few costs in litigating geographical indications claims, holders of geographical indications protected under Article 22 face significant enforcement costs as a result of their burden of proof. This cost may be prohibitive in many cases, especially for producers in developing countries. Consequently, it is argued that protection under Article 23 is more effective, easier to access and cheaper to actualize. Last but not the least, pro-extension Members have repeatedly emphasized that an increase in protection will be bound to provide substantial benefit to agricultural economies and hence to developing countries by proxy.

Extension: The Harmful Repercussions

The concept of strengthening the protection accorded to geographical indications has always been a source of concern for countries such as the US, where several locally manufactured products have names originally adopted from European nomenclature. A similar phenomenon occurred in other countries with European immigrants, such as Canada and the Latin American countries, where immigrant business owners of European descent were familiar with geographical names from their homeland that were associated with quality products and contrived to utilize them to promote their own products. The arguments put forth against geographical indication-extension range from those that contest the validity of designating certain terms as geographical indications, to those highlighting the inconveniences arising from such extension. One of the primary arguments put forth by the US and its allies is that many of the terms the EU claims to be geographical indications, such as "feta" cheese, are perceived as generic names in their countries. In fact, many U.S. companies feel that instead of reducing the value of a particular good, imitation enhances the value of the original product; that it is through the advertising and marketing by US companies that the public has become acquainted with terms such as 'Parmesan' and 'Roquefort'. As Tyler Cabot had explained rather succinctly, "*The only reason we now want Parmesan cheese is because [American] companies have made it, produced it, advertised it and distributed it. It doesn't matter if you protect some rock in the middle of France, if nobody knows what the value of it is.*"[16]

Another strategy of Members opposing geographical indications-extension is to emphasize that Article 23 does not offer an absolute protection as is often claimed by the pro-extension Members. To begin with, many products may not qualify for protection and/or more likely, exceptions in Article 24 will undoubtedly dilute the expectations of economic gain. Existing use is preserved through Article 24.4 (in the case of wines and spirits)–a provision that would apply to geographical indications of other products if they were included within the coverage of Article 23. Secondly, terms that have already become generic (e.g. Cheddar cheese) would be exempt from protection (Article 24.6). Other exceptions to Article 23 can also diminish, if not prohibit altogether the protection of some indications. Another line of argument relates to the prohibitive costs inflicted upon producers as a result of extension. If the EU proposal were to be adopted, several companies (primarily American) will be compelled to completely change the names of their existing products and it is not unlikely that consumer confusion may result from such re-naming, thereby defeating the very purpose of extension. Moreover, one cannot ignore either the substantial administrative costs that will be one of the many fall-outs of such re-naming and the resulting re-labeling. Furthermore, costs of the re-naming efforts are likely to face a considerable increase owing to the new marketing campaigns that would be necessary to promote the same product under a new name. It is suggested that geographical indications -extension will result in the "*disappearance of terms customarily used to identify used to identify products*" which "*will increase search and transaction costs for consumers, at least in the short to medium term.*"[17] In response to this, proponents note that only those labels will change that are considered infringing and not within the scope of exemptions under Article 24. The consumer confusion on account of new labels is thus unlikely to be anything more than a short-term disruption and effective marketing and promotion by the legal owners of geographical indications could ease the adjustment process by a considerable extent.[18]

Geographical indications opponents further argue that in essence the practice is protectionism that serves to cordon off future market access opportunities for emerging industries. For example, geographical indications would be a reason for serious trade restrictions in emerging industries, such as dairy and processed agricultural industries. Hence, allowing only certain products to carry a given geographical indication will unfairly reduce competition and encourage monopolization, and arguably, sanctioning such monopolies will ultimately lead to higher prices for consumers for the products that are permitted to maintain that indication.[19] In addition, critics attack the motives of the EU in pressing for stronger geographical indications protection, by dubbing EU's stance on as a response to reduction of agricultural subsidies, with geographical indications monopoly rents allegedly intending to become the 'new agricultural subsidies'. In the words of Justin Hughes, "*In a possible world of reduced agricultural subsidies, control of valuable geographical indications would at least allow European farmers to compete better in high-end food categories and secure at least some monopoly rents from well-known food names."* [20] Geographical indications opponents also seek to debunk the notion of homogeneity of geographical indications products, arguing that much of Europe's production of such products is carried on a large-scale, industrialized manner and that the image of the family-based traditional farm unit projected is nearly a caricature that no longer corresponds to reality.[21]

THE NECESSITY FOR REASONABLE EXTENSION OF PROTECTION

There remain few parties to this dispute under discussion who are yet to acknowledge the implications of stronger geographical indication protection. It serves economic policies and fosters national developments, with special emphasis in relation to the agricultural industry. In fact, there exists a direct correlation between providing for a greater level of protection as established by Articles 23 and 24 and a direct increase in the current benefits for local economies, particularly those based primarily on agriculture or those exhibiting local traditions in manufacturing different products. Stronger protection would attract investment in regional products, while the same on an international scale would limit future competition, thereby leading to an immediate increase in the incentive to create and register new products and brand names based on geographic origin. Regional foods could be marketed internationally with less risk that their niche would be overwhelmed by domestic competition. Extension would especially help developing countries gain market power because geographical indications frequently protect the type of products common to developing countries. For a good to be entitled to bear geographical indications, it must have special qualities attributable to the good's geographical source. Logically, this would occur most frequently in those countries where there are unique pockets of nature that have not been adulterated by extensive development. Moreover, geographical indications goods tend to belong to the indigenous rural, agricultural and handicraft sectors of the economy, thereby further implicating the interests of developing countries. Mexico's experience with regard to Tequila is a prime example of the considerable financial benefits that can arise from the exclusive rights granted through geographical indications–increased Tequila exports combined with the production monopoly inherent in geographical indications have caused a sharp rise in the price of domestic inputs and thus generated considerable profits for Mexican producers. Nor do such benefits need to be restricted to developing countries and 'old world' countries alone. Extended geographical indication protection may prompt an introspection in even 'new world' countries to find local products capable of competing with geographical indication products, the expansion of the Australian wine industry in the past decade offering a prime example. The bilateral agreement with the European Union in 1994 had compelled Australian wine-makers to stop using the names of French regions like Burgundy or Chablis to describe their wines. However, it did not lead to a decrease in production and competition as feared by opponents of stronger protection. On the contrary, the signing of this agreement signified a huge leap forward for Australian wine industry by compelling reliance on regional names like Coonawarra and Barossa and grape varieties like Chardonnay and Shiraz. Such is the story behind Australia's emergence as a major player in the world wine industry, with Australian wines having outsold the French in both Britain and the United States during more than one financial year. Nor have imports of European wines in Australia grown during the past decade, which goes on to prove that apprehension over the remaining of national products and the risk of a decrease in competition is not necessarily a cause for real concern. The aforementioned argument of protection offered under Article 23 proving to be a source of great benefit for local economies finds general acceptance in the global arena. However, what is often 'dusted under the carpet' is the inadequacy of protection under Article 22. In addition to subjecting plaintiffs to superfluous legal costs, Article 22 renders the issue of 'misleading' indications subject to judicial discretion. One of the primary goals of the WTO Agreements is the establishment of a fair and predictable legal framework within which international trade can flourish. Thus subjecting the determination of what constitutes a 'misleading' indication to judicial discretion cannot help but undermine such a lofty goal. Moreover, due to the burden of proof being placed on the plaintiff and the consequent costs of litigation, plaintiffs may choose not to engage in legal proceedings if the infringement is done on a small enough scale that the cost of litigation would outweigh the market detriment. The current system thus creates a loophole within itself in the form of an incentive for manufacturers to engage in low-impact infringements that are unlikely to be brought to the attention of a court. The author would like to submit herein that when plaintiffs have the legal right to exclude defendants' marks from the market, the unnecessary costs created by the discriminatory provisions of the TRIPS Agreement should not be allowed to stand as impediments. However, the sole problematic area *vis-à-vis* extension of Article 23 that is susceptible to the charge of excessive protectionism is the prohibition even on the use of the correctives such as 'like', 'type' or 'style' etc. Members opposing extension argue that this makes it more difficult for consumers to find substitute goods. There can often arise situations where the authentic good is unavailable due to its cost or some other limitation ad under such circumstances, consumers should have easy-to-find alternatives. Surely this merits consideration, particularly given that firstly, geographical indication-certification inevitably leads to such products being sold at a premium and secondly that the entire debate on geographical indication protection originates from the need to eliminate consumer confusion. The prohibition on "Roquefort-style cheese' or 'Indian Scotch' needs to be justified in terms other than consumer confusion, which is something that the pro-extension lobby has been unable to do. Thus the argument for extension fails at the point where it extends beyond consumer protection to the realm of protectionism. A reasonable extension of protection, which would eliminate the hassles of Article 22, while permitting the use of correctives, is more defensible both from a logical as well as legal point of view–the potential benefits seem endless, ranging from promotion of sustainable development of local rural communities by encouraging a quality agricultural and industrial policy and employment growth in decentralized regions, to supporting the establishment of other economic activities such as tourism, and contributing in the preservation of traditional knowledge and biodiversity.

CONCLUSION AND OBSERVATIONS

There appears to exist no adequate legal defense for the unwillingness to extend protection under Article 23 to a broader range of products. To begin with, the hierarchy between product categories embedded in Articles 22 and 23 resulted from a political compromise that can no longer be offered as an excuse. In fact, the author would herein like to suggest that the discrepancy between Articles 22 and 23 and the requirement of consumer confusion in Article 22 have together become pivotal in defeating the very purpose of a uniform, predictable system of world trade envisioned by the WTO Member States. Moreover, none other than the developing countries are at present being compelled to bear most of the encumbrances of such disparity. A reasonable extension of protection that would remove the burden of proof from petitioners by prohibiting *per se* use of geographical indications while allowing the use of correctives would be an optimal solution for producers as well as consumers. Promoting the use of geographical indications may be the best way of demonstrating their benefits to the nations that still remain to be convinced. Replacing confusion with substantial clarity in the law relating to geographical indications, both on the national as well as on the international fronts, is definitely a prime requirement. In the national scenario at least, the practice of offering similar extensions across the board are already in vogue in some of the countries, so making the rest of the nations to see the logic behind such a move should not be too difficult. Any fear on the part of any of the nations opposing extension of getting overwhelmed with applications must be mitigated with speed and assurance. On the one hand, it is imperative to make negotiations on extensions mandatory for the global community as a whole, but at the same time, care must be taken so as not to tie it up with any other commitment that can potentially jeopardize the very purpose of such negotiations. Giving priority to agricultural products can act as a beneficial incentive for the group of nations having an economy based on agriculture.[22] The author believes that the discussions that have taken place on geographical indication-extension since the start of the Doha Round qualify as more than exhaustive, with all the necessary technical level consultations having been carried out under the supervision of the WTO DG In 2005. The time has now come, following the GC decision of August 2004, for the GC to decide appropriate action on such extension and to adopt guidelines for the negotiations on the said topic, provided the WTO Members are truly willing to reach a fair overall balance. Among the steps that can be prescribed, the obvious ones include application of Article 23-protection to geographical indications for all products, *mutatis mutandis* application of the exceptions contained in Article 24 to all products rather than only to wines and spirits and the establishment of a multilateral register[23] under paragraph 4 of Article 23 and opening the same to geographical indications for all products.[24] What is necessary most of all is the cultivation of the urge to fight usurpation of geographical indications for products falsely marked as well as 'genericisation' of geographical indications and the only feasible option available to achieve such a goal is none other than geographical indications -extension. A close look at the Indian scenario ought to reveal that the Indian counterpart of Article 23 in the Geographical Indications of Goods (Registration and Protection) Act, 1999 (Geographical Indications Act) does not restrict itself to wines and spirits, but, rather, leaves it to the discretion of the central government to decide which products should be accorded higher levels of protection. This approach has deliberately been taken by the drafters of the Indian Act with the aim of providing Article 23-type stringent protection to Geographical indication of Indian origin. However, an absence of obligations on the part of the other WTO members to ensure Article 23-type protection to all Indian Geographical indication dilutes the effect of the said provision to a considerable extent, thereby leaving scope for misappropriation of such geographical indications in the international arena. Around 30 geographical indications of Indian origin, including Darjeeling (tea), Pochampalli, Ikat (textiles), Chanderi (sarees), Kancheepuram silk (textiles), Kashmir Pashmina (shawls), Kondapalli (toys), and Mysore (agarbattis) have already been registered with the Geographical Indications Registry, with many more being there in the pipeline. However, issues like effective enforcement of geographical indications in the domestic and export markets and the apprehension of the inherent commercial potential of Indian geographical indications remaining unrealized in the absence of effective policies and strategies on marketing and promotion thereof are yet to be addressed, which makes it more prudent for Indian policy-makers to carefully ponder the socio-economic cost-benefit analysis of geographical indications-extension through meticulous empirical research before making any decision thereto.[25]

NOTES

1. The Lisbon and Madrid Agreement also seek to demarcate the scope of the term; for an account of the evolutionary history of the concept, see E. Guiterrez, *Geographical Indicators: A Unique European Perspective on Intellectual Property*, Hastings International and Comparative Law Review, 29 (Fall 2005).
2. Having said that, the Agreement does not prevent the Members from going beyond the minimum obligations laid down under Section 3, thereby allowing them to address services through their respective national legislations, as has already been done by nations like Liechtenstein, Peru and Switzerland.
3. Italian Toscano oil can provide a suitable illustration of such value addition, having been sold at a premium of 20% since its registration as a GI in 1998; see Why do Geographical Indications Matter to Us?, available at *www.ec.europa.eu/trade/issues/sectoral/intell-property/argu_en.htm* (last visited on 9.3.2008).
4. IP/C/W/211.
5. As of August 1, 2006, only 25 states were parties to the Lisbon Agreement.
6. Dr. Dwijen Rangnekar, Geographical Indications: A Review of Proposals at the TRIPS Council: Extending Article 23 to Products other than Wines and Spirits, UNCTAD-ICTSD Project on IPRs and Sustainable Development, 2003.
7. A number of wine regions have homonymous names due to the fact that immigrant from European countries often named their new places after locations in their motherland. Eg. Rioja wine from Spain and Rioja Wine from Argentina. Article 23.3 attempts to protect both indications, while ensuring that consumers are not misled.

8. Felix Addor, The Way Ahead–What Future for Geographical Indications? Extension of the more effective protection of Article 23 of the TRIPS Agreement to all products, available at *http://www.wipo.int/meetings/en/2005/geo_pmf/presentations/doc/wipo_geo_pmf_05_addor.doc* (last visited on. 10.3.2008).
9. Irene Calboli, Expanding the Protection of Geographical Indications of Origin under TRIPS: "Old" Debate or "New" Opportunity? *Marquette Intellectual Property Law Review*, Vol. 10 (2005).
10. Viewed as a parallel strategy to GI-extension, this proposal intends to prohibit the use of specific geographical names currently used by producers other than the right-holders in the country of origin.
11. *Ibid.*
12. WTO Doc WTO/MIN(03)/W/24 of 14 September 2003.
13. WTO Doc WT/L/579 of 2 August 2004.
14. Dr. Tanapoj Ekkayokkaya, Extension of GI Protection: TRIPs Standard and New Development for Protecting GI, available at *http://www.aseminfoboard.org/content/documents/061107_WG_Intellectual Property_04TanapojEkkayokkaya.pdf* (last visited on 10.3.2008).
15. (IP/C/W/386, para 3): "If the extension discussion were purely one of intellectual property policy, it would make sense to treat all products in the same manner legally. However, we note that the WTO TRIPS Council discussions take place in the context of trade policy and the additional protection provided geographical indications for wines and spirits resulted from the Uruguay Round of multilateral trade negotiations."
16. Tyler Cabot, Naming Rights: Is America the Home of the Free but Not of the Brie?, WAHINGTON POST, May 21, 2003, at F01.
17. (IP/C/W/289, page 7).
18. Lina Monten, Geographical Indications of Origin: Should They Be Protected and Why?–An Analysis of the Issue From the U.S. and EU Perspectives, *Santa Clara Computer and High Technology Law* (*Journal*), (January, 2006)
19. *Ibid.*
20. Justin Hughes, Champagne, Feta and Bourbon: The Spirited Debate About Geographical Indications, *Hastings Law* (*Journal*), (December, 2006).
21. Justin Hughes, Champagne, Feta and Bourbon: The Spirited Debate About Geographical Indications, *Hastings Law* (*Journal*), (December, 2006).
22. Dr. Tanapoj Ekkayokkaya, Extension of GI Protection: TRIPs Standard and New Development for Protecting GI, available at *http://www.aseminfoboard.org/content/documents/061107_WG_Intellectual Property_04TanapojEkkayokkaya.pdf* (last visited on 10.3.2008).
23. Besides providing a comprehensive shop mechanism covering all WTO members, such a register would also facilitate implementation of existing

obligations by governments and the beneficiaries of the register would include all stakeholders in GIs.

24. Felix Addor, The Way Ahead–What Future for Geographical Indications? Extension of the more effective protection of Article 23 of the TRIPS Agreement to all products, available at *http://www.wipo.int/meetings/en/2005/geo_pmf/presentations/doc/wipo_geo_pmf_05_addor.doc* (last visited on 10.3.2008).
25. Kasturi Das, Protection of Geographical Indications: An Overview of Select Issues with Particular Reference to India, available at *http://www.centad.org/cwp_10.asp* (last visited on 10.3.2008).

Controversies in a Harmonized Global Patent System: A Study of the WIPO Patent Agenda

*Debosmita Nandy**

INTRODUCTION

A single global patent system, with a central office issuing patents that are valid and enforceable in any country of the world has always remained a cherished dream for many. Towards this goal, there have been attempts of standardization of the patent law by the World Intellectual Property Organization (WIPO) during the 1980s, but it failed due to inadequate political pressure within the body. Trade Related aspects of Intellectual Property Rights (TRIPS) achieved the same goal to some extent by establishing a new, much higher harmonization floor, through the World Trade Organization (WTO's) trade sanction system, which resulted in imposing developed country's patent standards on the whole of developing world at one go. Patents on pharmaceuticals and living organisms became mandatory, while the possibility of adding development initiatives was radically curtailed. The majority of the developing countries had to accept TRIPS as part of WTO's single undertaking, since the other option was to opt out of the whole multilateral trading system. The rapidly growing importance of patents is reflected in the present trend of using intellectual property rights (IPRs) as the means of control over a globalized economy. As production of tangible goods is being increasingly moved to developing countries to take advantage of their lax environmental standards and cheap labour, strong IPR protection becomes absolutely crucial for the developed nations. The different patent system prevalent all over the world posed hardship for the multinationals that always wanted a simplified global patent framework, with standards to their liking. With the broad standards being taken care of under the TRIPS, it was now the turn of the WIPO to bring in harmonization in the procedural and substantive

* Final year, National University of Juridical Sciences, (NUJS) Kolkata.

aspects of patent law, through the "Agenda for the Development of the International Patent System" (Patent Agenda) of 2001. This paper is an attempt to discuss the issues and controversies revolving around the proposed reforms in the global patent law with special focus on the perspective of the developing countries.

PATENT LAW STANDARDS UNDER WIPO

The WIPO is one of the specialized agencies of the United Nations system of organizations, with presently 184 nations as member-states and headquarters in Geneva, Switzerland. The Convention Establishing the WIPO was signed at Stockholm on July 14, 1967 and amended on September 28, 1979. The predecessor to the WIPO was the BIRPI, French acronym for *United International Bureau for the Protection of the Intellectual Property*, set up in 1893 to administer the Berne Convention for the Protection of Literary and Artistic Works, 1886 and the Paris Convention for the Protection of Industrial Property, 1883 (Paris Convention). Both of these conventions provided for the establishment of international secretariats, which were placed under the supervision of the Swiss Federal Government. The few officials who were needed to carry out the administration of the two conventions were located in Berne, Switzerland.

At the 1967 diplomatic conference in Stockholm, when WIPO was established, the administrative and final clauses of all the then existing multilateral treaties administered by BIRPI were revised to remove the supervisory authority of the Swiss Government, and to give it the same status as all the other comparable intergovernmental of the United Nations system. WIPO became a specialized agency of the United Nations (UN) when an agreement was signed to that end between the United Nations and WIPO, which came into effect on December 17, 1974.[1] The agreement between the United Nations and WIPO recognizes that WIPO is, subject to the competence of the United Nations and its organs, responsible for taking appropriate action in accordance with its basic instrument and the treaties and agreements administered by it, *inter alia*, for developing a balanced and accessible international intellectual property system, which rewards creativity, stimulates innovation and contributes to economic development while safeguarding the public interest.[2] The WIPO has been divided into specialized organs namely the *General Assembly*, *Conference*, *Coordination Committee* and *International Bureau* to carry out its functions, like harmonization of national legislation in the field of intellectual property, conclusion of international agreements designed to promote protection of intellectual property, offering legal-technical assistance to its member states and promotion of research in this arena. The WIPO Convention provides for only the umbrella framework for the organization, while the substantive intellectual property standards are established by separate treaties, each of which has different contracting States. WIPO currently administers 23 such international treaties relating to various aspects of intellectual property rights.The WIPO patent system has been based on two main treaties, namely, the Paris Convention, which established the substantive standards and the Patent Cooperation Treaty (PCT), which laid down the requisite procedural standards. Under the Paris Convention, countries were able to adopt different standards especially in areas of technology relating to societal interests, such as public health. In addition to these, the Budapest Treaty on the Deposit of Microorganisms establishes a system for the international recognition of deposits of microorganisms in specified institutions for the purposes of patent disclosure. The increasing participation of developing countries in WIPO had defeated almost all the expansive proposals mooted by the developed countries, while at the same time allowing some progress in advancing developing countries' agenda for the reform of the Paris Convention.

During the 1980s, the United States (US), being unable to promote its own Intellectual Property (IP) standards through WIPO, propagated the opinion that the WIPO administered treaties provided rights without remedies. Moreover, due to the lack of uniform standards and an enforcement mechanism in WIPO, key industry players in the United States, persuaded their government that WIPO had failed to secure the appropriate levels of intellectual property protection, and lobbied to initiate an IPR standardization process within the General Agreement on Tariffs and Trade (GATT) system. An obvious advantage of GATT vis-à-vis WIPO was the possibility of applying trade sanctions to countries found as non-compliant under the disputes settlement mechanism and, the possibility of negotiating higher standards of IPR protection with the developing countries in exchange for concessions in other trade areas, such as textiles and agriculture. Though forum shifting of IPRs to the WTO and subsequent adoption of the TRIPS meant fulfillment of the long cherished dream of a unified IP law of the developed world, the role played by WIPO in this regard cannot be overlooked. While TRIPs placed states under obligations, WIPO helped them to achieve them through legal assistance. In close cooperation with the WTO secretariat, WIPO had been instrumental in the implementation of TRIPS standards in developing countries, often taking the opportunity to draft and recommend TRIPS-plus legislation. In this role, WIPO has pushed its own pro-patent agenda rather than serving the best interests of its clients. West African countries were advised to implement TRIPS well ahead of their commitment as Least Developed Countries (LDCs), and against using the flexibility TRIPS allows in compulsory licensing or parallel imports. In Cambodia, WIPO somehow failed to inform the government that, as an LDC, it was not obliged to grant patents on pharmaceuticals before 2016.[3] WIPO realised that for effective implementation of a world standard intellectual property system, it should work in cooperation with the WTO. For this reason, the WIPO Assembly entered into an Agreement in 1995 which provided for:[4]

(a) Accessibility of laws and regulations in the WIPO collection by WTO members and their nationals,

(b) Accessibility of the computerised database to WTO members and their nationals,

(c) Accessibility of laws and regulations in the WIPO collection by WTO Secretariat and the Council for TRIPs,

(d) Transmission of laws and regulations by the WTO Secretariat to the International Bureau, WIPO

(e) Availability of techno-legal assistance by the WIPO to the developing states of the WTO, not being members of WIPO, and

(f) Exchange of non-confidential information between WTO Secretariat and International Bureau on a regular basis.

Furthermore, with the adoption of the WIPO Copyright Treaty and the Performances and Phonograms Treaty in 1996, and of the Patent Law Treaty (PLT) in 2000, WIPO showed its ability to respond to developed countries' demands. Though initially it was seen as lacking in enforcement, the technical expertise that had developed over the years was gradually being perceived by developed countries as indispensable in promoting the TRIPS standards, through extensive technical assistance to developing countries. TRIPS revived the dream of having a unified global patent throughout the world, and the developed countries decided WIPO to be the best forum for the necessary further negotiations. Thus emerged the WIPO Patent Agenda in September 2001, sparking off long negotiations, which have continued till date.

ANALYSIS OF THE WIPO PATENT AGENDA

The TRIPS Agreement introduced the principle of minimum intellectual property standards, which has played a critical role in the overall strategy of developed countries to attain higher standards of intellectual property protection in areas of their interest. The implication of this principle is that each subsequent bilateral or multilateral intellectual property agreement can only create higher standards but not derogate from the existing minimum standards. With the TRIPS standards firmly established, the Patent Agenda can only aim at higher standards.The main complaint about the current patent system is the burdensome, complex and costly procedures for obtaining patents internationally, due to the current territorial nature of the patent system. The main emphasis in the so-called *"improvement of the patent system"* is to facilitate acquiring patent protection in foreign countries by making the system more user-friendly, cost-effective and secure in the present scenario of globalization. The main purpose of the Patent Agenda, as set out by the WIPO Director-General is, therefore, to create mechanisms and programmes whereby inventors and industry have access to internationally effective patent protection systems which enable them to obtain, maintain and enforce their patents globally.[5]Following is a discussion on the three pillars of the Patent Agenda.

The Patent Law Treaty (PLT)

The PLT, adopted in 2000, aims to harmonize the procedure of filing for, obtaining and maintaining patents by means of a set of standard formal requirements for national patent offices. Article 2 provides.[6]

> *"[n]othing in the Treaty or in the Regulation is intended to be construed as prescribing anything that would limit the freedom of a Contracting State to the PLT to prescribe such requirements of the applicable substantive law relating to patents as it desires".*

It also provides a clear linkage to the PCT for current and any future patent law harmonization in Article 16. One controversial aspect of the PLT is the relaxation of the conditions for admission of a patent application and the determination of the application date, which is crucial for the assessment of novelty and inventive step, as well as to establish the right to a patent grant in case of rival claims by different inventors. Article 5(1) of the PLT allows the applicant to submit minimal information, *an express or implicit indication to the effect that the elements (received by the patent office) are intended to be an application* and *a part which on the face of it appears to be a description*[7]. This provision opens the possibility of deliberate submission of an application prior to the actual conception of an invention, e.g. when an inventor has a hypothesis but not an experimental verification as well as to subsequently introduce different or additional subject matter and claims while benefiting from an earlier filing date. Moreover the lax requirements of Article 5(1)(ii) relating to minimal identification of the applicant may give rise to uncertainty, and also fraud and manipulation regarding ownership of the patent. The patent office also has the responsibility of inviting the applicant to provide the elements missing in the application without any fixed term, thereby dragging the patent application process almost indefinitely. Moreover, non-compliance with formal requirements is not be a ground for revocation, unless fraudulent intention is proven by the complaining party. Thus it can be seen that in contrast to the proclaimed goal of the Patent Agenda, the provisions of the PLT are likely to increase rather than reduce patent offices work in dealing with applications at the initial phase of procedures.

The Patent Cooperation Treaty (PCT)

The PCT was concluded in 1970, amended in 1979 and 1984 and sought to establish a single system under which applicants can file one international patent application, which would be valid in all contracting states designated by the applicant. While patents are not granted by this system, it allows for international publication, a global 'prior art' search and even an international examination of the application. It provides the applicant with an option to withdraw his application if the result makes granting of his patent unlikely. The Treaty has only three mandatory obligations:[8]

(i) a regularly filed PCT application must have the effect of a regularly filed national application, thereby making the patent valid in the countries mentioned by the applicant in his application

(ii) a PCT application cannot be processed by national authorities before the expiry of a certain time limit, generally 20 months, unless expressly mentioned by the applicant

(iii) a PCT contracting state cannot require compliance relating to the form or contents of a PCT application that differs from the requirement provided by the PCT, except in certain circumstances.

So it is perceived that the PCT is a great success upon which a truly international patent system can evolve, though the treaty itself was not originally designed as a harmonizing instrument. According to its Article 27(5):

> *"Nothing in this Treaty and the Regulations is intended to be construed as prescribing anything that would limit the freedom of each Contracting State to prescribe such substantive conditions of patentability as it desires.*

In particular, any provisions in this Treaty and the Regulations concerning the definition of prior art is exclusively for the purposes of the international procedure and, consequently, any Contracting State is free to apply, when determining the patentability of an invention claimed in an international application, the criteria of its national law in respect of prior art and other conditions of patentability not constituting requirements as to form and contents of applications".

The reform in PCT is geared towards introducing amendments to the treaty to simplify the procedures and formalities. Other reform objectives include avoiding duplication of examination tasks by national offices and PCT authorities, remedy the overload of patent offices, lessening of the cost of filing patent application, and facilitate grant of same patent for countries more than one. It was also agreed upon to align the PCT to the maximum possible extent with the provisions of the PLT and the ongoing substantive harmonization work being carried out by WIPO's Standing Committee on the Law of Patents and have technical assistance programmes for the developing countries, particularly in the field of information technology. This reform initiative was started at the behest of the United States, who along with many other developed countries wanted to make PCT decisions binding on member countries so that they no longer have the freedom to assess merit of an international patent application independently. During the first session of the Committee on Reform of the Patent Cooperation Treaty (the Committee) held in Geneva on May 2001, it was settled that the reform of the PCT system should be of the basic and general objectives. Though the initiative to reform the PCT has found substantial support from both developed and developing countries, but there is no consensus on several aspects of the reform, including its scope. Colombia and Brazil especially are opposed to the grand objective of grant of international patents, since it erodes most of the flexibility of national legislations, and along with it, their sovereignty.

THE DRAFT SUBSTANTIVE PATENT LAW TREATY (SPLT)

The SPLT is the political core of the Patent Agenda as it deals with the substance of patents, like what can and cannot be patented, under what conditions and with what effect. If such matters are not harmonized, there can never be a world patent, no matter how uniform and streamlined the formalities and procedures become. Not surprisingly, the SPLT is the most difficult piece of the puzzle for WIPO. Patent laws have historically always been governed by the national authorities, and individual governments are very reluctant to give up their freedom to decide on the rules of patentability. Although a number of treaties, beginning as far back as the Paris Convention in 1883, have created a regime of mutual recognition between national patent systems, there has been very little substantive harmonization at a global level.

The negotiations and discussions on the SPLT are taking place in the WIPO Standing Committee on the Law of Patents (SCP). This work is aimed at initially creating uniform substantive patent law standards relating to issues of prior art, novelty, utility and inventiveness, requirements relating to sufficient disclosure, drafting and interpretation of claims, grounds for refusal of an application, and for revocation and invalidation of a patent.After this first phase of work, further harmonization is envisaged in areas where the US and the European Union (EU) do not agree so far, e.g. the first to file versus first to invent principles and post-grant opposition proceedings, which have been kept aside for negotiations at the latest stage.

Neither the Paris Convention nor the TRIPS Agreement defines what an "invention" is, thus allowing for different interpretations at the national level. The draft SPLT, with its objective of harmonizing patent laws, would bring in a uniform standard for the term *invention,* thereby eroding much of the space given to many countries to exclude patentability of biological materials. Another significant issue on which some developing countries expressed their concern at the meetings was whether an invention should show a 'technical character' in order to be patentable. US argued that requiring a technical character would unnecessarily limit the innovations in new fields of endeavour, such as information technology and biotechnology. It is clear that the main objective behind this argument is to export to the rest of the world the US policy of patentability of software, business methods and research tools.'Software' is patentable in the US, as held by the Supreme Court in *Diamond v. Diehr* and *Diamond v. Bradley*[9], resulting in patents being granted to softwares, which involve only manipulation of data and no physical transformation. EU and other countries do not grant patent protection due to lack of 'industrial application' of softwares. India, for example protects computer programs under its Copyright Act. 'Business methods' include methods applied to business activities such as marketing techniques and financial schemes and strategies, generally supported on computer software and networks. In the US, the *State Street Bank v. Signature Financial Group* case opened the way for the controversial patenting of business methods. Because of their low inventive standard and broad coverage, 'business method' patenting initiated a plethora of litigation focused on technical methods long in use, but patented only recently.'Research tools' are methods or substances e.g. Expressed Sequence Tags or ESTs used to undertake research in specific fields. Patents on genes, for instance, restrict their use as tools to identify possible therapeutic molecules. Access to these tools, and consequentially, the progress of science, may be slowed down, mainly in developing countries and in public research institutions, due to the need to obtain multiple licences and the escalation of research costs from license fees. [10]

Thus it can be seen that dropping the requirement of 'technical character' of inventions would substantially expand the scope of the patent system, beyond its basic intent of promoting technical progress. Such a step will go well beyond the TRIPS Agreement, which only prescribes patenting in 'fields of technology' and the current PCT, according to which the invention must be of 'technical character'. It is to be noted that many countries that want to keep 'industrial application' as a separate requirement have objected to this proposal. Many would undoubtedly agree that the most controversial provision of the draft Treaty is the one that prohibits Contracting Parties from imposing any further conditions in granting of a patent other than those specifically provided for in the treaty. This is a very sensitive issue, since many developing countries have argued in WIPO and WTO time and again for the need to establish an obligation on the patent applicant to disclose the origin of any biological materials claimed. It is believed that such an obligation may help to limit or remedy the misappropriation of genetic resources and traditional knowledge, since it would permit patent offices to obtain more complete information on the 'prior art', and may also facilitate to establish effective mechanisms for benefit sharing. It is observed that traditionally, US had been instrumental in granting numerous patents to such properties of *neem, turmeric* etc which are considered indigenous knowledge in India. Article 102 of the US Patent Code provides separate standards for 'prior art' requirement within US, where it should be known or used by anyone, and outside US, where it should be patented or described in a printed publication. Since most of the traditional knowledge is usually not documented, it has become extremely difficult for the developing countries to prevent biopiracy. Article 8 of the draft treaty, as stood after the tenth session in 2004,[11] imposes a uniform standard whereby all information, which has been made available to the public anywhere in the world *in any form* before the date of the claimed invention will qualify as being 'prior art'.

The only freedom given to the contracting parties in Article 2 relate to infringement, measures regarding preservation of essential security interests or compliance to international obligations and public interest, very much in the lines of Article 27.2 and Article 27.3 of the TRIPS. Preserving flexibility in framing national patent laws is not an end in itself but a necessary condition to allow countries to adapt, as far as permitted under existing international obligations, patent standards to their own needs and circumstances. In this context, the proposed harmonization raises, from the perspective of developing countries, a few concerns.

Adaptation of Patent Law to Local Conditions

There is a growing opinion that the regulation of patents and other IPRs cannot be reasonably made with a unique, universal standard. Different socio-economic conditions and levels of development of different countries require different intellectual property systems. A recent report by the World Bank shows that the patent system may entail considerable short-term costs for developing countries, mainly due to administrative costs and problems with higher prices for medicines and key technological inputs, while long term benefits seem uncertain and costly to achieve in many nations, particularly for the poorest countries[12] The said report concludes that "one size does not fit all" and that countries should be left with the flexibility to adapt the levels of intellectual property protection as their economies grow. The flexibility provided by TRIPS recognizes the fact that it is in the development needs of some countries that there should be lower IP standards. The Commission on Intellectual Property Rights (CIPR) also opined that higher IP standards should not be imposed on the developing countries without proper assessment of their development impact. It stressed on the fact that IP system should facilitate, and not hinder, the application of the rapid advances in science and technology to the benefit of developing countries.[13] History shows that all the developed countries adopted IPR regime suited to their needs and amended it as they progressed in the developmental path. But this benefit of such adjustment is being denied to other countries under the TRIPS Agreement and more so, if the SPLT is adopted.

Impact of Harmonization in Developing Countries

The agenda for development of the international patent system launched by WIPO is premised on the assumption that "a robust and dynamic industrial property system, and particularly the patent system, supports and encourages technological innovation, brings more and better products onto the market for the benefit of people, and promotes investment and technology transfer"[14] But reality does not corroborate this ambitious vision. The new international framework on patents established by the TRIPS Agreement has affected the conditions for access to and use of technology in developing countries. Reverse engineering and other methods of imitative innovation have been restricted by use of product patents, thereby making technological catching-up more difficult. It is a known fact that strengthened patents improves the negotiating position of right-holders to determine the royalties to be paid and other conditions for the transfer of needed technologies, in case they agree to part with them at all.[15]

Many argue that a strong IP regime attracts Foreign Direct Investment (FDI), but it is also true that FDI depends a lot on factors such as market size, growth prospects, resource endowment and political conditions, and not solely on patent protection regime.

CONCLUSION

There is no doubt that the multinational companies, supported by the US, EU and other developed countries are the main beneficiaries of higher, uniform and harmonized intellectual property standards worldwide. While substantive harmonization may facilitate compliance with laws in different countries by any applicant, Small and Medium Enterprises (SMEs) and individual inventors will not benefit much from this harmonization. This is evident because the Patent Agenda does not include any specific component aiming at reducing the barriers for the use of the patent system by SMEs and individuals, such as reduction of registration fees and, particularly, of the substantial litigation costs required to defend their rights or protect them against infringement.

Harmonization of patent standards is not welcome globally, particularly when countries like the US have been granting patents for minor trivial developments, or for substances already existing in nature and which have been merely been discovered and not invented.

Like the TRIPS Agreement, which was not designed to respond to development concerns but to satisfy industrial demands of the developed countries, the Patent Agenda has been launched without any analysis of its effect on the developing and least developed countries. It is quite clear that the benefits and costs of patents significantly vary according to the levels of economic and technological development of a society. And it is of no dispute that the costs for developing countries of introducing or increasing the levels of IPRs protection are higher than the benefits that they can extract from such protection. Developing countries are also to be blamed to a great extent for even allowing this negotiation to materialize, since there was hardly any participation by them in the initial stages. Any amount of proactive role played by some of the more powerful developing countries would have definitely stalled all efforts of such substantive patent law standardization. Presently coordinated and sustained efforts should be maintained by the developing world to preserve the flexible framework envisioned by the TRIPS in crucial areas like patentability and what constitutes an invention. It is imperative that the developing countries now consider the Patent Agenda in the light of their developmental needs and exert their sovereignty with regards to domestic patent legislations. It is not to be denied that a uniform standard regarding the patent requirements, especially prior art, is essential even from a developing country perspective. But the whole framework proposed by the WIPO does more harm than any visible benefit, since the harmonization is being done on the terms of the dominant countries and reflect their political priorities. On 22nd June 2007, after a one-year hiatus, it was decided that the WIPO would renew its agenda on patent policy issues in 2008 following members' informal approval.[16]It would be pertinent to mention here that a 45-point Development Agenda, aiming at establishment of a new development-based framework for norm-setting activities, consideration of access to knowledge and technology issues, enhancing technology transfer to developing countries and introducing a new evaluation and impact assessment framework in WIPO was proposed by Argentina and Brazil and supported by 12 developing countries, including India in October 2004. On 4th October 2007, it was adopted by the WIPO, with the goal of lessening the gap of knowledge between the developed countries on one hand and the developing and least developed countries on the other hand.[17] It has already been perceived as an immense victory for the developing world amidst the uncertainty of the Patent Agenda. Thus the author would like to conclude by rejecting the WIPO Patent Agenda, being insensitive to growing needs of the developing countries and suggesting that the member states take necessary steps in the forthcoming negotiations to prevent any more economic and intellectual colonization by the developed countries in the guise of harmonization of IP laws.

NOTES

1. See *www.wipo.int/treaties/en/agreement/index.html* last visited on 2nd August 2007.
2. See generally, *http://www.wipo.int/ip/en/iprm/pdf/ch1.pdf,* last visited on 14th September 2007.
3. See *http://www.grain.org/briefings/?id=159* last visited on 12th August 2007.

4. Myneni S. R, *Law of Intellectual Property* (Hyderabad: Asia Law House, 2001) 44.
5. See generally, Correa M C and Musungu S F, *The WIPO Patent Agenda: The Risks for Developing Countries,* Trade-Related Agenda Development and Equity Working Papers, South Centre, November 2002, available in *http://www.mihr.org/?q=node/*view/125 last visited on 3rd October 2007.
6. See WIPO document PT/DC/47 for the text of the Treaty.
7. See Article 5(1) (i) and (iii) of the PLT, emphasis added.
8. See WIPO document PCT/R/1/2 for the text of the Treaty.
9. See Correa M C and Musungu S. F., *The WIPO Patent Agenda: The Risks for Developing Countries,* Trade-Related Agenda Development and Equity Working Papers, South Centre, November 2002, available in *http://www.mihr.org/?q=node/view/*125 last visited on 3rd October 2007.
10. *Ibid.*
11. See WIPO document SCP/10/2.
12. World Bank, *Global Economic Prospects and Developing Countries,* 2001, World Bank, Washington D.C, 129.
13. CIPR, Integrating Intellectual Property Rights and Development Policy, London, 2002, available at *www.iprcommission.org* last visited on 14th September 2007.
14. See WIPO document A/36/14 for the Memorandum of the Director-General.
15. See Correa M C and Musungu S.F., *The WIPO Patent Agenda: The Risks for Developing Countries*, Trade-Related Agenda Development and Equity Working Papers, South Centre, November 2002, available in *http://www.mihr.org/?q=node/view/125* last visited on 3rd October 2007.
16. See *http://ip-watch.org/weblog/wp-trackback.php?*p=667 last visited on 3rd October 2007.
17. See Hiddleston Sarah, "U.N. Patent Agency Adopts Development Agenda", *The Hindu*, 5th October 2007, 5.

Intellectual Property Disputes and Arbitration

Mallika Taly & Sidharth A. Menon**

INTRODUCTION

There is not much scope for a normative debate on the reasons for the existence of Intellectual Property Rights. The rights of the author, creator, discoverer are to be considered supreme as opposed to that of the non-authors, non-creators and non-discoverers. They are to be accorded all the benefits that arise out of the commercialization of an entity that is the result of application of their respective intellects. We have come to be, in a modern market based economy, where expansion in terms of traditional geographical terms is either not possible or not viable at the moment. As of now, businesses in terms of market expansion perceive intellectual property rights in general and patents in particular to be the final frontier.[4] In the light of these facts the resolution of I.P. Disputes becomes all the more relevant. In a world where knowledge is power, patents will be the smart bombs of tomorrow's business wars.[5] Rhetoric apart, it has to be accepted that the rights over any intellectual property is valuable and throughout the history of mankind the path of anything valuable has been fraught with dispute. It is the functional duty of law to regulate these disputes. In this paper we shall discuss the compatibility of Intellectual Property Disputes and Arbitration as a mode of resolution of such disputes. There are certain features that are unique to I.P. Disputes, different from other disputes that usually come before a court. The questions raised in this paper shall seek to address whether these unique features of an I.P. disputes are in anyway more suitable to be resolved through way of arbitration rather than traditional dispute resolution mechanisms. The exclusion of intellectual property from Alternate Dispute Resolution Mechanisms in most countries was originally by design, rather than by accident. In various nations for public policy reasons, intellectual property cases could not be resolved using

* The authors are fourth year B.A LL.B (Hon's) students from National University of Juridical Sciences, (NUJS), Kolkata.

ADR.[6] Having said so, it wouldn't be unfair to harbor hope that 40 years after the establishment of the World Intellectual Property Organization there would have been change in this regard.

INTELLECTUAL PROPERTY DISPUTES-PECULIAR PROBLEMS & SOLUTIONS

Technical Nature of Disputes

Intellectual Property issues have their own dimension, jurisprudence and political economy.[7] Even a brief look into the field of Intellectual Property Rights and resolution of disputes arising thereof can lead to a wide range of queries and arguments. This can be due to various reasons, one of which is the existence of various different kinds of intellectual property, making it very difficult to find a generalized method for solving Intellectual Property disputes. It is simply not possible to identify a thumb rule that will apply uniformly. For example, patent disputes on one hand would require a particular kind of expertise to solve while geographical indicators will require quite another. The diversity that exists in the nature of the dispute will be the first of many quandaries that must be overcome while considering a solution. Under the scheme of allotment of administration of intellectual property rights under the existing framework we see a similar dilemma. The Department of Industrial Policy and Promotion is the nodal agency for coordinating the process of administration between Department of Higher Education, Department of Information Technology and Department of Agriculture and Cooperation. Thus the magic combination that will work in all situations is an elusive one. When we consider the specific issue of arbitration of Intellectual Property disputes it cannot be blindly applied under all conditions. Even staunchest proponent of ADR would accept that there are situations where it would be safer to continue resolving the dispute through litigation. I propose in the course of this article, to attempt to unearth the pre-conditions that would tip the balance in favor of the practice of arbitrating Intellectual Property disputes.

As mentioned before, there are certain barriers that stand in the way of considering Intellectual Property disputes in the same way as any other normal disputes. One basic distinguishing feature of Intellectual Property disputes is that they are highly technical in nature. This bring into picture incidental difficulties. Technical expertise is required in order to deal with the dispute effectively. The cost of litigation increases as it involves massive research by both the parties to establish their claim. This again increases the length of the proceeding, as this research would have to be presented as evidence before the court. All this would work to the detriment of the parties especially in an Intellectual Property disputes. Arbitration has the potential to remove with one sweep many of these impediments. This potential was recognized by the World Intellectual Property Organization and they have enacted rules with regards to arbitration of Intellectual Property disputes. Article 2 of the WIPO arbitration rules state that: *"Where an Arbitration Agreement provides for arbitration under the WIPO Arbitration Rules, these Rules shall be deemed to form part of that Arbitration Agreement and the dispute shall be settled in accordance with these Rules, as in effect on the date of the commencement of the arbitration, unless the parties have agreed otherwise."*

Most corporation involved in an Intellectual Property disputes often discover that the stakes are too high and decide to stick to the know evil of litigation in fear of encountering an unknown or unpredictable situation. Such conditions arise mostly in patent and trademark cases where even the entire business of the company might be at risk. The counter question to be asked under these circumstances is whether it would be prudent to leave such grave matters in the hands of judges who might lack expertise to reach a reasoned decision. The technical nature of the dispute makes it mandatory for it to ideally be dealt with by a board with at least one person having the technical expertise in that specific field. Such a dispute would more often than not be based on a question of fact as opposed to a question of law. Unlike most other disputes a person deciding an Intellectual Property disputes will not be faced with merely the task of assessing what is right and wrong and a decision can be made only with technical knowledge. Such a board would also facilitate the inclusion of persons with knowledge of the law thus helping in reaching a balanced decision.

Even among Intellectual Property disputes we could locate a dichotomy that exists based on the extent of technical complexity. We could say that patents and other related disputes are relatively more complex than copyright or trademark disputes. This distinction is however blurred as for example even software is accorded copyright protection in most instances and they are highly technical in nature. This classification is based on the argument that the resolution of disputes concerning intellectual property rights of a less-technical nature will require less complicated litigation. It has to be stated however that neither the classification nor the contention is viable mainly because of the reason that such distinctions are too obscure and even if it stands to be of any use will have to be made on a case to case basis. The fact to be considered when choosing between litigation and arbitration should be whether a judge in a conventional court would have the required knowledge to understand and thereby make a decision.

The Limitations on Intellectual Property Disputes and their Arbitrability

There are two arguments made by the scholars who oppose the view that Intellectual Property disputes should be arbitrable. Firstly, what is commonly known as "validity issues."[8] A dispute involving a validity issue questions the validity of a patent, copyright, trademark etc. This means that since conferring a patent or any other intellectual property rights is done by a public authority the validity of such titles cannot be questioned by a private individual and that such issues can be decided only by a court. However, designating a conventional court to deal with such matters would not be always be in the best interest of the parties. For example a patent is granted after a search procedure done by a group of experts in a searching office to check that the entity in question qualifies as an 'invention', the requirements are widely accepted to be an inventive step, commercial viability and usefulness. The person judging the case should be capable of comprehending the intricacies of these procedures when dealing with a validity issue. This might not be efficiently achieved if such cases are brought before a conventional court. Yet Germany[9] and Japan[10] prevent arbitration of a dispute on a validity issue. Secondly, that public policy must be taken into account. Earlier it was considered that since the society has a right to enjoy the fruits of Intellectual Property Rights disputes concerning the same should not be considered behind closed doors by an arbitration tribunal. Intellectual Property disputes often tend to be international in nature. Once limited to a set of relatively anemic treaties that lacked an effective means of international enforcement, international Intellectual Property law has, in the last decade, been transformed by the arrival of a dense array of new institutions and agreements. This dense array of institutions has in turn transformed both the substance and the process of international IP lawmaking.[11] India is a signatory to the Paris Convention, the Berne convention and the Patent Cooperation treaty. Intellectual Property disputes often tend to be international in nature. It is therefore more viable to arbitrate to prevent waste of time and resources in the event of jurisdiction being denied by municipal courts in the concerned country. On the other hand, considering the public policy that exists in every single country would be cumbersome while deciding whether to arbitrate a dispute or not. The public policy in certain countries places a restriction on arbitration of certain kinds of disputes. These restrictions are however based on few general principles and can be easily dealt with. Most nations, which exercise constraint on the power of the parties to refer anything to arbitration, do so with respect to certain specific disputes. The stand taken by different nations on the extent and limitations of the Arbitrability of Intellectual Property dispute has been discussed below.

THE INTERNATIONAL PERSPECTIVE

The World Intellectual Property Organization (WIPO) strongly advocates the use of methods of Arbitration and Mediation for settlement of Intellectual Property Disputes. The WIPO-recognized definition of arbitration states that arbitration is "a neutral procedure in which the dispute is submitted to one or more arbitrators who make a binding decision on the dispute."[12] The WIPO Arbitration Rules[13] are a standing testament to the belief that Intellectual Property issues can and should be settled amicably, through arbitration.

Germany

In Germany, Arbitration matters are dealt with under the last part of the Code of German Civil Procedure known as the "*Zivilprozessordnung*."[14] It lays down the rule for selection of arbitrators, rules for enforcement of awards, requirements for subject matter being at the disposal of the parties, etc. Two primary forms of Intellectual Property Disputes have been seen to arise in Germany namely, validity issues and handled by the Federal Patent Court in the first instance and by the Federal Supreme Court as the second and final instance, infringement matters by the civil courts with special chambers which are competent at the first, second and third instance[15]. With regard to validation issues, the grant of a patent requires an act from the Patent Office which is a public authority, thus this poses a limitation on the capacity of arbitrators to decide the issue, and thus only the Federal Courts have jurisdiction over validity issues. Decidedly, arbitration may be undertaken in infringement matters. Patent rights are assignable, they can be licensed, and of-course, the patentee can renounce his patent rights, thus in Germany, patent infringement matters have no limitation in the field of Arbitration as validation or invalidation issues do.[16]

Japan

The law concerning Arbitrability in Japan is akin to that in Germany. The validity or invalidity of an Intellectual Property Right cannot be a subject of arbitration as it needs to be granted by a Public Office. However, there is no binding opinion on whether or not disputes regarding infringement are arbitrable. While an arbitral award in itself cannot invalidate or validate a patent, for example, if arbitration proceeding are undertaken, the arbitral award will be taken into consideration by the Patent Office in its decision.[17]

Switzerland

The law governing arbitration in Switzerland is known as *lex arbitri.* It is seen as a starting point for the arbitration process, allowing plenty of room for the implementation of other legal regimes concerning arbitration.[18] The Swiss Intercantonal Arbitration Convention of March 27, 1969 governs Swiss domestic arbitration, this document along with the Swiss Private International Law Act of December 18, 1987, Chapter 12 of which deals specifically with rules for international arbitration, provide, specifically for settlement of Intellectual Property Disputes by Arbitration.[19] Thus, all aspects of intellectual property rights are arbitrable in Switzerland without restriction; the Arbitrability of Intellectual Disputes has always been recognized in Switzerland.

United States of America

The view in the United States on the Arbitrability of Intellectual Property Rights Disputes were that by their very nature, Intellectual Property Rights precluded competitors from using the knowledge acquired by the holder of the patent, copyright, trademark, etc. The Courts in and around the year 1983[20] took the view that since this type of monopolization affected public policy, it is for public courts and not private arbitral tribunals to decide the matter[21]. Once such example in 1984 was the Mitsubishi Motors Corporation Case[22], the Honorable Supreme Court of the United States held that the validity of intellectual property rights (patents, trademarks, etc.) is classically non-arbitrable subject matter. However, later this view changed. Section 294(a) of the US Patents Act states: "A contract involving a patent or any right under a patent may contain a provision requiring arbitration of any dispute relating to patent validity or infringement arising under the contract. In the absence of such an agreement, the parties to any existing patent validity or infringement suit may agree in writing to settle such dispute by arbitration". Thus, firmly establishing that Intellectual Property Disputes are arbitrable in the United States.

THE ARBITRABILITY OF INTELLECTUAL PROPERTY DISPUTES IN INDIA

Advantages and Disadvantages of Arbitration Over Litigation

To quote Aristotle, "The arbitrator looks to what is equitable, the judge to what is law; and it was for this purpose that arbitration was introduced, namely, that equity might prevail." It is the flexibility of the Arbitration process that makes it perfectly suited for the settlement of Intellectual Property disputes. The essence of arbitration laws lies in the discretion of the parties to a dispute to choose their own forum for redressal. Arbitration has been the preferred method for dispute resolution for centuries the world over. In Rome there was no struggle between court and tribunals, for the settlement of disputes, it was first the Roman senate and then the Emperor who acted as arbitrators[23]. Arbitration, called "compromise" or "compromissum" was a mode of terminating controversies much favored in civil law[24]. In India, the history of Arbitration finds its beginnings in ancient times. The Ancient Smritis refer to tribunals other that the statutory courts set up by the King. There were three popular forms of courts in these times: the *Puga* (assemblies) *Kulani* (village council) and *Sreni* (corporations). It has been observed that all three of the above courts were, for all practical purposes, arbitration tribunals[25]. The panchayats set up during the pre-British period were proceeding before five persons, who act as the sole and final judges of the matter referred to them by the parties for decision. The corresponding word for 'arbitrator' and 'arbitration' are in-fact *'Panch'* and *'Panchayat.'*[26]

The maturity of arbitration in India leaves us with a wholesome law the prime advantage of which is that it allows amicable resolution of disputes. Arbitration can only be undertaken when an agreement to arbitrate is reached by both parties. The terms of the agreement must be certain and definite, it must be in clear language as it is intended to oust the jurisdiction of the court while seeking recourse in arbitration[27]. The requirement of *consensus ad idem* to bring a dispute before an arbitral tribunal assures a certain degree of amicability during the proceedings. It is even practice for the courts to "suggest(ed) to the parties that having regard to their close relationship... it would be desirable to explore the possibility of settlement or have the dispute resolved through arbitration."[28]

The advantages of choosing arbitration over litigation for settlement of disputes are in abundance. Cost effectiveness, and speed are the oft-cited reasons for undertaking arbitration, this is because Arbitration.[29]

- Is less formal than litigation,
- Allows for less discovery,
- Judicial rules of evidence typically do not apply[30],
- The arbitrator's award is final[31], binding and enforceable in court[32], and
- There are limited appeal rights[33].

Mr. Hornickel, one of the fourteen participants of the Intellectual Property Round-table discussion on IP and Arbitration organized by the American Arbitration Association aptly pointed out that "One [advantage of using arbitration or mediation] is having an answer in one or two years, even if it's not the answer you want. That's better than litigating for five or more years to get the answer you do want."[34]

Overview of Arbitration Laws and their Suitability to IP Disputes

Having discussed the suitability of Intellectual Property disputes for resolution by arbitration I now turn to whether the law concerning arbitration in India is suited to resolve Intellectual Property disputes. There are no laws in place, in India that directly either allow or disallow the settlement of IP disputes through arbitration, like there are in Switzerland or the United States of America. However, there have been instances where Intellectual Property disputes have been brought before an arbitration tribunal, albeit in conjunction with or pursuant to another dispute. For instance in M/s. V.H. Patel and Company and Ors. v. Hirubhai Himabhai Patel and Ors.[35] the Court had recommended that the parties before it go to arbitration for the amicable settlement of the issues arising from the dissolution of their partnership. One of these issues was concerning the usage of the Trademark of the erstwhile partnership firm. The infringement of Intellectual Property Rights carries with it, in most cases, criminal liability. The Copyright Act, 1957 provides for imprisonment for a term which shall not be less than six months but which may extend to three years and with fine which shall not be less than fifty thousand rupees but which may extend to two lakh rupees[36] in case of infringement of Copyright. The Act also sets up a Copyright Board but this Board deals only with very specific issues[37] and cannot be said to provide holistic remedy in case of a dispute. The Patents Act, 1970 provides for a penalty for offences such as Contravention of secrecy provisions relating to certain inventions[38] and making an unauthorized claim to patent rights.[39] The Trade and Merchandise Marks Act, 1958 provides for criminal liability for falsifying and applying for false Trademarks[40], falsely representing a Trademark[41], *interalia*.[42] One of the most precious assets of any Business are its Intellectual Property Rights, patents, copyrights, trademarks, trade secrets and technical knowledge. Thus when an infringement occurs along with criminal liability, an offender is required to recompense the true holder of the Intellectual Property Rights, as it is bound to have caused loss in business or other such private wrong. The Arbitration and Conciliation Act, 1996 provides for such an eventuality. In Kamini Kumar Basu v. Birendra Nath Basu[43] a complaint was pending before the Court under Sections 465,467,193 and 194 of the Indian Penal Code. An agreement was executed whereby the dispute was referred to arbitration. The law as it stands today does not allow dropping criminal charges in lieu of arbitration in the case of a non-compoundable offence, in case of a compoundable offence, the permission of the Court is a necessity. Under Section 320(2) using a false trade or property loss or mark or counterfeiting a trade or property mark used by another or knowingly selling, or exposing or possessing for sale or for manufacturing purpose, goods marked with a counterfeit property mark are compoundable offences and thus require permission from the Court if they are to be dropped in favour of arbitration proceedings. If the criminal complaint and civil dispute subsist, the civil claims will not become void just because the criminal complaint is dropped.[44] The chief concern while discussing whether or not Intellectual Property disputes in a country can be referred to arbitration is whether or not the laws dealing with the subject-matter that can be referred to an arbitral tribunal will allow such disputes to be considered.

Supplementary concerns are, for example, finding the right arbitrators. One of the advantages of choosing arbitration over litigation is the ability of the parties to choose their own arbitrators. A distinction must be made between arbitrators with expert experience and experts deciding a dispute. If an expert it chosen, the process is no longer that of arbitration. However, an arbitrator with expert knowledge or experience is always desirable during the arbitral process, especially when the dispute takes on a highly technical or complex character as Intellectual Property disputes are ant to do. In India, in the absence of any specific bar on IP disputes being sent for arbitration, the laws allow for disputes to be referred as such, it is determinedly so.

CONCLUSION

The winds of change the world over are gently carrying Intellectual property disputes towards arbitration for their resolution. Can India measure up? While the laws in India certainly make it possible settle these disputes through alternative dispute resolution mechanisms, the question still remains a matter of policy, the answer to which lies with the Indian parliament. As has been discussed before Intellectual Property disputes are best suited for arbitration and the arbitral process is more than equipped to handle Intellectual Property disputes. India requires all Intellectual Property to be registered by pubic authorities setup under the specific Acts. Here the objections raised by persons opposed to arbitration of Intellectual Property disputes find validity. Validity issues can not be arbitrable in India, however, infringement matters most certainly can be. Perhaps it is time to take a leaf out of Germany's "*Zivilprozessordnung*" and allow the arbitration of disputes regarding the infringement of Intellectual Property disputes in India, even if arbitration cannot be used for all issues as it is in Switzerland.

NOTES

1. Grantham, W.(1996), *"The Arbitrability of International Intellectual Property Disputes"*, 14 Berkeley *J Int'l L*, 173.
2. Caron, D.D. (2003), *"The World of Intellectual Property and the Decision to Arbitrate"*, 19 Arbitration International 441-449.
3. Available at *http://www.wipo.int/amc/en/arbitration/rules/index.html*, last visited, 16th August, 2007.
4. Ghosh, S. (2007), *"The Merits of Ownership; or How I Learned to Stop Worrying and Love Intellectual Property Law", Harvard Journal of Law and Technology,* available at: *http://ssrn.com/abstract=304480*, last visited on 1st October.
5. Rivette, K. *et al.*, *Rembrandts In The Attic: Unlocking the Hidden Value of Patents* (Boston: Harvard University Press, 1999) p. 200.
6. Yeend, N.N. (2007), *et al*, *"ADR & Intellectual Property: A Prudent Option": The Journal of Law & Technology. http://www.svmediators.com/article_adr.pdf,* last visited 1st October.
7. Biadgleng, ET (2007), *"IP Rights under Investment Agreements: The TRIPS-Plus Implications for Enforcement and Protection of Public Interest"* (August 2006) available at *http://ssrn.com/abstract=943013,* last visited 1st October.
8. Caron, D.D. (2003), *"The World of Intellectual Property and the Decision to Arbitrate"*, 19 Arbitration International 441-449.
9. Pagenberg, J. (2007), *"The Arbitrability of Intellectual Property Disputes in Germany"*, available at *http://www.wipo.int/amc/en/events/conferences/1994/pagenberg.html,* last visited on 1st October.

10. Briner, R. (2007), *"The Arbitrability of Intellectual Property Disputes with Special Emphasis on the Situation in Switzerland"*, available at http:// *www.wipo.int/amc/en/events/conferences/1994/briner.html,* last visited on 1st October.
11. Raustiala, K. (2007), *"Density & Conflict in International Intellectual Property Law"*. University of California at Davis Law Review. available at *http://ssrn.com/abstract=914606,* last visited 1st October.
12. WIPO ADR Procedures, available at *http://www.wipo.int/amc/en/center/wipo-adr.html,* last visited on 1st October, 2007.
13. WIPO Arbitration Rules, available at *http://www.wipo.int/amc/en/arbitration/rules/,* last visited on 1st October, 2007.
14. Cohn, E.J., *"New Regulations in the German Code of Civil Procedure, Journal of Comparative Legislation and International Law"*, 3rd Ser., Vol. 17, No. 1 (1935), pp. 73-81.
15. Pagenberg, J. (2007), *"The Arbitrability of Intellectual property Disputes in Germany"*, available at *http://www.wi(2007) po.int/amc/en/events/conferences/1994/pagenberg.html,* last visited on 1st October.
16. *Ibid.*
17. Briner, R. (2007), *"The Arbitrability of Intellectual Property Disputes with Special Emphasis on the Situation in Switzerland"*, available at *http://www.wipo.int/amc/en/events/conferences/1994/briner.html*, last visited on 1st October.
18. Redfern A. *et al*, *Law and Practice of International Commercial Arbitration,* (London: Sweet & Maxwell 1991), p. 70.
19. Briner, R. (2007), *"The Arbitrability of Intellectual Property Disputes with Special Emphasis on the Situation in Switzerland"*, available at *http://www.wipo.int/amc/en/events/conferences/1994/briner.html*, last visited on 1st October.
20. McConnaughay, P.J. (2007), *"ADR of Intellectual Property Disputes"*, available at *http://www.softic.or.jp/symposium/open_materials/11th/en/PMcCon.pdf,* last visited on 1st October.
21. Plant, D. (1994), *"Arbitrability of Intellectual Property Issues in the United States"*, 5 *Amer. Rev. of Int'l Arb.*, 11, 20.
22. Mitsubishi Motors Corporation v. Soler Chrysler-Plymouth Inc. available at *http://www.usdoj.gov/osg/briefs/1984/sg840160.txt,* last visited on 1st October, 2007.
23. Law Commission of India, Seventy-sixth Report on the Arbitration Act, 1940.
24. Story, Equity Jurisprudence, 2nd Edition, p. 1001, as cited in Chandabssappa v. Baslingayaya AIR 1927 Bom., 565, 567.
25. Law Commission of India, Seventy-sixth Report on the Arbitration Act, 1940.

26. Singh, S.D., *Law of Arbitration*, (Lucknow: Eastern Book Company, 1994), p. 3.
27. Ganpatrai Gupta v. Moody Bros. (1950) 85 CLJ 136.
28. M/s. V.H. Patel and Company and Ors. v. Hirubhai Himabhai Patel and Ors., (2000) 4 SCC 368.
29. Kowalchyk, A. W. (2007), *"Resolving Intellectual Property Disputes Outside of Court: Using ADR to Take Control of Your Case"*, available at *http://findarticles.com/p/articles/mi_qa3923/is_200605/ai_n17185910,* last visited on 1st October.
30. According to Section 19 of the Arbitration and Conciliation Act, 1996, the parties are free to decide the procedure to be undertaken during the proceedings and the tribunal has the power to independently determine rules of evidence. This section corresponds to Article 19 if the UNCITRAL Model Law.
31. Section 35 of the Arbitration and Conciliation Act, 1996, it corresponds to Paragraph 7 of Schedule I of the Arbitration Act, 1940, and is in compliance with Article 35 of the UNCITRAL Model Law.
32. Under Section 36 of the Arbitration and Conciliation Act, 1996, the award of an Arbitral Tribunal is enforceable as if it were a decree of a Court.
33. Section 37 of the Arbitration and Conciliation Act, 1996, it corresponds to Section 39 of the Arbitration Act, 1940.
34. *"Intellectual Property Roundtable: A Discussion of IP and ADR, November 10, 2004 Cleveland, Ohio"*, available at *http://findarticles.com/p/articles/mi_qa3923/is_200502/ai_n13635376*, last visited 1st October, 2007.
35. M/s. V.H. Patel and Company and Ors. v. Hirubhai Himabhai Patel and Ors., (2000) 4 SCC 368.
36. Section 63 of the Copyright Act, 1957.
37. Section 16 of the Copyright Act, 1957.
38. Section 118 of the Patents Act, 1970.
39. Section 120 of the Patents Act, 1970.
40. Section 77 of the Trade and Merchandise Marks Act, 1958.
41. Section 82 of the Trade and Merchandise Marks Act, 1958.
42. Chapter X: Offences, Penalties and Procedure of the Trade and Merchandise Marks Act, 1958.
43. Kamini Kumar Basu v. Birendra Nath Basu, AIR 1930 PC 100.
44. Sukhdeo Rao v. Mangal Chand (1917), 2 PLJ 630 as cited in Singh, S.D., *Law of Arbitration,* (Lucknow: Eastern Book Company, 1994) p. 36.

Understanding Originality in Copyright Law and the Development of an Indian Position on the Protection of Compilation of Facts

*Swayambhu Mukherjee**

INTRODUCTION

The debate between 'creativity' and 'sweat of the brow' or 'industrious creation' schools, coupled with the newly articulated 'skill and judgment' test, centers round the question of whether creativity is a prerequisite for a finding of originality in copyright law. It is one that has originated primarily because of the fact that copyright statutes the world over have chosen not to define the word "original" even though it is a prerequisite for a work to be granted copyright protection. The "sweat of the brow" doctrine, which holds the field in the U.K., suggests that labour or industry alone, even in the absence of a substantial amount of creativity, can be sufficient to bestow copyright upon the author. For example, the labour that is required to compile a database is sufficient to provide copyright protection to the author, as long as it has not been copied from some other pre-existing work. Even though the work involved in compiling such a database is automatic and mechanical in nature, not involving the use of the creative faculties of the author, this does not affect the copyrightability of the work in question. The American school of thought, the creativity school, holds that there cannot be any copyright in the absence of any creativity. According to this line of thought, the test of originality demands that there be at least some amount of creativity involved in the production of the work. To be subject to copyright protection, the work in question must be minimally creative and not be copied. *"More precisely, the creativity requirement subsumes the not–copied requirement."*[1] Labour alone is not enough; the essence of

* Final year, B.A LL.B (Hon's), National University of Juridical Sciences (NUJS) Kolkata.

creativity has to be present. This school believes that merely mechanical rearrangements of pre-existing material are not original even if they have not been copied. The views held by this school have been articulated in a number of cases, for example, *Tele-Direct Publications Inc. v. American Business Information Inc.*[2] and *Feist Publications v. Rural Telephone.*[3] In *Tele-Direct,*[4] for example, it was stated that *"compilations of data are to be measured by standards of intellect and creativity....the word author conveys a sense of creativity and ingenuity."* The Canadian school of thought, comprising proponents of the 'skill and judgment' test, seems to suggest that the exercise of skill and judgment by an author is what gives a work its originality and copyrightability, as opposed to labour alone. It also suggests that creativity alone is not what gives a work its originality.[5] In essence; the debate between the 'creativity' and 'sweat of the brow' or 'industrious creation' schools is *"a far deeper theoretical encounter between two different and incompatible versions of the very meaning and purpose of copyright law."*[6] The 'sweat of the brow' school believes that the purpose of copyright law is to protect the interests of the author and allow him to enjoy the fruits of his labour. On the other hand, the creativity school belongs to the public interest model of copyright law, for which the production and circulation of works in the name of public interest is the key concern.[7] The skill and judgment school, on the other hand, would say that *"[W]hen an author must exercise skill and judgment to ground originality in a work, there is a safeguard against the author being overcompensated for his or her work. This helps ensure that there is room for the public domain to flourish as others are able to produce new works by building on the ideas and information contained in the works of others."*[8] At the end of it all, one can say that the aim of copyright law is to resolve this conflict or tension. This was articulated first by Lord Mansfield in the case of *Sayre v. Moor,*[9] when he wrote, *"We must care to take guard against two extremes equally prejudicial; the one that men of ability who have employed their time for the service of the community, may not be deprived of their just merits, and the reward of their ingenuity and labour, and the other, that the world may not be deprived of any improvements, nor the progress of the arts be retarded. The challenge facing this court, and copyright law generally, is to find a fair and appropriate equilibrium that achieves both goals."* A similar view was articulated by Binnie, J., in *Théberge v. Galerie d'Art du Petit Champlain Inc.,*[10] when he said, *"The Copyright Act is usually presented as a balance between promoting the public interest in the encouragement and dissemination of works of the arts and intellect and obtaining a just reward for the creator or, more accurately, to prevent someone other than the creator from appropriating whatever benefits may be generated."*

ORIGINALITY IN CANADIAN JURISPRUDENCE

Originality as a criterion for copyright seems to be omnipresent: in almost all copyright legislations, it is incorporated. For example, the Canadian Copyright Act,[11] in Section 5, provides that copyright shall subsist in *"every original literary, dramatic, musical and artistic work."* The word 'original' first encompassed the 'sweat of the brow' doctrine, which has been the traditional commonwealth position,[12] and then Canada adopted the *'Feist'*[13] standard followed in the U.S., before finally reaching the 'skill and judgment' test in the *C.C.H* case.[14] To start with an analysis of this journey, we can first look at the *U & R Tax Services* case.[15] Decided in 1995, this case adopted the 'sweat of the brow' theory of copyright protection. It was held, *"industriousness as opposed to creativity is enough to give a work sufficient originality to make it copyrightable."*[16] However, this position changed within a couple of years, with the decision of the Federal Court of Appeal in the *Tele-Direct* case.[17] This case adopted the creativity standard as part of the Canadian jurisprudence.[18] One of the reasons given in support of this position was that if Canada did not adopt this standard, it would fail to meet its North American Free Trade Agreement obligations.[19] This case essentially adopted the *'Feist'* ruling[20] and made it a part of Canadian copyright law. In fact, *"the court expressly found assistance in the U.S. experience."*[21]

Tele-Direct was followed by *C.C.H.* in the Federal Court of Appeal.[22] According to the Federal Court of Appeal in this case, the only pre-condition to copyright in "Anglo-Canadian Law" was that a work be *"independently produced and not copied from another person."*[23] Skill, judgment, labour, knowledge and so forth were all possible indicators of originality but were not required for an independently produced work to receive protection.[24] This case was followed by the *C.C.H* case in the Canadian Supreme Court,[25] which gave shape to the Canadian law as it stands today. However, before going into the details of this case, the case of *Theberge v. Galerie D'Art du Petit Champlain*[26] needs to be studied as it provides the backdrop to this case.

In *Theberge*,[27] the majority of the court, for the first time in Canada, provided an articulation of the balance to be struck between the rights of the creators and the rights of users to works which were copyright protected.[28] More importantly, the Supreme Court shifted away from its previous author-centered approach to an idea that copyright involves a balance between two sets of interests, *"public interest in the encouragement and dissemination of works of the arts and intellect and obtaining a just reward for the creator."*[29] The decision of the Canadian Supreme Court in *C.C.H Canadian Ltd. v. Law Society of Upper Canada*[30] was, in essence, a sequel to the *Theberge* case in that it built upon the concept of copyright law as a balancing act between author's rights and public interest. It should be noted here that this position was first articulated in the *Theberge* case, and later reiterated in the case of *Desputeaux v. Chouette*,[31] before being given a concrete shape in the *C.C.H.* case.[32]

THE C.C.H DECISION: DEVELOPING THE 'SKILL AND JUDGMENT' STANDARD

C.C.H Canadian Ltd. v. Law Society of Upper Canada[33] was the result of concerted efforts by Canadian law book publishers to crack down on what they thought to be copyright infringing activities arising from the 'document delivery' services of the Great Library of the Law Society of Upper Canada. The publishers argued that their products, which included edited reasons for judgments, head notes, case summaries and the like, were protected by copyright, and that the L.S.U.C had violated the provisions of S. 30.2 of the Canadian Copyright Act. The L.S.U.C. contended that copyright did not exist in many of the works of these publishers. It was in this context that the question of what can be termed 'original' under Canadian copyright law came up.

It was held that in Canada, the standard for originality could be best understood and interpreted by using a "skill and judgment" test. It was decided that in order to receive copyright protection, a work must, firstly, "*be more than a mere copy of another work.*"[34] Secondly, it must reflect "*an exercise of skill and judgment.*"[35] This involves the exercise of some kind of intellectual effort. While rejecting the creativity and the sweat of the brow standards, the court said that while the creativity standard is too heavily loaded in favour of public interest, the "sweat of the brow" standard favours the rights of the author over public interest. In fact, it was held that the "*sweat of the brow approach... fails to allow copyright to protect the public's interest in maximizing the production and dissemination of intellectual works.*"[36] And, in elaborating upon the "skill and judgment" standard, McLahlin, C.J., stated that "*the exercise of skill and judgment... must not be so trivial that it could be characterized as a purely mechanical exercise.*"[37] Thus, the *C.C.H.* case provides a new standard for originality, one that requires an independent production of work involving skill and labour. However, the most important implication of the ruling flows not from the standard that it has framed but from the fact that it has identified public interest as a relevant criterion in formulating the standard that is to be applied in determining copyrightability. In fact, it is the first case that has been decided with public interest, and not author's rights, in mind.[38]

SWEAT OF THE BROW: THE TRADITIONAL COMMONWEALTH POSITION

Moving on from the jurisprudence of *C.C.H.*, one comes across the traditional Commonwealth jurisprudence that once held the field in Canada. The 'sweat of the brow' doctrine is generally regarded as the traditional Commonwealth approach to determine originality in authorship for the purposes of copyright law,[39] and this is not without reason. The 'sweat of the brow' doctrine has been operative in England for more than two hundred years now, and this situation does not look like changing. In fact, this rule was affirmed in the U.K. on the same date that the '*Feist*' case[40] was taken up for hearing by the U.S. Supreme Court, in *Waterlow Directories Ltd. v. Reed Information Services Ltd.*[41]

One of the earliest cases on this doctrine and its applicability in public source databases arose in the year 1776, in the case of *Taylor v. Bayne*.[42] This had piracy of the plaintiff's road book as its subject matter. This contention was upheld, and an interdict was granted. In Sayre & *Ors. v. Moor*,[43] the defendant had copied and made alterations to the plaintiff's sea charts. The defendant's charts were of a better quality than the plaintiff's. In this case, the court refused to grant an injunction. Reflecting on the aim of copyright law, Lord Mansfield wrote, "*We must care to take guard against two extremes equally prejudicial; the one that men of ability who have employed their time for the service of the community, may not be deprived of their just merits, and the reward of their ingenuity and labour, and the other, that the world may not be deprived of any improvements, nor the progress of the arts be retarded. The challenge facing this court, and copyright law generally, is to find a fair and appropriate equilibrium that achieves both goals.*"[44] In *Kelly v. Morris*,[45] the defendant had copied some portions from the plaintiff's directory. An injunction was granted against those parts that were copied. In this case too, it was recognised that the plaintiff had a copyright in the facts that he had published. Again, in *Morris v. Ashbee*,[46] the subject matter of the dispute was a business directory, from which the plaintiff had copied some information. An injunction was granted in this case as well. Similarly, in *Morris v. Wright*,[47] the defendant had used the plaintiff's directory for the purposes of verification. A preliminary injunction was first granted, and then this was maintained.

In *Weatherby and Sons v. International Horse Agency and Exchange Ltd.*[48] it was held that the plaintiff was entitled to succeed in an action to restrain the defendant from infringing his copyright in his stud book with its list of brood mares. Significantly, it was held that an action would lie even though no damage was shown. In *Independent Television Publications Ltd. v. Time Out Ltd. & Elliott*,[49] the dispute was with respect to a television programming where a licensing scheme was available. It was held that an injunction could be granted in this case for a copyright infringement. Importantly, this was a case about a sole source database.

The debate about whether mere industriousness should be enough to give a work sufficient originality to make it copyrightable stems from the fact that copyright acts generally remain silent on this point. As a result, various countries across the globe have adopted various positions on this point. In the U.K., the legislature enacted the Copyright, Designs and Patents Act in 1988, and this is currently in force. Yet, despite being enacted in the 1980s, by which time the creativity versus sweat of the brow debate had acquired serious proportions, this act chose to stay silent on this issue. However, even after the coming into force of this act, the 'Sweat of the Brow' doctrine has been reaffirmed in the U.K. This happened in the case of *Waterlow Directories Ltd. v. Reed Information Services Ltd.*[50] In this case, the defendant entered names from the plaintiff's directory into a word processor and sent letters to them to invite them to be included in the defendant's directory. The court applied the principle that a compiler cannot copy facts appearing in a prior copyrighted directory to create another directory. It was held that a publisher may use or refer to a prior copyrighted work only *"for the purpose of directing him where to call"* in order to rediscover the facts appearing in the work. An injunction was granted against the defendant. However, this distinction between lawfully looking at facts in a directory and unlawfully writing them down without rediscovering them appears theoretically troublesome and somewhat trifling on the practical level.[51] This was recognized by the court in the *Waterlow* case when it said that this issue may need further consideration, especially when *"the person takes names and addresses and reproduces them on envelopes or letters"* rather than on to a computer.[52]

It is noteworthy that even though British law has only followed the "Sweat of the Brow" doctrine, the creativity theory also originated in a British court, in the year 1900. This happened in the case of *Walter v. Lane*,[53] where the issue was whether the report of a speech could be given copyright protection and whether the reporter could be considered to be the author for the purposes of copyright law. Lord Robertson's dissenting judgment in this case is often considered to be the paradigmatic "creativity" judgment.[54] According to Lord Robertson, it was difficult to see "*how, in the widest sense of the term author, we are in the region of authorship.*"[55] Lord Robertson's understanding is based on an affirmation of the specificity of the labour of authorship, and, therefore, on a distinction between mental products per se and the specific works of authorship.[56] Thus, for him, there has to be an effort of the mind, even if it is very pedestrian.

The majority judgment in this case went along with the "sweat of the brow" doctrine. This was delivered by Lord Halsbury, and his pronouncement is often considered to be the paradigmatic "sweat of the brow" judgment.[57] For Lord Halsbury, what is at stake is not "authorship" in any special sense, but rather the "grievous injustice" involved in the misappropriation of another's effort. Thus, Lord Halsbury's expansive conception of the word "author" is a part and parcel of a view of copyright as a remedy for misappropriation of one's labour.[58] For Lord Halsbury, no skill of any kind is a prerequisite for any finding of copyrightability. "*If I have not insisted upon the skill and accuracy of those who produce in writing or print spoken words, it is not because I think less of those qualities, but because, as I have endeavoured to point out, neither the one nor the other are conditions precedent to the right created by statute.*"[59] This judgment captures the essence of the "sweat of the brow" school of thought as it exists in the U.K.

THE LAW IN THE U.S.

In the U.S., too, the application of copyright law in cases involving compilation of facts was initially similar to the law as it existed in the U.K.[60] This was brought about by a reliance on English cases such as *Kelly v. Morris*,[61] *Morris v. Ashbee*[62] and *Morris v. Wright*.[63] Proof of this can be found in American decisions such as Leon *v. Pacific Tel. & Tel. Co.*,[64] *Jewelers Circular Publishing Co. v. Keystone Publishing Co.*[65] or *Sampson & Murdock Co. v. Seaver-Radford Co.*[66] However, it was suggested by a number of critics that the "sweat of the brow" theory went against the constitutional scheme of things in the U.S., because the U.S. Constitution only empowered the Congress to enact laws to protect the writings of authors.[67] Nimmer, for example, was of the view that facts could not originate with the author, irrespective of the labour involved in collecting or compiling those facts. For him, this meant that they could not be given copyright protection. What could be protected was the manner in which they could be expressed under copyright law.[68]

This view was upheld in a number of cases, for example, *Rosemont Enterprises, Inc. v. Random House*,[69] *Miller v. Universal City Studios, Inc.*,[70] *Hoehling v. Universal City Studios, Inc.*,[71] *Gardner v. Nizer*,[72] and *Greenbie v. Noble*.[73] Moreover, "*placing published facts off limits conflicted with the policy of encouraging subsequent authors to build upon the efforts of their predecessors by using previously published facts in the creation of new and useful works.*"[74] This contentious issue finally came up for a decision before the Supreme Court in *Feist Publications Inc. v. Rural Telephone Service Co.*[75] This case has been discussed in detail in the following paragraphs.

FEIST IN THE AMERICAN SUPREME COURT[76]

Feist was a publishing company that specialized in the publication of an area-wide telephone directory. For North West Kansas, out of eleven telephone companies, only Rural had denied Feist the permission to use its listings by refusing to grant it a license. The refusal was motivated by a desire to extend its monopoly in providing telephone services to a monopoly in yellow-pages advertising. "*Unable to license Rural's white pages listings, Feist used them without Rural's consent. Feist began by removing several thousand listings that fell outside the geographic range of its area-wide directory, then hired personnel to investigate the 4,935 that remained. These employees verified the data reported by Rural and sought to obtain additional information. As a result, a typical Feist listing includes the individual's street address; most of Rural's listings do not. Notwithstanding these additions, however, 1,309 of the 46,878 listings in Feist's 1983 directory were identical to listings in Rural's 1982-1983 white pages. Four of these were fictitious listings that Rural had inserted into its directory to detect copying.*"[77]

Rural sued Feist for copyright infringement, stating that Feist could not use the information contained in its directory, and that Feist personnel were under a legal obligation to travel door-to-door or conduct a telephone survey in order to rediscover the information for themselves. This argument was based on the "Sweat of the Brow" doctrine. It was rejected by a unanimous decision of the U.S. Supreme Court. The Court in *Feist*[78] held that only the elements of original selection and arrangement used in a directory or other compilation are eligible for copyright protection and that subsequent compilers may freely take the underlying facts in copyrighted compilations for use in their own publications. This essentially means that there can be no copyright over facts and data that are contained in databases. What can be protected are the selection, arrangement and compilation of data. In the ratio of the judgment, it was expressly mentioned that facts in themselves are not copyrightable because of the fact that they are not original to the author. To qualify for copyright protection, a work must be original to the author. *"Original, as the term is used in copyright, means only that the work was independently created by the author (as opposed to copied from other works), and that it possesses at least some minimal degree of creativity. To be sure, the requisite level of creativity is extremely low; even a slight amount will suffice."*[79]

The divergence with the British 'sweat of the brow' position starts here. While the Commonwealth position seeks to protect the labour of the author, by ensuring, among other things, that a person will have to discover facts anew before publishing them in his database (this was relied upon by counsel for Rural in their arguments) the American Constitution allows for the framing of a law only to protect original works.[80] Since facts cannot be called original, it was held that facts could not be given protection by the Copyright Act as that would be unconstitutional. As a result, the creativity test was framed by the Feist court, in keeping with the Constitutional mandate. And, as the judgment itself mentions, factual compilations may be protected as they may possess the required originality, as opposed to facts themselves. The choices as to selection and arrangement, so long as they are made independently and entail minimum amount of creativity, are sufficiently original for the Congress to protect them with enactments. However, this protection is also subject to the limitation that copyright protection extends only to those works which are original to the author, and not the work as a whole. The facts themselves do not become original through association. This decision is important for another reason. It seeks to preclude the creation of a monopoly in facts lying in the public domain, thereby placing public interest ahead of proprietary interests in the creation of such a monopoly.

DEVELOPMENT OF INDIAN JURISPRUDENCE ON ORIGINALITY AND THE PROTECTION OF COMPILATION OF FACTS

Now we come to the position in India. In India, database rights and copyright in databases is an emerging field, and not too many cases have been decided on this or other related subjects. The ones that had been decided earlier indicated that the law in India should be similar to that followed in the United Kingdom. Historically, the two countries have shared similar copyright laws and many cases seem to indicate that the jurisprudence in both countries is roughly identical, with an emphasis on protecting a man's labour. For example, S. 3A protects databases in the U.K. by classifying it as a literary work. This section reads *"a collection of works, data or other materials which are arranged in a systematic or methodical way, and are individually accessible by electronic or other means."*[81] In India, too, databases have been treated as literary work. S. 2(o) of the of the Copyright Act reads, *"literary work includes computer programs, tables and compilations including computer databases."*[82]

RELIANCE ON ENGLISH JURISPRUDENCE

The similarity in approach could be seen in a number of decisions too. For example, in the case of *Macmillan and Co. v. K.J. Cooper*,[83] it was held that for a work to be entitled to copyright protection, *"independent labour must be apparent"* and that *"it is necessary that labour, skill and capital should be expended sufficiently to impart to the product some quality or character which the raw material does not possess and which differentiate the product from the raw material."*[84] This view, which formed a part of the common Anglo-Indian jurisprudence of its time, was later accepted in a number of cases such as *Camlin Pvt. Ltd. v. M/s National Pencil Industries*,[85] *Mishra Bandhu Karyalaya v. S. Koshal*,[86] *S.K. Dutt v. Law Book Co.*,[87] *V. Errabhadra Rao v. B.N. Sharma*,[88] and *C. Cunniah & Co. v. Balraj & Co.*[89].

In *Camlin Pvt. Ltd. v. M/s National Pencil Industries*,[90] it was held that *"in order to be covered by the Copyright Law, any work in which copyright is claimed must originate from the author who must have expended his skill and labour and the work must be something which has not been copied by the author from anyone else. It is only then that it can be said to have been originated from the author."*[91] In coming to this conclusion, this case relied upon two English cases: *Leslie v. J. Young and Sons*,[92] and *Ladbroke (Football) Ltd. v. William Hill (Football) Ltd.*[93] In both of them, there was an emphasis upon the labour expended in the creation of the work sought to be protected. This approach had been adopted by the Indian Courts too. More than anything else, the Indian approach seemed to be to try and ensure that the fruits of a man's labour are not appropriated by someone else. As a result, the law as it then stood would protect facts in a compilation simply because of the labour that had been expended in collecting it. If someone else wanted to use those facts, he had to discover them anew. He could only look at a previously existing database to find out where to call in order to gather that data afresh This is different from the American approach. In the U.S., it has been decided that facts cannot be protected; facts could not originate with the author, irrespective of the labour involved in collecting or compiling those facts. This was in keeping with the Constitutional mandate in that country to protect the original writings of authors.[94]

Indian jurisprudence on this point was also different from Canadian law as stated by the Canadian Supreme Court in *C.C.H.*[95] The Canadian position focuses more on the skill and judgment used in the creation of a work of authorship and less on the labour used in creating it while determining whether a work is eligible to receive copyright protection. This position also seeks to strike a balance between *"public interest in the encouragement and dissemination of works of the arts and intellect and obtaining a just reward for the creator."*[96] In fact, in the *C.C.H.* case, the "Sweat of the Brow" test was rejected for this reason alone. Speaking on the "sweat of the brow" test, McLahlin, C.J., stated, *"Sweat of the brow standard fails to allow copyright to protect the public's interest in maximizing the production and dissemination of intellectual works."*[97]

As opposed to the promotion of public interest by encouraging the dissemination and creation of intellectual works, the "Sweat of the Brow" standard seeks to ensure that the fruits of a man's labour are not appropriated by someone else. This is what sets it apart from the Canadian, and, to an extent, the American position as well. The law as it stood in India was more of a private law than a public one, and was roughly similar to the position in the U.K. The presumption we can draw from this is that Indian jurisprudence had been relying too heavily on the English understanding of what laws should be like, and this had an adverse effect on the development of Indian jurisprudence in this field. This was brilliantly articulated by Mr. Rajeev Dhawan in an article[98] where he propounded the concept of the *"Black Letter Law Tradition."* He suggested that the modern legal system in India developed under the aegis of British rule and, as a result, could not shake off the colonial influences that led to its creation. This has been the case even after independence, and, as in all other fields, copyright law has also been shaped by English jurisprudence. *"Mature versions of Black Letter Law Tradition were kept alive by contacts with English jurisprudence and English legal education........Mainstream scholarship in Indian law continues to espouse the narrow Black Letter Law Tradition. It is concerned with a knowledge of statute and case law."*[99] The emphasis, as has been rightly pointed out, is on knowledge of statute and case law, rather that a thorough understanding and development of the same. As a result, the Indian law in most fields only served to reflect the English position, and the concept of sweat of the brow in protecting compilations of facts is no exception.

THE EASTERN BOOK COMPANY CASE: A RADICAL SHIFT IN THE INDIAN POSITION

The Indian position underwent a radical change with the Supreme Court's ruling in *Eastern Book Company v. D.B. Modak*,[100] wherein it was opined that in matters relating to the compilation of certain facts, the standards that are required are a minimum level of creativity and the exercise of skill and judgment. This pronouncement means that the Court has now adopted a combination of the U.S. and Canadian positions as the Indian position on this issue. The Court stated, "*No doubt the appellants have collected the material and improved the readability of the judgment by putting inputs in the original text of the judgment by considerable labour and arranged it in their own style, but that does not give the flavour of minimum, requirement of creativity. The exercise of the Skill and judgment required to produce the work is trivial and is on account of the labour and the capital invested and could be characterized as purely a work which has been brought about by putting some amount of labour by the appellants. Although for establishing a copyright, the creativity standard that applies is not that something must be novel or non-obvious, but some amount of creativity in the work to claim a copyright is required. It does require a minimal degree of creativity.*"

CONCLUSION

It has to be said that this judgment is a step in the right direction, and is in accordance with the spirit of copyright law, which seeks to protect that which is the creation of a man's intellect, not that which is the fruit of his labours. Works that have necessitated the expenditure of time, labour and money alone cannot be classified as original literary works. Moreover, facts do not originate with the author, and therefore, protecting facts through copyright law goes against the concept of copyright as an intellectual property right. Such protection would also be in violation of the letter and spirit of the Berne Convention for the Protection of Literary and Artistic Works, 1886. In the long run, a separate statute needs to be enacted for compilations of facts, and this should have a separate yardstick for determining originality, which is different from that given to literary works as per existing copyright statutes. This should keep in mind the fact that databases are different in nature from other literary works in that there is very little scope for originality in them, because facts cannot originate with an author, but compiling them needs labour, money and skill. Moreover, such a law should also keep in mind the fact that some protection should be given to compilations of facts, so as to serve as an incentive for the publishing industry, but that this protection should not be too stringent or excessive, because that would deter the creation of a strong public domain of facts.

NOTES AND REFERENCE

1. Drassinower, A. (2008), Sweat of the Brow, Creativity, and Authorship: On Originality in Canadian Copyright Law, (2003-04) 1 U.O.L.T.J. 105, at page 108, available online at *www.uoltj.ca / articles / vol1.1-2 / 2003-2004.1.1-2.uoltj.Drassinower.105-123.pdf,* last visited on 18th March, 2008.
2. Tele-Direct Publication Inc. v. American Business Information Inc., [1998] 2 F.C. 22.
3. Feist Publication v. Rural Telephone, 499 U.S. 340 (1991) 1282.
4. Tele-Direct Publication Inc. v. American Business Information Inc., [1998] 2 F.C. 22.
5. C.C.H Canadian Ltd. v. Law Society of Upper Canada, [2004] S.C.C. 13.
6. Drassinower, A. (2008), Sweat of the Brow, Creativity, and Authorship: On Originality in Canadian Copyright Law, (2003-04) 1 U.O.L.T.J. 105, at page 108-109, available online at www.uoltj.ca/articles/vol1.1-2/2003-2004.1.1-2.uoltj.Drassinower.105-123.pdf, last visited on 18th March.
7. Mazeh, Y. (2008), Canadian Originality and the Tension Between the Commonwealth and the American Standards for Copyright Protection: The Myth of Tele-Direct, (2003) 16 I.P.J. 561, as given in Drassinower, A., Sweat of the Brow, Creativity, and Authorship: On Originality in Canadian Copyright Law, (2003-04) 1 U.O.L.T.J. 105, at page 107, available online at *www.uoltj.ca / articles / vol1.1-2 / 2003-2004.1.1-2.uoltj.Drassinower.105-123.pdf,* last visited on 18th March.
8. C.C.H Canadian Ltd. v. Law Society of Upper Canada, [2004] S.C.C. 13, at paragraph 23.
9. Sayre v. Moor, (1785) 102 E.R. 139, at p. 140.
10. Theberge v. Galerie D'Art du Petit Champlain Inc., 2002 S.C.C 34.
11. R.S.C. 1985, c. C-42, available online at http://laws.justice.gc.ca/en/c-42/ last visited on 18th March, 2008.
12. Drassinower, A. (2008), Sweat of the Brow, Creativity, and Authorship: On Originality in Canadian Copyright Law, (2003-04) 1 U.O.L.T.J. 105, at page 109, available online at www.uoltj.ca/articles/vol1.1-2/2003-2004.1.1-2.uoltj.Drassinower.105-123.pdf, last visited on 18th March, 2008.
13. Feist Publications Inc. v. Rural Telephone Service Co., 499 U.S. 340 (1991) 1282.

14. C.C.H Canadian Ltd. v. Law Society of Upper Canada [2004] S.C.C. 13
15. U&R Tax Services Ltd. v. H & R Block Canada Inc., 62 C.P.R. (3d) 257.
16. *Ibid*. at p. 264.
17. Tele Direct (Publications) Inc. v. American Business Information Inc. [1998] 2 F.C. 22; 76 C.P.R. (3d) 296.
18. *Ibid*., at pp. 303, 308.
19. Craig, C.J., The Evolution of Originality in Canadian Copyright Law: Authorship, Reward and the Public Interest, (2005) 2:2 U.O.L.T.J. 425, available online at www.uoltj.ca/articles/vol2.2/2005.2.2.uoltj.Craig.425-445.pdf, last visited on 18th March, 2008.
20. Feist Publications Inc. v. Rural Telephone Service Co., 499 U.S. 340 (1991) 1282
21. Craig, C.J., The Evolution of Originality in Canadian Copyright Law: Authorship, Reward and the Public Interest, (2005) 2:2 U.O.L.T.J. 425, at p. 428, available online at *www.uoltj.ca / articles / vol2.2 / 2005.2.2.uoltj.Craig.425-445.pdf,* last visited on 18th March, 2008.
22. [2002] 2 F.C. 451.
23. *Ibid*. at paragraph 36.
24. *Ibid*., at paragraph 53.
25. C.C.H. Canadian Ltd. v. Law Society of Upper Canada, [2004] S.C.C. 13.
26. Theberge v. Galerie D'Art du Petit Champlain [2002] S.C.R. 336.
27. *Ibid.*
28. *Ibid.*
29. *Ibid*., at paragraph 30-31.
30. C.C.H. Canadian Ltd. v. Law Society of Upper Canada, [2004] S.C.C. 13.
31. Desputeaux v. Chouette [2003] S.C.C. 17.
32. C.C.H Canadian Ltd. v. Law Society of Upper Canada, [2004] S.C.C. 13
33. *Ibid.*
34. *Ibid.*
35. *Ibid*., at paragraph 24.
36. *Ibid*., at paragraph. 24.
37. *Ibid*., at paragraph 25.
38. Craig, C.J., The Evolution of Originality in Canadian Copyright Law: Authorship, Reward and the Public Interest, (2005) 2:2 U.O.L.T.J. 425, at p. 439, available online at *www.uoltj.ca / articles / vol2.2 / 2005.2.2.uoltj. Craig.425-445.pdf,* last visited on 18th March, 2008.
39. Drassinower, A., Sweat of the Brow, Creativity, and Authorship: On Originality in Canadian Copyright Law, (2003-04) 1 U.O.L.T.J. 105, at page 109, available online at *www.uoltj.ca / articles / vol1.1-2 / 2003-2004.1.1-2.uoltj.Drassinower.105-123.pdf,* last visited on 18th March, 2008.

40. Feist Publications Inc. v. Rural Telephone Service Co., 499 U.S. 340 (1991) 1282.
41. Waterlow Directories Ltd. v. Reed Information Services Ltd. (1990) 20 I.P.R. 69; [1992] F.S.R. 409 (Ch. 1990).
42. Taylor v. Bayne, (1776) 10 Mor. Dict. 8308 (Scot.).
43. Sayre & Ors. v. Moor, (1785) 102 E.R. 139.
44. *Ibid.*, at p. 140.
45. Kelly v. Morris, (1866) L.R. 1 Eq. 697.
46. Morris v. Ashbee, (1866) L.R. 7 Eq. 34.
47. Morris v. Wright, (1870) L.R. 5 Ch. App. 279.
48. Weatherby and Sons v. International Horse Agency and Exchange Ltd. [1910] 2 Ch. 297.
49. Independent Television Publications Ltd. v. Time Out Ltd. & Elliott, [1984] F.S.R. 64 (C.A. 1983).
50. Waterlow Directories Ltd. v. Reed Information Services Ltd., (1990) 20 I.P.R. 69; [1992] F.S.R. 409 (Ch. 1990).
51. Arden, Thomas P., The Conflicting Treatments of Compilations of Facts under the United States and British Copyright Laws, *A.I.P.L.A.Q.J.* Vol. 19: 267 No. 4 1991, available online at www.mbc.com/db30/cgi-bin/pubs/TPA-Conflicting_Treatments.pdf, last visited on 18th March, 2008.
52. Waterlow Directories Ltd. v. Reed Information Services Ltd., (1990) 20 I.P.R. 69; [1992] F.S.R. 409 (Ch. 1990).
53. Walter v. Lane, [1900] A.C. 539.
54. Drassinower, A., Sweat of the Brow, Creativity, and Authorship: On Originality in Canadian Copyright Law, (2003-04) 1 U.O.L.T.J. 105, at page 113, available online at *www.uoltj.ca/articles/vol1.1-2/2003-2004.1.1-2.uoltj.Drassinower.105-123.pdf,* last visited on 18th March, 2008.
55. Walter v. Lane, [1900] A.C. 539, at p. 561.
56. Drassinower, A., Sweat of the Brow, Creativity, and Authorship: On Originality in Canadian Copyright Law, (2003-04) 1 U.O.L.T.J. 105, at pages 114-116, available online at *www.uoltj.ca/articles/vol1.1-2/2003-2004.1.1-2.uoltj.Drassinower.105-123.pdf,* last visited on 18th March, 2008.
57. *Ibid.*, at p. 113.
58. *Ibid.*
59. Walter v. Lane, [1900] A.C. 539, at p. 549.
60. Arden, Thomas P., The Conflicting Treatments of Compilations of Facts under the United States and British Copyright Laws, A.I.P.L.A.Q.J. Vol. 19: 267 No. 4 1991, available online at *www.mbc.com/db30/cgi-bin/pubs/TPA-Conflicting_Treatments.pdf,* last visited on 18th March, 2008.

61. Kelly v. Morris, (1866) L.R. 1 Eq. 697.
62. Morris v. Ashbee, (1866) L.R. 7 Eq. 34.
63. Morris v. Wright, (1870) L.R. 5 Ch. App. 279.
64. Leon v. Pacific Tel. & Tel. Co., 91 F.2d 484, (9th Cir. 1937).
65. Jewelers Circular Publishing Co. v. Keystone Publishing Co., 281 F. 83, 88-90 (2d Cir. 1922).
66. Sampson & Murdock Co. v. Seaver-Radford Co., 140 F. 539, (1st Cir. 1905).
67. U.S. Constitution. Art. I, §8, cl. 8.
68. Nimmer on Copyright §2.03[E], pp. 2-34.1—2-34.2 (1988).
69. Rosemont Enterprises, Inc. v. Random House, Inc. 366 F.2d 303, 310 (2d Cir. 1966), cert. denied, 385 U.S. 1009 (1967).
70. Miller v. Universal City Studios, Inc., 650 F.2d 1365, 1370-72 (5th Cir. 1981).
71. Hoehling v. Universal City Studios, Inc. 618 F.2d 972, 974, 979-80 (2d Cir.), cert. denied, 449 U.S. 841 (1980).
72. Gardner v. Nizer,391 F. Supp. 940, 943-44 (S.D.N.Y. 1975).
73. Greenbie v. Noble, 151 F. Supp. 45, 67-68 (S.D.N.Y. 1957).
74. Rosemont Enterprises, Inc. v. Random House, Inc. 366 F.2d 303, 310 (2d Cir. 1966), cert. denied, 385 U.S. 1009 (1967)., as given in Arden, Thomas P., The Conflicting Treatments of Compilations of Facts under the United States and British Copyright Laws, *A.I.P.L.A.Q.J.* Vol. 19: 267 No. 4 1991, available online at www.mbc.com/db30/cgi-bin/pubs/TPA-Conflicting_Treatments.pdf, last visited on 18th March, 2008.
75. Feist Publications Inc. v. Rural Telephone Service Co., 499 U.S. 340 (1991) 1282.
76. *Ibid.*
77. *Ibid.*, at para. 6, per O' Connor, J.
78. Feist Publications Inc. v. Rural Telephone Service Co., 499 U.S. 340 (1991) 1282.
79. *Ibid.*, at para 10, per O' Connor, J.
80. *Ibid.*, at para 11, per O' Connor, J.
81. The Copyright, Designs and Patents Act, 1988.
82. The Indian Copyright Act, 1957.
83. Macmillan and Co. v. K.J. Cooper, A.I.R. 1924 P.C. 75
84. *Ibid.*
85. Camlin Pvt. Ltd. v. M/s National Pencil Industries, A.I.R. 1986 Del. 444.
86. Mishra Bandhu Karyalaya v. S. Koshal, A.I.R. 1970 M.P. 261.
87. S.K. Dutt v. Law Book Co., A.I.R. 1954 All. 570.

88. V. Errabhadra Rao v. B.N. Sharma, A.I.R. 1960 A.P. 415.
89. C. Cunniah & Co. v. Balraj & Co., A.I.R. 1961 Mad. 111.
90. Camlin Pvt. Ltd. v. M/s National Pencil Industries, A.I.R. 1986 Del. 444.
91. *Ibid.*, at p. 448.
92. Leslie v. J. Young and Sons, [1894] A.C. 335.
93. Ladbroke (Football) Ltd. v. William Hill (Football) Ltd., (1964) 1 All E.R. 465.
94. U.S. Constitution. Art. I, §8, cl. 8.
95. C.C.H Canadian Ltd. v. Law Society of Upper Canada [2004] S.C.C. 13.
96. Theberge v. Galerie D'Art du Petit Champlain, [2002] S.C.R. 336, at para. 30-31.
97. C.C.H Canadian Ltd. v. Law Society of Upper Canada, [2004] S.C.C. 13.
98. Dhavan, R., Introduction, at p. xiii, Galanter, M., Law and Society in Modern India, Oxford University Press, London, 1st edn., 1993.
99. *Ibid.*, at p. xx-xxi.
100. Eastern Book Company v. D.B. Modak, (2008)1 S.C.C. 1 .

UNEMPLOYMENT AND JOBLESS GROWTH IN INDIA UNDER THE ERA OF GLOBALISATION

*V. S. Adigal**

INTRODUCTION

Inequality, Inflation and unemployment are three major problems that the capitalist economies have been facing continuously all the time and none of them have succeeded in overcoming these problems. Therefore these problems are taken as in-built features of the capitalist system. In the less developed capitalist economies such as India. We have the fourth problem viz.. Absolute Poverty, i.e. denial of minimum subsistence to a large section of the population. Of these four problems, admittedly, the problem of unemployment is the most serious, because inequality and poverty are derived from and in fact, intensified by unemployment. Though the term unemployment is used in a general sense in relation to non-utilisation of all the 4 factors of production viz.. Land, Labour, Capital, and Enterprise, the term is most commonly and more specifically used in relation to labour. Unemployment of labour is considered as the most serious problem in comprison to unemployment of other factors of production, because labour being a human factor, it's unemployment or idleness has the social, economic and political impacts. In fact, The Human Development Report (1993) talked of the "humanising role" of employment when it said, "Employment empowers people economically by giving them purchasing power for goods and services. It empowers them socially by offering a productive role that enhances their dignity and self-esteem. And it can empower them politically if they being to influence decision-making in the workplace and beyond." (UNDP-HDR. 1993. P. 34). It is for this reason that all over the world today there is talk of the Right to work being treated as a fundamental right. The left parties in India in fact incororate this in their national manifestoes.

* Principal & Head Department of Business Economics, Manjunath College of Commerce, Kanchangaon, Khambalpada, Thakttrli (East), Dist-Thane-421201

MEANING AND DEFINATION

Unemployment of labour is defined as a situation in which any person, being not below the age of 15 years: physically and mentally fit: (capacity of working): willing to work and ready to accept the market wage: is not able to secure a job.

Thus unemployment is a situation of joblessness. This is also called involuntary unemployment. It leaves out from its scope those who are children below 15 years: those who are physically or mentally unfit: those who are voluntarily unemployed by being not ready to work or by demanding a wage higher than what the market offers. While it includes Rural, Urban, Educated, Open, Cyclical etc. Unemployment, it excludes such important types of unemployment as disguised/hidden unemployment and under-employment. Unemployment has been one of the most serious and unmanageable problems faced by India. Unemployment refers to a situation in which people who are willing able to work remain jobless.

According to Samuelson "employed people are those people who perform any paid work, but as well as those who have jobs but are absent from work because of illness, strikes or vacations".

"Unemployment includes those people who are not employed but are actively looking for work or waiting to return to work".

"Unemployment refers to a situation when a person who is willing to work fails to get a job at the prevailing wage rate. It implies involuntary idleness".

"By unemployment we mean that state of affairs when in an economy there are large number of able bodied persons of working age, who are willing to work, able to work, but can not find employment at the current prevailing wage rate".

The concept of unemployment is restricted only to able bodied adults belonging to the age group of 15-60 years who constitute the working population. Unemployment is measured as a ratio between the unemployed and the total labour force. The term labour force includes all persons who have been working or seeking jobs or available for work.

Under Employment

"A person is considered to be underemployed if he is forced by unemployment to take a job that he thinks is not adequate for his purpose or not commensurate with his training".

Under employment refers to a situation when the capacity of a person is not fully and properly use. If a B.Com graduate is appointed as peon a in a bank his talents in accountancy remain under utilized. When a person does not get a full time work, it is also called under employment. In other words what they earn from the present job is very little or insufficient and they live below the line of poverty. Casual laboures is agricultural sector, hawkers petty traders workers in service and repair shops etc in urban area fall under this criteria.

Criteria of Unemployment

Prof. Rajkrisha presents four criteria to determine whether a person is unemployed or under employed.

1. Time criterion: If a person is gainfully occupied during the year for a number of hours (or days) less than some normal or optimal hour (or days) defined as full employment hour (or days).
2. Income criterion: If the earns an income per year less than some desirable minimum.
3. Willingness criterion: If he is willing to do more work than he is doing at present on terms to which he is accustomed and
4. Productivity criterion. If he is removable from his present employment in the sense that his contribution to output is less than normal productivity and there fore his removal would not reduce the output.

ESTIMATES OR EXTENT OF UNEMPLOYMENT IN INDIA

There are conceptual and statistical difficulties in estimating the magnitude of unemployment in India. The Planning Commission, the census Reports, the National Sample Surveys (NSS) and the Committee of Experts on Unemployment (Bhagwati Committee) have all estimated the magnitude of unemployment in India. But none of them is accurate.

Unemployment in India (1971)
Report of Bhagwati Committee (1973)

	Total number of Unemployed (in Milli ons)	*Total labour force Force (in millions)*	*Unemployment as a Percentage of Total labour force*
Rural	16.1	146.8	10.9
Urban	2.6	32.0	8.1
Total	18.7	180.4	10.4

Thus, according to the Bhagwati Committee 16.1 million were unemployed in rural areas and 2.7 million in urban areas in 1971. By March 1978, 21 mn people were unemployed of which 16.5 mn were in rural areas and 4.5 mn in urban areas.

Estimates of Unemployment during Plan Periods

	Period	*Backlog of unemployment at the beginning of the plan (in million)*
I Plan	(1951-56)	3.3
II Plan	(1956-61)	5.3
III Plan	(1961-66)	7.1
Annual Plans	(1966-69)	9.6
IV Plan	(1969-74)	10.1
VI Plan	(1980-85)	14.0
VII Plan	(1985-90)	12.02
VIII Plan	(1992-97)	28.0

The table shows that the backlog of unemployment increased at the end of every Five–Year Plan except in the 6th and 7th Plan. Recently the NSS has introduced the following concept relating to unemployment.

National Sample Survey

Usual Principal Status (UPS): A person is unemployed if he/she was not working but was either seeking or was available for work for the major part of the reference year.

Current Weekly Status (CWS): A person is unemployed if he/she had not worked even one hour during the week, but is seeking or available for work.

Current Daily Status (CDS): Unemployment is measured in terms of aggregate of all unemployment days of all persons during the reference.

Unemployment Rates in India (Period 1993-94 to 2004)

	Rural			*Urban*		
Status	*Male*	*Female*	*Total*	*Male*	*Female*	*Total*
Usual-principal status	24	22	23	46	86	53
Current weekly status	47	45	46	57	90	64
Current daily status	90	93	91	81	117	88

Source: Nsso's 60th Round survey on employment and Unemployment Conducted in January-June 2004.

Unemployment Rates: number of persons (or person days) unemployed per 1000 persons (or person days).

In the above table UPSS and CWS which are treated as measure of chronic unemployment rate remain very high during the period 1993-94 to 1999-2000. The CDS which is considered as comprehensive measure of both chronic and invisible unemployment has also increased during the same period. Unemployment rates for both male and female have increased. Female unemployment rate in terms of current daily status is higher than that of male. Unemployment rates on the basis of current daily status are much higher than those on the basis of usual status.

Extent of Educated Unemployment

According to the Ministry for Labour and Employment, the umber of educated unemployed was around 2.44 lakh in 12951. It rose to 68 lakh in 1992. Educated unemployment prevails in rural area also. At present rural areas have about 40 per cent of the educated but more than half of the educated are unemployed. The noticeable feature of educated unemployment is that the rate of unemployment among the highly educated population is much higher than unemployment rate among people with low level of education.

Trend

(i) Incidence of unemployment is much higher in urban than in rural areas. However the differences has been considerably reduced.

(ii) Unemployment rates for women are higher than those for men Underemployment is of much higher proportion among the former than the latter.

(iii) There has been a shift from wide spread underemployment towards greater open unemployment.

(iv) There is large scale interstate difference in unemployment rate.

The states like Kerala, West Bengal, Tamilnadu and Assam show higher rate unemployment while poorer and less literate states like M.P U.P Bihar and Rajasthan have relatively lower rates of open unemployment.

(v) Employment among women witnessed a rapid rise compared to men in urban areas. This is an indicator of the growing informalisation of the economy.

(vi) Unemployment rate among the younger age group (15-29) remains very high.

Economic planning began in India in 1951 and the Ninth Five Year Plan commenced in 1997 and will end in 2002. Indian planners have always emphasied the importance of employment. However, at the end of each plan, there has been an increasing backlog of unemployed. While the growth of population and demographic reasons have been advanced for this trend, the fact remains that it is the failure of planning-economic and social-that is responsible for the huge size of the unemployment in the country. The situation has gone from bad to worse. At the end of the Seventh Five Years Plan, members of the Planning Commission observed that "The gravest crisis Indian political, economic and social order faces today is the mounting unemployment. Nothing exposes the barrenness of pure growth rate approach than the empirical results of the decade of the eighties in India. The GDP has shot up from 3.5 per cent to 5.3 per cent in the period, but the employment growth rate has fallen from 2.82 during 1973-78 to 1.55 per cent during 1983-88. In agriculture it has declined from 1.8 per cent to an insignificant 0.07 per cent in the 15 year period ending 1988." The Eighth Plan (1992-1997) in its Approach Paper observed: "The central thrust of the eighth plan is employment. The plan will seek to give operational content to the commitment to guarantee the right to work to every citizen through appropriate development programmes." The failure of the government to tackle the problem of unemployment from time to time, compelled it however, to talk of self-employment rather than the state's responsibility of providing gainful employment to all able-bodied persons in the country.

WORSENING SITUATION

The Ninth Five Year Plan (1997-2002) came at a time when the economic, social and political situation was precarious and one of the most daunting challenges facing the nation was to provide employment for the additions to the labour force and to reduce the backlog of unemployment. Despite an expected reduction in the growth rate of population to 1.59 per cent per annum by the end of the Ninth plan, the growth of labour force reaches a peak level of 2.54 per cent per annum during the period. This will be the highest growth of labour force in the country in our history and in fact it will be the highest that India would ever experience in the future. This is because of the change in the structure of population in the age-group 15-19 years. The data indicate that the population increased to a level of 1027 million by 2001. The age structure of the population changes in response to fertility behavior experienced in the past, and projected in the future. The proportion of the population in the most active working age group 15-59 years goes up significantly during the plan period. The requirement of work opportunities will increase by 53 million in the Ninth Plan, followed by an increase of 59 million in the five year period of 2002-2007, and a mild reduction to 56 million in the next five year period 2007-2012.

Projection of Unemployed for 1990-2000	*(in millions)*
Backlog of unemployed in the beginning of 1990	28
New entrants to the labour force during 1990-95	37
Total unemployed during the Eighth Plan (1+2)	65
New entrants to the labour force during 1995-2000	41
Total unemployed for the Ninth Plan (3+4)	106

The largest number of persons unemployed n the world will be in India as per the projection of the United Nations. Tremendous efforts will therefore be necessary in the Ninth Plan period itself if the nation is to be saved in the post-Ninth Plan period that is in the twenty-first century.

CAUSES FOR THE CATASTROPHE

The situation will be alarming in the country just a few years from now. Unfortunate part of the story is that only a few have even recognised the nature and the seriousness of the problem. Even those who have recognised the problem do not have either a rational solution to the problem or the solution that they offer in the form of Free Market economic policies of Privatisation, Libralisation, Marketisation and Globalisation, can only aggravate the situation. International economic and social analyses have preferred to describe the situation as "India will be sitting dangerously on the unemployment bomb". What has gone wrong?

(a) *Growth of Population:* This is one of the many factors. From about 252 million in 1911 (251 million in 1921) India has grown to 846 million as per 1991 census. In 2002 the figure will be reach 1027.61 million: in 2007 it will be 1107.51 million: and in 2012 it will be 1200.67 million. To provide employment to the teeming millions is a stupendous task.

(b) *Lesser Economic Growth:* The absorption of labour in the economy depends on the growth of the economy and level of development. Inspite of economic planning from 1951, economic growth has been much smaller than what India needed and which we could have achieved under different conditions.

(c) *Wrong Priorities in the Plans:* Though Jawaharlal Nehru adopted what he called "the socialist pattern of society", in fact it has created an economic climate for the capitalists to grow at the cost of the nation, taking advantage of the public sector and the infrastructure.

(d) *Capitalist Part of Growth and Development:* The most serious cause of the present state of economic, social and political crisis in the country is the growth path that was accepted and adopted in the fifties. Though it was called a mixed economy tilting towards the left and being to the left of the middle, in fact, except for the public sector being established and some important sectors of the public sector being under the control of the state, the economy was charted a clear course for capitalist development. Capitalist cannot and does not provide employment to all those eligible to be employed. This is a truth established by economic history. Karl Marx not only established this fact but went on to point out that the levels of employment will necessarily fluctuate from year to year in the capitalist system due to the chaotic nature of production relationship. He asserted that in order to face the ups and downs of production, the capitalist will necessarily have to create a Reserve of the Unemployed which will expand and shrink as the capitalist economy reaches the stages of prosperity and depression. His analysis of "the Reserve Army of the Unemployment" is a marvelous contribution to the study of the capitalist economy with particular reference to employment of labour.

(e) *New Economic Policy:* In 1981 loan of $ 5 billion and the conditionalities that the Government of India has fallen a victim to, has led to the dictates of the IMF and the WB. This has ushered in an era of what is called NEP and SAP (Structural Adjustment Programme) and this goes in the name of "Privatisation, Libralisation, Marketisation and Globalistion". Monopolies and Multi-National Corporation and Trans-National Corporation have been given an entry into our economy and this has led to many dangerous consequence. One of the important effects is on employment of labour. Labour and capital are complimentary only upto a stage, and thereafter, they become substitute of one another. In advanced capitalist economies capital in the form of new machinery is used to display labour and therefore capital substitute labour. But when they produce the new machines they create new production centers which to some extent takes care of the displaced labour in normal times (not in depressionary period). If such a policy is adopted in India and such less developed economies of Asia, Africa and Latin America, the substitution of labour by capital for outstrips the absorption of labour through new job creations, more so when importations of machinery and technology occur. This is exactly what happened in India because the Giant Corporations in the private sector including the MNCs have taken to capital intensive production techniques. For example, even in the manufacture of such goods as salt, match sticks, soaps and detergents whose manufacturing technologies have not undergone much change, sophisticated production lines been set up to the detriment of labour employment.

(f) *Displacement of Small Units:* As a part of the NEP more particularly after 1991, the small viable units which existed for a long time and which had been given some support by the state, have been displayed. These were completely labour intensive units of great importance to the economy for employment generation.

(g) *Unorganised Sectors:* The attempt of the Government under the NEP is to encourage disruption of the organised units of production and push them into unorganised units. This has happened in the cotton textile industry in the country and in Maharashtra itself including in Mumbai, dispersal of some of the important operations from the organised industries has taken place and Malegaon, Bhiwandi, etc., are becoming such centers. The workers are forced either to give up their employments or alternatively move to distant places increasing their journey get daily wages, lump sum wages, etc. They have lost the social security benefits such as PF, Gratuity, ESIC, Pension. There is tremendous uncertainty of the future not only in employment but in respect of their old age. Women workers are particularly made targets so that they discontinue. The MNCs have adopted this as a systematic policy of labour market which in USA and Europe goes by the name "hire and fire", "exit policy" and so on. The Casualisation of employment is the labour market policy in regard to employment of the bulk of labour though managerial and executive staff is employed in small numbers with attractive pay packets and perquisites, the salaries being stated annually as Rs. 4 to 5 to 10 to 15 lakhs. A big number of employees and officers are accepting VRS to take up such managerial jobs. This is happening in the service sector such as banking, City Bank, for example, recruit only a small number of employees for some of the banking operations, and use agency firms for other banking operations such as giving of credit, recovery of loans, and so on. They render banking service to a microscopic section of the community with an urban-bias, not opening accounts of persons with income lesser than about Rs. 1 lakh a year. Their main attention is credit card system and overdraft facility to such executive account holders. The banks are paid commission by the shops and establishment when the bank account holders use the credit cards. Such practices are adopted in courier services, educational institutions, tours and travels, transport and communications and so on. these have the effect of completely dislocating the existing organised service, such as, nationalised banks, post and telegraph, MTNLs, airlines who function under the control of of the International Air Traffic Authority (IATA), grant-in-aid educational institutions, and so on. The state has permitted some of these MNCs to function in such a manner that they exercise power. without any responsibilities or social commitment. This is popularly called in Europe and the USA as "JOBLESS GROWTH".

EFFECTS OF UNEMPLOYMENT

(a) *Poverty:* Unemployment causes poverty. Conditions of unemployed people remain miserable and they suffer from all kinds of hardships. They are not able to meet ever the basic needs without which one can not survive. Thus they suffer from absolute poverty.

(b) *Underutilisation:* India is gifted with surplus man power. But such a labour force is not effectively utilised due to lack of opportunities. Those who are employed are not fully and properly utilized. Thus there is unutilisation or underutilization of the factor labour which reduces the overall productivity.

(c) *Pressure on Agriculture:* The rural sector is overcrowded. Agriculture is the main source of income and employment for the rural masses. Due to lack of other opportunities more and more people look upon agriculture as a shelter resulting in unfavorable land man ratio. The precipitate availability of land declines. This resulted\s in sub division, fragmentation, underemployment and lower productivity.

(d) *High Dependency Ratio:* Besides children (0-15) and old persons (above 60). Persons who are unemployed in the age group of 15 to 59 will become dependents. The large scale unemployment in rural and urban sector adds more and more unproductive consumers and thereby keeps the dependency ratio at a higher level.

(e) *Inequality:* Unemployment divides the society into two group namely haves and have nots. Employed people enjoy a higher status in the society while the unemployed people suffer miseries.

Social Effects

(a) *Psychological Pressure:* Unemployment produces adverse effects. An unemployed person is looked upon as useless and ill treated. Continuous unemployment makes the people disillusioned and pessimistic. It will have adverse effects on their behavior.

(b) *Evil Effects on Family:* The prosperity of a family depends upon the income from the Brea winner of the family. If the bread winner looses the job, the entire family suffers. It creates conflicts among the family members and the unemployed member has to face uncomfortable situation. Sometimes unemployed person is ignored, insulted and humiliated by his own family member. Thus it affects the harmony and unity among the family members.

(c) *Anti-social Effects:* Unemployed youth, if not taken care of, may be easily misguided and exploited by the anti-social elements. In order to earn their daily bread, they may indulge in anti-social activities.

THE WAY OUT

Has India followed the correct path of economic development? Will the NEP and SAP adopted since the middle of the eighties and intensified from 1991 help in reducing, if not eliminating unemployment of labour? The initial argument in the 1980s was that Nehruvian economic policies have led India to a control raj which has been responsible for all the problems that India was facing. To get out of the crisis, the only way out was to adopt NEP and SAP. Though it began when Shri Rajiv Gandhi become PM, it was intensified during the regime of shri Narsimha Rao. The government threw open the economy to the MNCs in the name of inviting foreign capital for investment in developmental activities. Where have the MNCs come? are they on developmental path? Admittedly. MNCs have entered into the consumer goods sector manufacturing and selling such goods as soft drinks (Coca Cola, pepsi): liquors and beers: food stuffs (jams, ketch-ups, sausages, masalas and spices): Wafer and chips: ball pens and refills: TVs, Music systems, wrist waches: telephones: friges and washing machines: and other electronic goods. Even in respect of infrastructure, their entry has been mostly in electricity projects and communications. The MNCs have purchased Indian production units or eliminated them by competition, advertisement wars and other aggressive marketing tacties. They have come in with their capital intensive technologies and their operations are in areas which are not directly relevent to the common-man. With all kinds of concessions, exemptions in duties and incentives, they have expanded the output in respect of some lines of production even through importations. The increase in output and profit has been brought about by increasing the rate of capital per unit of output and lowering the rate of labour per unit of output. This has led to large scale unemployment of existing labour and no new generation of new employment. With this policy therefore. the industrial sector cannot provide employment opportunities. The following measures are necessary:

(a) Unfold the NEP and make the reforms really meaningful to Indian conditions by laying down conditions under which the MNCs if at all permitted, will operate;

(b) Re-orient Plans for introducing Decentralised pattern of development with emphasis on rural centers and small towns:

(c) Labour intensive techniques to be adopted emphasizing local employment and a wage structure that will ensure a decent minimum standard of living and prevent migration of labour;

(d) Ensure participation of the people in the process of economic development of the areas in which they live and work;

(e) Greater attention on agricultural development is necessary. This is because keeping in mind the level of education and training of those who are waiting for employment, mass employment around the rural centers alone would be possible. This will need equitable land distribution and a proper land reforms policy on the lines of West Bengal, as may be suitable to the states concerned;

(f) Encouraging small entrepreneurs to produce the goods that the common-man would need everyday;

(g) Eliminating child labour completely and if necessary compensating the families whose incomes suffer on account of ban on child labour.

REFERECES

Economic Policy;-A Critique–Sundaram

Bhalla & Sheila (1997), "Trends in Poverty, Wages and Employment in India", *Indian Journal of Labour Economics,* Vol. 40, No. 2.

Rao V. M. (1998), "Economic Reforms & Poor Emerging Scenario", *EPW*, Vol. xxxiii No. 29-30, July 18.

Kurian (2000), "Widning Regicnal Disparities in India some Indicators", *EPW* Vol. xxxv, (7) Feb. 12-18.

Dr. Mrs. Paranjpe M.S. (2007), "Uneven Distribution of Education in Maharashtra", Rural Urban, Gender & Caste Inequalities, *EPW*, Jan 20th.

Sundar Raj (2000), *"People's Participation in Rural Development"*, Vol. 48(5) Feb.

Sen Amartya, "Employment Technology & Development".

Rao Hanumanta and Linneman Hans, *"Economic Reforms and Poverty Alleviation in India"*, Edited Sage Publications New Delhi.

Krishnan Gopal (2000), Jobless in Punjab, *Economic Times,* Punjab Vision

Thomas V. Y. Wang and Xibo Fan (2000), "Measuring Education Inequality: Gini Coefficients of Education", Working Paper 2525, World Bank, Washington D.C.

Tilak J.B.G. (1999), Investment in Human Capital in India: An Interstate Analysis of Stock and Flow of Human Capital,' *Journal of Indian School of Political Economy*, Vol. xi, No. 1.

Governmant of India (2001a), Various Reports, NSS 55th Round, National Sample Survey Organisation, Ministry of Statistics and Programme Implimentation. New Delhi.

————(2001 b), Employment and Unemployment Situation among Social Groups in India. 1999-2000 Report No. 469, NSS 55th Round.

Indian Economy-Dutt Sundaram S. Chand & Co. New Delhi, 2006.

Health Infrastructure in India: Present Challenges and Future Prospects

Dinesha P. T., Jayasheela** & V. Basil Hans****

INTRODUCTION

Health is one of the vital indicators reflecting the quality of human life. It is a basic need along with food, shelter and education and is a precondition for productivity and growth. That there is a positive correlation between the health status of people and the economic development of the country is a well-established fact. It is also one of the key variables that determine "growth with a human face" even as health economics has emerged as an important area of research (Hans, 1997). There are three principal ways by which health programmes can affect the pace of economic development in the developing countries: *One*, increasing the number of man-hours of work available, *two* increasing the quality of productivity of the existing work force, and *three*, changing the attitudes towards innovations and entrepreneurship. Though health has been considered a fundamental human right since the Alma Alta Declaration (1978), yet expenditure on health in India is often lower than expected and the condition of health infrastructure in the country is not in a better condition good enough.

Keeping the above facts in view this paper has the following objectives; (i) to understand the status of health indicators in India, (ii) to understand the problems faced by health infrastructure and (iii) to consider policy alternatives.

* Junior Research Fellow Department of Economics, Mangalore University, Mangalagangothri–574 199, Karnataka, *Email: talk2dineshpt@rediffmail.com*

** Reader in Economics, and Coordinator Chair in Rural Banking and Management, Mangalore University, Mangalagangothri–574 199, Karnataka, *Email: jayasheela_mu@yahoo.com*

*** V. Basil Hans is HOD of Economics, St Aloysius Evening College, Mangalore–575 003, Karnataka. *Email: vbasilhans@yahoo.com*

STATUS OF HEALTH IN INDIA

As per the United Nations Development Programmme's (UNDP) Global Human Development Report (HDR) 2007, India ranks at 128 among the countries with medium human development out of 177 countries of the world. In terms of Gender Development Index (GDI), India ranks 113 out of 157 countries. India's HDI rank clearly reflects low relative achievement in the level of human development and it also indicative that the country has done better in terms of per capita income than in other components of human development. The condition of India's neighbours like China and even Sri Lanka with respect to health indicators including HDI values is far better than India (GOI, 2008).

The following table clearly shows the deplorable condition health indictors. The status of health indicators in India is in deplorable condition. As the Table 1 reveals that crude birth rate in India is 23.5, total fertility rate is 2.5, life expectancy at birth in India is 63, infant mortality rate is 57 and maternal mortality rate is 301. From these figures we can understand the unhealthy condition of health status of our country. Again the serious matter of concern is that, even the improvement in health indicators since Independence is slow.

Table 1
Selected Indicators of Health in India

Details	*1951*	*1981*	*1991*	*Current level*
Crude birth rate (Per 1000 population)	40.8	33.9	29.5	23.5 (2006)
Crude death rate (Per 1000 population)	25.1	12.5	9.8	7.5 (2006)
Total fertility rate (Per 1000 woman)	6.0	4.5	3.6	2.5 (2005)
Maternal mortality rate (Per 100,000 live births)	NA	NA	437 (1992-93)	301 (2001-03)
Infant mortality rate (Per 1000 live births)	146 (1951-61)	110	80	57 (2006)
Child (0-4) mortality rate (Per 1000 children)	57.3 (1972)	41.2	26.5	17.3 (2005)
Couple protection rate (per cent)*	10.4 (1971)	22.8	44.1	48.2 (1998-99)
Life expectancy at birth				
Male		55.4 (1981-85)	59.0 (1989-93)	62.3 (2001-05)
Female		55.7 (1981-85)	59.7 (1989-93)	63.9 (2001-05)

Note: Dates in brackets indicates year for which latest information is available, *National Family Health Survey, N A: Not Available.

Source: GOI, *Economic Survey of India* 2007-08, pp. 252 and *Office of the Registrar General of India*.

Though there has been a steady increase in health care infrastructure available over the plan period (Table 2), progress is not satisfactory, as, there is a shortage health centers and infrastructure to the existing population norm. Further, almost 50 per cent of the existing health infrastructure is in rented buildings. Poor upkeep and maintenance and high absenteeism of manpower in rural areas have also eroded the credibility of the health delivery system in the public sector (GOI, 2008).

Table 2
Trends in Health Care

	1951	*1991*	*2005/06*
SC/PHC/CHC*	725	57,353	171567(March 2006**)
Dispensaries and Hospitals (all)	9,209	23,555	32156(1-4-2006***)
Beds (Private and Public)	1,17,198	5,68,495	9,14,543 (Jan 1 2002-CBHI****)
Nursing Personnel	18,054	1,43,667	1481270(2005***)
Doctors (Modern System)	61,800	2,68,700	660801(2005***)

*SC/PHC/CHC: Sub centre, Primary Health Centre and Community Health Centre,** RHS: Rural Health Statistics, ***National Health Profile 2006, ****CBHI: Central Bureau of Health Statistics.
Source: *GOI, Economic Survey of India,* 2007-08, pp. 254.

Another serious matter of concern of health sector is the disparity in the condition of health indicators between the states. The Table 3 shows that condition of Kerala with respect to Life expectancy at birth, Infant Mortality Rate, Birth Rate as well as Death Rate are far better than other states. Condition of states like Assam Uttar Pradesh, Rajastan is worse than other states in some indicators.

PROBLEMS IN THE HEALTH INFRASTRUCTURE

Following are the some of the reasons for the poor growth of health infrastructure in India.

Inadequate Financial Resource

The paucity of financial resources because of poor allocations has often proved to be a major obstacle in the execution of health programmes. Public health investment on health infrastructure in the country over the years has been comparatively low. India spends about 5.1% of its GDP on health, but 82% of total health care expenditure is spent by the private sector and almost all of this represents private out of pocket expenditure (Acharya and Ranson, 2005). Moreover, with shrinking budgetary support and fiscal shortage most state governments are finding it difficult to expand their public facilities to cater to the growing health care needs of their population. Thus, the state health sector only partially serves the needs of rural and urban poor in the informal sector.

Table 3
Selected Indicators of Human Development for Major States

	Life expectancy at birth (1998-2002)			*Infant Mortality Rate*			*Birth rate (per 1000)*	*Death rate (per 1000)*
State	*Male*	*Female*	*Total*	*Male*	*Female*	*Total*	*2003**	*2003**
Andhra Pradesh	62.0	64.6	63.5	59	59	59	20.4	8.0
Assam	57.7	58.1	57.9	69	65	67	26.3	9.1
Bihar	61.4	59.5	60.8	59	62	60	30.7	7.9
Gujarat	62.4	64.4	63.4	54	61	57	24.6	7.6
Haryana	64.7	65.4	65.2	54	65	59	26.3	7.1
Karnataka	62.8	66.2	64.5	51	52	52	21.8	7.2
Kerala	70.8	75.9	73.5	11	12	11	16.7	6.3
Madhya Pradesh	57.0	56.7	56.9	77	86	82	30.2	9.8
Maharashtra	65.0	67.4	66.2	32	54	42	19.9	7.2
Orissa	58.4	58.5	58.5	82	83	83	23.0	9.7
Punjab	67.4	69.5	68.5	46	52	49	20.6	7.0
Rajasthan	60.5	61.6	61.1	70	81	75	30.3	7.6
Tamil Nadu	64.2	66.3	65.2	44	41	43	18.3	7.6
Uttar Pradesh	59.4	58.5	59.1	69	84	76	31.3	9.5
West Bengal	63.3	64.8	63.9	45	46	46	20.3	6.6
India	61.6	63.3	62.5	57	64	60	24.8	8.0

Source: Office of the Registrar General of India, Ministry of Home Affairs, *Provisional.

So lack of adequate finance has become the strong reason for the under development of the infrastructural facilities.

Inadequate Buildings

Health sector also faces the problem of shortage of buildings for health centres. Many health centres are functioning in buildings whether government or rented which have limited available space. In rural areas about 49.7 per cent of the sub-centres, 78.0 per cent of the PHCs and 91.5 per cent of CHCs are located in the government buildings. The rest are located either in rented buildings or rent free Panchayat/Voluntary Society buildings. As on September 2005, overall 60,762 buildings are required to be constructed to house sub-centres. Similarly, for PHCs 2948 and for CHCs 205 additional buildings are still required (Laveesh Bhandari and Siddhartha Dutta, 2007). Besides these there is no sufficient availability of residential accommodation in remote rural areas, which are acting as a great deterrent in motivating medical officers to work in such areas.

Inadequate Physical Infrastructures

Health facilities in India face many operational difficulties. These include inadequate funding for drugs supplies, diagnostic facilities, laboratory equipment, urinals, latrines, bathrooms, ambulances, phone, fax etc and these are in extremely hopeless condition which a very sad reflection on the functioning of health centres and a general deterioration of physical infrastructure. Lack of adequate hospitals and clinical persons is another problem. According to HDR 2002, in India there is only one hospital for every 68,881 population and one hospital bed for every 1498 population and 51.8 doctors for every one lakh population. This clearly reveals the poor condition of health infrastructure in India (Karne, 2007).According to a survey by the Jan Swasthya Abhiyan, only 38% of all PHCs have all the critical staff. A survey by the International Institute of Population Sciences found that only 20% of PHCs have a telephone. So not only is the infrastructure inadequate, we don't even have the staff to use the existing infrastructure (Srinivasan, Sandhya, 2005).

Absence of Effective Personnel and Materials Planning

In most of the hospitals there is no personnel planning resulting in the under utilisation of resources. The hospital authorities must ensure that the existing staff in the various departments has been deployed consistent with the workload and are according to the prescribed norms. Periodic studies of the functioning of hospitals are needed to enable the administrators to mange them effectively.

Absence of Good Transport Facilities

Another problem of health infrastructure is the lack of good transport facilities between the villages and hospitals. The data reveals that only 73.9% of villages are well connected with the roads to health centres (Laveesh Bhandari and Siddhartha Dutta, 2007). According to the National Council for Applied Economic Research (NCAER), nearly 20% of cases rural households travelled more than 10 km for treatment. In Meghalaya, in 54.56% and in Orissa 33.47% of rural illness cases, patients travelled more than 10 km. Studies shows that in Andrapradesh nearly 75% of PHC's are located at agency area where the villagers are scattered widely. It has become very ardous for the tribal and the down trodden people to reach the PHC's as there are no link roads in most of the villages (Himanshu Sekhar Rout, Prashant Kumr Panda, 2007).

Imbalance Between the Rural and Urban Areas

There has been an imbalance in the availability of medical facilities and health manpower in rural area and urban areas. The National Health Policy (NHP) 1983 envisaged a three-tier structure of primary, secondary and tertiary healthcare facilities to bring the services within the reach of the rural population. In spite of the three-tier system of rural health infrastructure the condition of rural health infrastructure has been deplorable. A Review of Rural Health Care Infrastructure Development by the Central Council of Health and Family Welfare in April 1999 revealed not only in the establishment but also in the amount of man power required.

Table 4
Rural Health Care Infrastructure 2000-01

Service (per population)	*Existing*	*Required*
Primary Heath Centres 1 per 20,000-30,000	22,842	24,717
Sub Centres 1 Per 3,000-5,000	137,311	148,303
Community Health Centres 1 Per 100,000	3,043	7,415

Source: Srinivasan, Sandhya (2005).

Table 4 clearly shows the mismatch between the existing and required health infrastructure. For instance, if we should have one CHC for every 100,000 rural populations, we need at least 7,415 CHCs, but we have less than half of what we should have. In the 3,043 CHCs that we do have, only 440 have a paediatrician, only 704 have a physician only 780 have a gynaecologist and 781 a surgeon.We need 76,622 midwife nurses (one per PHC and seven per CHC). We have planned only for 44,143 and only 27,336 are in place.

In the case of other rural healthcare personnel too there are similar and dramatic differences between what we *need,* what is *allocated,* and what is *actually in place* : we have only 71,053 male multipurpose workers compared to the 13,73,311 planned and the 148,303 needed; 137,407 auxiliary nurse midwives compared to the 160,153 planned and 173,020 needed; 19,927 male health assistants compared to the 22,842 planned and the 24,717 needed; 19,855 lady health visitors compared to the 22,842 planned and the 24,717 needed; 21,118 pharmacists compared to the 25,885 planned and the 32,132 needed; and 13,262 lab technicians compared to the 25,885 planned and the 32,132 needed (Srinivasan, Sandhya ,2005).

Studies reveal that one of the reasons for the reluctance of doctors to serve in SCs, PHCs and CHCs is lack of adequate drug suppliers and paramedical support services, which place them in an embracing position *vis-à-vis* the patients. Lack of communications and other facilities in rural areas is also a reason for doctors to flee or keep away from the country side.

SUGGESTIONS TO IMPROVE THE CONDITION OF HEALTH INFRASTRUCTURE

India does have a systematic health policy. What need to be done are its effective implementation, monitoring and evaluation for promoting holistic health and economic welfare of the people. The following suggestions are made to improve the health of the health infrastructure.

Creating New Infrastructure and Strengthening Existing Infrastructure

The availability and accessibility of good quality health-care services need to be extended to larger population. In the long run, new infrastructure (hospitals and essential equipments in the hospital) need to be created to make quality services available to a larger population and wider area. It is possible to restructure and rationalise the existing health care institutions to improve their service delivery and enhance outreach in the short run. Besides creating new infrastructure existing health infrastructure should be strengthened with appropriate infrastructures like beds, laboratories, ambulances, telephones, medicines etc.

Refocus on Government Expenditure

A major chunk of the resources needs to be deployed for development of health infrastructure and amenities. Government expenditure should cover both healthcares for the poor and health promotion and disease prevention for all. There should be a shift from the current emphasis on curative, advanced and urban services to increase funding for preventive services and better services in the rural areas. Government expenditure on healthcare services should be increased and spread across regions based on the principle of 'equity'.

Filling up the Vacant Posts

Vacant posts should be filled up with the appropriate staff. If a state finds it difficult to fill up vacant specialist positions in hospitals simple medical graduates should be recruited so that the people get at least minimum services. Convenient and standard residential accommodation needs to be provided for at least the key staff as a motivation for them to stay on so, as to ensure the availability of services to the people. The mismatch between manpower and infrastructure facilities should be done away with so as to enhance efficiency as a whole.

Use of Technology

Technological innovations make it possible for delivery of health care facilities at cheaper cost. A detailed plan for use of information technology in health care delivery, referral, training and administration should be formulated and implemented. There should be emphasis on continuous training for both medical and paramedical professionals (Thomas, 2007).

Supporting Involvement VO/NGO's

Committed and reputed NGO's may be involved in the development of primary health care system by handing over certain proportion of infrastructural facilities namely SC or PHC along with building , funds and staff with relatively more management freedom to VO/NGO's depending upon their capability of funds, staff etc, after ascertaining their credibility. Initiatives in health care by private sector and NGOs can be encouraged through appropriate tax breaks and other healthy incentives.

Constructing Buildings in Ideal Location of Hospitals and Staff

There is an urgent need to provide adequate buildings for hospitals to provide good service. Besides the construction building for hospitals, houses for the staff should be constructed to increase the morale and efficiency of the personnel working there. While opening a new health centre care may be taken in selecting such a site which should be easily accessible to largest number of people in the block.

Proper Supply of Drugs and Other Health Equipments

Steps may be taken to ensure adequate and timely supply of medicines and equipment to health centres. They should maintain adequate stock of drugs. For efficient discharge of curative functions the health centres should be provided sufficient equipments like x-ray and laboratory facilities, oxygen cylinders, operation tables, indoor beds and surgical instruments etc.

CONCLUSIONS

The past sixty years have witnessed the development of a vast health care infrastructure and manpower aimed at providing health care to the population. Several programmes for health care are evolved and implemented both at national and state level. Even after these efforts, lower and middle strata of the society are being exploited by the private dominated health care industry. So, Health policy and strategies of its implementation in the New Millennium should be geared towards strengthening the state-run health infrastructure by increased allocation of funds and community involvement to ensure an efficient and effective referral system. There is a need to provide greater resources for the rural health services. More attention should paid to improve the health status of the population by providing additional resources to the provision of safe drinking water, education, nutrition better housing and sanitation etc. Since health is an important determinant of productivity countries like India, which depend on "human capital" for their rapid economic progress must accord higher value to having a healthier work force to hasten the progress of economic development. Further, addressing the health inequalities along with general health would not only bring about growth but also development with a human face.

REFERENCES

Acharya, Akash and M. Kent Ranson (2005), "Health Care Financing for the Poor. Community Based Health Insurance Schemes in Gujarat", *Economic and Political Weekly*, September, Vol. XL, No. 38, pp.17-23.

"INDIA 2006", Research, Reference and Training Division, Publication Division, Ministry of Information and Broadcasting.

GOI (2008), *Economic Survey of India*, 2007-08.

GOI (2006), *Economic Survey of India*, 2005-06.

Hans, V. B. (1997), *"Nature and Scope of Health Economics–A Survey of Literature"*, Unpublished M.Phil Dissertation, Mangalore University, Mangalagangothri.

Himanshu Sekhar Rout, Prashant Kumr Panda (2007), *"Health Economics in India"*, New Delhi, New Century Publications.

Karne, Manisha (2007), Public Health Care in India Issues and Problems, *Health Action*, December 2007. pp 8-11.

Laveesh Bhandari and Siddhartha Dutta (2007), "Health Infrastructure in Rural India", *India Infrastructure Report, 2007.*

Reddy, Byre V. J. and Manjunath S. J. (2006), "Health Inequalities in India", *Southern Economist*, Vol. 45, No. 1, May 1, pp. 61-63.

Srinivasan, Sandhya (2005), '*Public Health Infrastructure: What We Need and What We have*', Info Change India News & Features, June. *http://www.infochangeindia.org/HealthIbp.jsp*

Summary of the Report on Workforce Management Options & infrastructure Rationalization of PHC, Planning Commission, available at *http://planningcommission.nic.in/reports/peoreport/peoevalu/peo_NCAER.doc*

Thomas, George (2007), "Striking a Balance", *The Hindu*, Open Page, Sunday, March 11, pp. 15.

Social Sector and Dalits in India: A Review

P. S. Kamble, B.J. Kadam** & J.P. Patil***

INTRODUCTION

Government plays a very vital role in socio-economic development of the economy. It performs a number of duties, functions, responsibilities, which contribute in making conducive environment of the economy for speeding up socio-economic development. The role of government in the socialist economy and mixed economy is of more significance compared to capitalist economy. But as modern capitalist economies have become more or less mixed economies, consequently the role of government in the socio-economic development also has become so much important. This demands to undertake extensive and intensive efforts by the government in promoting social development especially in the countries having any type economy.

Reforms, in particular economic reforms movement has been launched in many countries of the world. It mainly intends in tackling of economic crises and making dynamic the process of economic development. More or less, economic reforms have not paid their attention towards enhancing the level of social development. Economic reforms consisting of privatization, liberalization and globalization create the situation of increased attention and attempts to be paid so as to mitigate their adverse effects and repercussions on the social development and maximization of social welfare.

The underdeveloped countries from Asian and African countries give priority to social development and social welfare maximization due to their socio-economic inequality to a great extent. To achieve the goal of socialistic pattern of society in the country like India more important

* Reader, Department of Economics, Shivaji University, Kolhapur-416004 (Maharashtra), *Email: pskamble2007@rediffmail.com*

** Research Students, Department of Economics, Shivaji University, Kolhapur-416004 (Maharashtra)

role and intention is desirable and expected. India is a country, which has been implementing economic reforms programme since 1991 comprising privatization, liberalization, globalization. It is a mixed economy. It has a significant disparity based on property, income, caste, creed, religion and other criteria. It is a country that has determined the goal of socialistic pattern of society as a planning goal. It has a prominent (more than 20% share in total population) class of Dalits, which is socially and economically very much backward. In this situation, it necessitates to study social development in general and the development of dalits in particular in the backdrop of economic reforms programme popularly known as New Economic Policy (NEP) being implemented since 1991 onwards. It is against this overall background, the present paper endeavours to examine the role played by the Union Government of India in achieving the social development in general and the development of the dalits in particular in the post NEP regime.

OBJECTIVES OF THE STUDY

Following are the major and important objectives of the present study.

1. To study growth and composition of Union Government finances in the post reform period.
2. To examine growth and pattern of social sector expenditure of the Government of India.
3. To analyse role played by the Government into consideration in the development of dalits.
4. To review the state of dalits in the post reform regime.
5. To identify problems before the dalits and suggest measures on the same.

HYPOTHESIS OF THE STUDY

Economic reforms neglect social development in general and socially deprived like dalits in particular. This necessitates to pay a special attention towards social development as well as development of dalits for speeding up economic growth and maximization of social welfare.

DATA BASE AND RESEARCH METHODOLOGY

The present study endeavours to review the state of social development and the development of dalits in the post reform period in the context of efforts made by the Union Government of India. For this, the present study has selected the latest period of seven years from 2000-01 to 2006-

07. This study mainly relies on secondary sources for data collection and collection of necessary information.

The data collection has been classified and tabulated in the light of objectives and hypothesis of the present study. To highlight the various trends and dimensions concerning the present topic, the data has been processed by using the appropriate statistical tools like Simple Growth Rate (SGR), Ratio Analysis, Mean as per the necessity.

PLACE OF SOCIAL SECTOR IN UNION GOVERNMENT FINANCES

Each and every country of the world desires and attempts to achieve rapid and all-round economic development. In the same way, India also endeavours to achieve rapid and overall economic growth. But it is not logical to attempt for only rapid economic development in the country like India, which has a wide socio-economic inequality and greater diversity based on region, class, caste, creed, religion and other criteria. This urgently demands to review the role played by the Union Government of India to achieve social development through the development of social sector, more particularly in the post reform period, which has severe repercussions on the finances of Government of India as well as social development. It is useful for us in assessing the state of social development along with the due consideration of the Union Government of India after 1991.

It will be better to begin with from very overall budgetary position of Union Government of India in the post NEP period. The necessary data is presented in Table 1 below.

Table 1
Overall Budgetary Position of Union Government of India

(Rs. in crore)

Year	*Total Revenue*	*Total Expenditure*	*Deficit / Surplus*
2000-01	325611	325611	–
2001-02	362453	362453	–
2002-03	414162	414162	–
2003-04	471368	471368	–
2004-05	497682	497682	–
2005-06	508705	508705	–
2006-07	563991	563991	–
SGR	73	73	–
Average	10	10	–

Source: GOI (2006), Budget at a Glance and Expenditure Budget, Vol. 1, Ministry of Finance, Feb. 28.

SGR: Simple Growth Rate.

It is observed from the data in Table 1, the finances of the Union Government of India has been rose rapidly and significantly. Its both Revenue as well as Expenditure showed a tremendous growth of 73 percent during 2000-01 to 2006-07 with an average of 10 per cent per annum. The government did not face deficit, which is a budgetary deficit. This does not mean, it has no fiscal crisis because it is one of the indicators of fiscal imbalance. But it is a good thing that the Union Government of India has been attempting to tackle the situation of fiscal crisis.

The composition of Government of India's Total Expenditure also shows tremendous growth with peculiar trends and features.

Table 2
Composition of Union Government of India

(Rs. in crore)

Year	*Revenue Expenditure*	*Capital Expenditure*	*Total Expenditure*
2000-01	277858	47753	325611
	(85.33)	(14.67)	(100)
2001-02	301611	60842	362453
	(83.21)	(16.79)	(100)
2002-03	339628	74535	414162
	(82.00)	(18.00)	(100)
2003-04	362140	109228	471360
	(76.82)	(23.18)	(100)
2004-05	384351	113331	497682
	(77.22)	(22.78)	(100)
2005-06	440295	68410	508705
	(86.55)	(13.45)	(100)
2006-07	488192	75799	563991
	(86.56)	(13.44)	(100)
SGR	76	59	73
Average	11 (83)	8 (17)	(10)

Source: Same as of Table 1.
Note: Figures into brackets indicate percentage share to Total.

It is revealed that Total Expenditure of Union Government of India consists of Revenue Expenditure and Capital Expenditure. Both the Revenue Expenditure as well as Capital Expenditure show a tremendous growth during the period into consideration. But the growth in Revenue Expenditure (76% SGR) was rapid than the Capital Expenditure (59% SGR) with an average of 11% and 8% growth rate respectively. Likewise, Union Government has mainly attempted to incur Revenue Expenditure (83% average share) by neglecting Capital Expenditure (17% average share) which has a special role in speeding up economic growth. This is not a good practice as far as the millennium goal of development is concerned.

Social sector has a special importance in achieving social development of a country like India, which has striking dimensions of social structure. This poses an urgent necessity of examining the efforts of the Union Government of India in the post reform regime. In the field of education and health, the increases proposed, except for primary education, are not exciting, considering the top most priority that is being held and for social sector development.[1]

Table 3
Total Expenditure of Government of India an Social Sector

(Rs. in crore)

Year	*Plan Expenditure*	*Non-Plan Expenditure*	*Total Expenditure on Social Sector*
2000-01	17865	7357	25222
	(71.00)	(29.00)	(100)
2001-02	20785	7677	28462
	(73.00)	(27.00)	(100)
2002-03	22699	6650	29349
	(77.00)	(23.00)	(100)
2003-04	25133	7203	32336
	(78.00)	(22.00)	(100)
2004-05	34370	8399	42769
	(80.00)	(20.00)	(100)
2005-06	46450	9519	55969
	(83.00)	(17.00)	(100)
2006-07	58181	8546	66727
	(87.00)	(13.00)	(100)
SGR	226	16	165
Average	32 (78.00)	2 (22.00)	24

Source: Same as of Table 1.

It is observed that the Union Government's expenditure on social sector shows a considerable growth of 165 per cent during 2000-01 to 2006-07. It is a thing of welcome that the Government of India has made a planned efforts to achieve social development through providing in plan expenditure. As a result, planned expenditure on social sector has shown a rapid growth of 226 per cent with an average of 32 per cent per annum during the period into consideration. Likewise, its share in Total Social Sector Expenditure was prominent, which stood at 78 per cent on an average. It is an indicator of definitionless and surety of attempts by the government concerned, but it is a little bit attempts, non-Plan Expenditure on Social Sector showed a mild growth with a insignificant relative share is a signal of further need to pay due attention towards this category expenditure for providing unexpected urgent and necessary expenditure obligations.

The analysis of the pattern of social sector expenditure made by Central Government reveals the priorities given by the Government to different social services in providing them. This also highlights the preference of the Government towards upliftment of the dalits, which a major and prominent community on the various grounds such as population, discrimination, backwardness, utility, social political stability and others. To achieve the millennium development goals, expenditures under social sector heads may have to be doubled in the next few years.[2]

Table 4
Social Sector Expenditure Pattern of Government of India

(Rs. in crore)

Year	*Health & Family Welfare*	*Education*	*Women & Child Develop-ment*	*Welfare of SC, ST, Minorities*	*Labour & Employ-ment*	*Total Expenditure on Social Sector*
2000-01	5255	7916	1381	1878	867	25222
	(21.00)	(31.00)	(5.00)	(7.00)	(3.00)	(100)
2001-02	5936	8020	1691	2268	831	28462
	(21.00)	(28.00)	(6.00)	(8.00)	(3.00)	(100)
2002-03	6503	9069	2133	2256	757	29349
	(22.00)	(31.00)	(7.00)	(8.00)	(3.00)	(100)
2003-04	7249	10144	2103	2139	819	32336
	(22.00)	(31.00)	(6.00)	(7.00)	(3.00)	(100)
2004-05	8086	13097	2448	2467	988	42769
	(19.00)	(31.00)	(6.00)	(6.00)	(2.00)	(100)
2005-06	10039	18336	3931	3009	1265	55969
	(18.00)	(33.00)	(7.00)	(5.00)	(2.00)	(100)
2006-07	12993	24114	4853	3487	1481	66727
	(19.00)	(36.00)	(7.00)	(5.00)	(2.00)	(100)
SGR	147	205	251	86	71	165
Average	21 (20)	29 (32)	36 (6)	12 (7)	10 (3)	24

Source: GOI (2006), Expenditure Budget, Vol. 1 and 2, Ministry of Finance, Feb. 28

It is revealed from Table 4 the Union Government of India has given priorities to Women and child development, Education, Health and Family Welfare as items of social sector, as a result expenditure on them showed a rapid growth i. e. 251%, 205%, 147% respectively. Hence, the items like Welfare of dalits, Labour & Employment remained too behind, which stood at 86%, 71%. Likewise, the relative share of Total Social Sector Expenditure received by them was also meagre and insignificant demanding the need for due attention in the future. The relative share of women and child development also indicates inadequate attempts made by the government concerned. The striking feature is that, Dalits form more than 20 percent of Total Population, but expenditure on them was just 7 percent of social sector development is to a greater extent neglect towards their development and upliftment.

Dalits is an important community, which has a long history of social religious exploitation, illiteracy, economic & social backwardness, poverty that demand due attention and precaution to attempt towards socio economic development. But it is a fact that much attention is not paid by the Government into our consideration. As economic reforms very severely affect this poor section of population that is so much necessary to develop and uplift them, but this lacks in the post reform period. The Government has made reservation for SC, STs and OBCs in services under its control. The quantum of reservation to SCs, STs and OBCs in direct recruitment on all India basis by open competition is 15%, 7.5% and 27% respectively.[3]

The examination of the composition of expenditure on the development of dalits (SCs, STs and Minorities) reveals the attempts of the Union Government of India towards assigning the dalits in providing self-sufficiency of their socio-economic development. The data on representation of SCs, STs in Central Government services reveals that instead of Ist and IInd class (A, B) posts their representation is higher (Jan 2001) in class III and IVth (C, D) employment. Likewise, the necessary reservation has not been filled up in many employments.[4]

Table 5
Composition of Expenditure on SCs, STs & Minorities

(Rs. in crore)

Year	*Revenue Expenditure*	*Capital Expenditure*	*Total Expenditure*
2000-01	1799	79	1878
	(96.00)	(4.00)	(100)
2001-02	2147	121	2268
	(95.00)	(5.00)	(100)
2002-03	2113	143	2256
	(94.00)	(6.00)	(100)
2003-04	2032	107	2139
	(95.00)	(5.00)	(100)
2004-05	2269	198	2467
	(92.00)	(8.00)	(100)
2005-06	2891	118	3009
	(96.00)	(4.00)	(100)
2006-07	3271	216	3487
	(94.00)	(6.00)	(100)
SGR	82	173	86
Average	12(95)	25(5)	12

Source: Same as of Table 4.

Capital Expenditure is more important for socio-economic development than Revenue Expenditure. But the data in Table 5 adequately reveals that the Government of India has attempted to provide social services to dalits at present and not in the future. Hence, socio-economic development of dalits is unsustainable in the present pattern of expenditure. Therefore, even though capital expenditure on the development of dalits showed a rapid growth, its relative share is very insignificant and meagre, which stood at just 5% on an average with 95% share for Revenue Expenditure. This suggests to provide for expenditure on capital account for a sustainable socio-economic development of dalits.

More than 75% of the dalits workers are still connected with land, 25% being the marginal and small farmers and balance over 50% are the landless labourers. In urban areas, they work mainly in unorganized sector. Out of the total dalit population of 138 million, the number of dalits in services falling in the domain of reservations does not exceed 1.1 million, a mere 0.8 percent.[5] But it is a fact that the Union Government of India has been making planned efforts for the socio-economic development of dalits in India during the post reform period under our study. The development of dalits is a item of economic planning process, no doubt a thing of welcome on the ground of surety and certainty. Likewise, there is a need for providing for the emergency expenditure on the development of dalits. The necessary data and information is given in Table 6.

Table 6
Plan and Non-Plan Expenditure on SCs, STs & Minorities

(Rs. in crore)

Year	*Plan Expenditure*	*Non-Plan Expenditure*	*Total Expenditure*
2000-01	1824	54	1878
	(97.00)	(3.00)	(100)
2001-02	2207	61	2268
	(93.00)	(7.00)	(100)
2002-03	2194	62	2256
	(97.00)	(3.00)	(100)
2003-04	2073	66	2130
	(95.00)	(5.00)	(100)
2004-05	2396	72	2467
	(97.00)	(3.00)	(100)
2005-06	2933	76	3009
	(97.00)	(3.00)	(100)
2006-07	3407	80	3487
	(98.00)	(2.00)	(100)
SGR	87	48	86
Average	12 (96)	7 (4)	12

Source: Same as of Table 4.

The levels of endeavours of the Union Government of India towards socio-economic development of dalits is necessary to examine in the post reform period, which is very much important in the backdrop of severe repercussions of economic reforms measures. Table 7 shows the necessary data and information about this important aspect.

As a measure of ensuring food security to the large mass of Indian population, public distribution system was instituted in India. The food distributed through PDS is subsidized by the Government with the FCI costs ever increasing, the impact of any reduction in subsidy has to hit the poor mainly dalits directily.[6]

Table 7
Levels of Expenditure on SCs, STs and Minorities

(Rs. in crore)

Year	*As % of GDP*	*As % of Total Expenditure*	*As % of Revenue Expenditure*	*As % of Social Sector Expenditure*
2000-01	0.08	0.57	0.67	7.44
2001-02	0.09	0.62	0.75	7.96
2002-03	0.09	0.54	0.66	7.68
2003-04	0.07	0.45	0.59	6.61
2004-05	0.07	0.49	0.64	5.76
2005-06	0.08	0.59	0.68	5.37
2006-07	0.08	0.67	0.71	5.22
SGR	--	7.01	5.97	-29.83
Average	0.01	1.00	0.85	-4.26

Source: Calculated on the basis of data collected.

Evidence available about population below the poverty line underlines the stark reality that the reform process did not help to reduce poverty. Dr. S. P. Gupta, Member of Planning Commission has underlined the inverse relationship between poverty and GDP growth by propelling out that population below the poverty line, which was 35.07% in 1993-94 increased to 37.23% in 1997.[7] The levels of expenditure on the development of dalits adequately indicate the endevarous of the Union Government of India during the period into our study. It is revealed that the Government into consideration even could not spend one percent share of GDP on the upliftment and development of dalits, which constitute more than 20 million population of India. The same is the case in the context of Total Expenditure, Revenue expenditure as well. Besides this, its share in social expenditure was considerably low, and at the same time, it significantly declined from 7% to 5% during 2000-01 to 2006-07. This should be assumed as a signal of inadequate efforts of the Union Government of India especially in the post reform period in which there was a need for increased attempts and attention.

The World Development Report has estimated that 1199 million were living in poverty in the world, the share of India in the World's total poor works out to be 34.95% a very grim scenario indeed.[8]

MAJOR CONCLUSIONS AND POLICY SUGGESTIONS

The in detailed study and through analysis of the topic about attempts of the Union Government of India towards development of social sector and dalits in the post reform period reveals some important conclusions. It is very much important in India to attempt for achieve the development of social sector in general and dalits in particular due to peculiar structure of the Indian society based on a wide disparity, socio-economic exploitation, discrimination based on caste, creed, religion, poverty, labour class, deprivation etc. As economic reforms, very badly affect economically and socially backward community people in the post reform period in India. In this backdrop, the assessment of role of the Union Government of India has a special significance. The government can do this through the development of social sector in general and dalits in particular.

The finances of the Union Government of India have been increased during the period 2000-01 to 2006-07 rapidly and significantly is a clear indicator of the extensive and intensive attempts to perform duties, responsibilities by the Government of India. The Union Government did not face the problem of budgetary deficit during the period into our consideration. But no doubt, the said Government is in fiscal crisis that can be indicated by revenue, fiscal and primary deficits. But the expenditure pattern of the Government of India is not conducive for rapid and all-round economic development due to its greater allocation of funds towards Revenue Expenditure than the Capital Expenditure. The development of social sector plays a pivotal role in the social development. The growth in expenditure on social sector shows considerable and not an adequate attempts made by the Union Government in achieving social development. But the efforts of the said government are definite, certain and sure as a result, it gave place to social sector in economic planning of India. It is also necessary to provide for social sector development for unexpected expenditure under non-plan category. It is a good thing that in the social sector the Union Government of India gave priority to the development of Education, Health and Family Welfare as items of social sector. But comparatively neglected the development of welfare of dalits, labour & employment and women & child development as well. It is urgent and necessary to pay due attention towards the development of dalits, which is an important community in India in many respects. They have been very badly affecting by the economic reforms programme in various ways. The Union Government of India has mainly attempted to provide various services and facilities at present and not much provided for the future development of dalits, which is sustainable. But it is a thing of welcome that the development of dalits is on the agenda of India's planning. It is adequately proved that the endeavours of the government into our consideration are inadequate in the background of the need for socio-economic development of dalits as well as severe consequences of provisions and decisions in the economic reforms programme being implemented. There is an urgent need for undertaking increased efforts by the government in that direction.

On the basis of the thorough study of the problem of the development of social sector and dalits, the following suggestions will be very much important which has policy implications for the Union Government of India. The government must give highest possible priority to the development of social sector in general and dalits in particular on the background of the peculiar social sector of India, its increased need in the era of economic reforms. For this, the government should make increased provisions in its budget by avoiding unnecessary expenditure. This will facilitate social stability and help in speeding up economic development of the economy. It is very much essential to provide for the upliftment and development of dalits in the regime of new economic policy, which have been hiting hard to this section of population. This should be important and part and parcel of budget of the central government and Indian planning. In the forthcoming budget and planning, the priorities should be given to the upliftment of dalits, labour and employment, women & child along with Education and Health through adequate provisions in the budget. A separate fund namely social development fund should be created, which will play a desirable role in that direction. While undertaking attempts to achieve the development of dalits, they should be provided for capital expenditure for the future and sustainable development of dalits. Due agency should be created like Social Commission that will examine progress of social development with emphasis on the development of dalits. Due incentives should be given to undertake research concerning various issues and aspects of social development and the development of dalits. Social budget should be an important component of the Government's public budget. It is necessary to take precaution of reviewing the distribution of benefits of rapid economic growth on the social background of the Indian economy.

CONCLUDING REMARKS

The development of social sector in general and upliftment and development of the dalits in particular has a special importance in India in the backdrop of social background of the economy as well as economic reforms programme being implemented in India since 1991. The present paper is a little bit attempts towards exploring the various issues and dimensions of social sector and the development of dalits in the context of India in the post reform era. It is difficult to capture each and every dimension of social sector and dalit development in a single paper. The purposeful research activity in the form of research projects, M. Phil. and Ph. D. dissertations and theses can play a very desirable and vital role in that direction. The insufficient information and database on social sector and dalits is a major obstacle in this type of studies.

NOTES AND REFERENCES

1. EPW, Research Foundation (2006), Budget Making a Chidambaram, *Economic and Political Weekly*, Mumbai, p. 1380.
2. *Ibid*, p. 1380.
3. Government of India (2004), India 2004, Government of India Publication, New Delhi, p. 710.
4. *Ibid*, pp. 710-11.
5. Teltumbde, Anand (1996), Impact of New Economic Reforms on Dalits in India, a paper presented in the International Seminar, University of Oxford, Oxford, UK, p. 2.
6. *Ibid*, p. 5.
7. Datta and Sundaram (2002), Indian Economy, S. Chand and Company Ltd., New Delhi, pp. 255-56.
8. *Ibid*, p. 256.

Service Led Growth in India: An Analysis

*Debesh Chandra Bhowmik**

INTRODUCTION

In colonial India, the British were very much interested in spreading the service sector economy rather than the expansion of producing sector in industry and manufacturing and even the agricultural sector was primitive in the mode of production. India, being an agricultural dominance, the growth pattern was not at all agriculture–led growth although agricultural surplus was utilized not for the overall development of the economy but for the development especially for the maintenance of kingdom. During the planning period, the agricultural sector and its resource were not properly utilized for the development of other sectors to speed up the growth rate of the Indian economy. Thus, the uneven growth patterns of the three sectors collapsed the main indicators of development and other key macro economic variables throughout the planning process. The investment was sharply fallen in agriculture in subsequent plans, on the contrary, planning for industrialization was not so strong in the planning models except in import substitution till 90s, and thence, the economy was biased in favour of tertiary sector development. Besides, in Indian mixed economy, mode of development was neither socialistic nor capitalistic. Since the reform, it is neither pro-poor nor export led growth, conversely the planning model favours the service led growth process.

In this paper, we will discuss the phenomenon of service led growth in Indian economy since independence and how far this sector could generate employment subsequently.

REVIEW OF LITERATURE

Service sector has been growing too fast during long course of time in India than the other sectors and it became the chief source of the GDP

* (International Institute for Development Studies, Kolkata), *Email-debeshbhowmik@rediffmail.com*

growth rate. This situation may be called as structural transformation. It is due to increase in domestic demand. The value additions in service sectors is skewed towards final consumption compared to other sectors of the economy and capital formation is the key driver of growth. There are some literature on the sectoral growth pattern in the theory of development in which Lewis (1955) and Preobrazhensky (1965) emphasised that industry is the engine of growth whereby transfer of resources takes from agriculture. Kuznets (1966) explained that a rise in productivity in agriculture is a precondition for economic growth where agriculture generates a surplus. The trade policies promote import substitution industries through favourable TOT for manufacturing, low effective protection for agricultural share in GDP is the basis of structural transformation. Clerk (1940) and Fisher (1939) asserted that the demand for manufacturing and services are more elastic than that of agriculture and therefore a shift away from agriculture towards services and manufacturing is expected in course of development. Park and Chan(1989) argued that there should be a positive and significant association between manufacturing and services at the advanced stages of industrialization. That is, during the course of development of manufacturing, the demand for services like trade, hotels, transport, banking, health, education, communication increase and raise productivity of industrial sector. Hence growth linkage between the two sectors is necessary. Johnston and Mellor (1961) and Krishna (1982) stressed that the two sectors-agriculture and industry are seen to be complementary to each other. But low industrial growth rate and rise in agriculture prices and subsequent rise in industrial prices failed the industry agriculture relationship (Chakraborty, 73, Mitra '77, Mundle '81). This diminishing growth linkage between the sectors was credited primarily to deficiency in demand for agricultural products, decline in share of agro-based industries coupled with slow employment growth. (Rangarajan 1982, Bhattacharjya and Rao 1986, Chowdhury and Chowdhury 1995). But still controversies arise, whether an increasing trend of relative share of tertiary sector is desirable in India. In this issue Bhattacharjya and Mitra (1990) stated that while the share of tertiary income has been increasing, its share in total employment has been much less. This mismatch along with a widening gap between growth rates of tertiary sector and commodity producing sectors would have negative repercussions on inflation, balance of payments and income distribution. In other words, a phenomenal growth in the relative share of services in gross national income was considered to be no indicators of development, and hence perceived to be warranted. Bhanumurthy and Mitra (2003) have found that a shift in value added mix towards industry and tertiary sector have caused a larger decline in the incidence of poverty in 90s compared to 80s. This result supports the findings of Ravallion and Datt (1966) who observed a significant role of sectoral composition of economic growth in reducing poverty in both rural and urban areas. World Development Reports (1992, 2006) showed that the pattern of world growth was such that service led growth dominated the entire period from 60s to 2004 because low income, middle income and even high income economies have lowered their shares of agriculture and industry in GDP but increased the share of service sector in GDP. Even globalization has speed up this process too in most of the countries of the world. Hence, it is a general tendency of the world economy towards a structural shift to tertiary sector at the cost of agriculture and industry. (Table 1).

Table 1
World Economy Towards Service Led Growth

	1965			*1990*			*2004*		
% share in GDP	*Ag*	*Ind*	*Serv*	*Ag*	*Ind*	*Ser*	*Ag*	*Ind*	Ser
China	38	35	27	27	41.6	31.3	15.2	53.0	31.8
India	44	22	34	31.3	27.3	41.1	21.1	27.2	51.7
Indonesia	51	13	36	19.4	39.1	41.5	15.4	43.7	40.9
Korea	38	25	37	8	37.3	54.6	3.3	36.3	60.4
Malaysia	28	25	47	15	41.5	43.5	9.1	48.5	42.4
Nepal	65	11	23	50.6	15.9	33.5	38.7	20.9	40.4
Philippines	26	27	47	21.9	34.5	43.6	15.3	31.8	52.8
Pakistan	40	20	40	26	25.2	48.8	23.1	24.6	52.3
Srilanka	28	21	51	22.9	27.3	49.8	17.8	26.8	55.4
Thailand	32	23	45	12.5	37.2	50.3	9.9	44.1	46
Australia	9	39	51	4	31	65	3	26	71
Argentina	17	42	42	13	41	45	10	32	59
Brazil	19	33	48	10	39	51	5	17	78
Germany	4	53	43	2	39	59	1	29	69
Greece	26	24	50	17	27	56	7	24	69
Japan	10	44	46	3	42	56	1	30	68
Kenya	35	18	47	28	21	51	16	19	65
Mali	65	9	25	46	13	41	38	26	36
Mexico	14	27	59	9	30	61	4	25	71
Nigeria	55	12	33	36	38	25	26	49	24
Paraguay	37	19	45	28	23	49	27	24	49
Saudi Arabia	8	60	31	8	45	48	5	55	40
Singapore	3	24	74	0	37	63	0	35	65
SouthAfrica	10	41	48	5	44	51	4	31	65
UK	3	46	51				1	27	72

Source: World Development Report-1992, 2006.

AN OUTLINE OF INDIAN SERVICE SECTOR

The tremendous growth of the tertiary sector in India since independence neither follows the Clerk-Fisher theory nor follows the Kuznets hypothesis towards sectoral development. In India, the continuous decline in the share of agriculture in GDP and sharp increase in the share of tertiary sector and slow increase in the share of industry in GDP were observed since 1950-51 up till now. The industrial share would not become the pivoting sector for development rather tertiary sector is the key sector in the growth process. The trend model log y = a + bt showed that the share of agriculture in GDP has been declining at the rate of 1.71% per year during 1950-51-2005-06. On the other hand, the share of industry in GDP has been stipulating at the rate of 1.05% per year during 1950-51-2005-06. But, the share of service sector in GDP has been increasing at the rate of 1.17% per year during the period of 1950-51-2005-06 respectively. Hence, agriculture share has been declining more steadily than the increasing shares of the both industry and tertiary sectors. But, the volatility of tertiary sectors is marginally higher than the industry and volatility of agriculture sector is too higher than both of them. These are uneven sectoral growth patterns that India has been confronting with the stages of development. The semilog linear models are shown below in Table 2 and their graphical representation is plotted in Figure 1 where the nature of trends are seen vividly.

Table 2
Trends of Sectoral Shares in India During 1950-51-2005-06

$\text{Log}(x_1) = 4.1498 - 0.0171\,t$ (310.06)* (-41.667)* $R^2 = 0.97$	Mean of x_1 = 40.419, SD = 10.838, Skewness = -0.0018, Kurtosis = 1.88, Coefficient of Variation = 26.81%
$\text{Log}(x_2) = 2.798 + 0.01057t$ (110.245)* (13.647)* $R^2 = 0.77$	Mean of x_2 = 22.601, SD = 4.042, C.V.=17.88% Skewness = - 0.654, Kurtosis = 2.44
$\text{Log}(x_3) = 3.2579 + 0.01172t$ (362.0084)* (42.667)* $R^2 = 0.97$	Mean of x_3 = 36.996, SD = 7.414, C.V. = 20.04% Skewness = 2.526, Kurtosis = 2.526

Where x_1 = share of agriculture in GDP, x_2 = share of industry in GDP, x_3 = share of service sector in GDP. * = significant at least 10% level.

The growth rate of the service sector during 1950-51-1980-81 was observed as 4.5% per year which increased to 7.3% per year during 1980-2005 and the contribution to growth of this sector increased at the rate of 4.5% per year during 1950-51-1980-81 which subsequently rose to 6.7% per year during 1980-81-1990-91,7.6% per year during 1990-91-2000-01, and 7.9% per year during 2000-01-2003-04

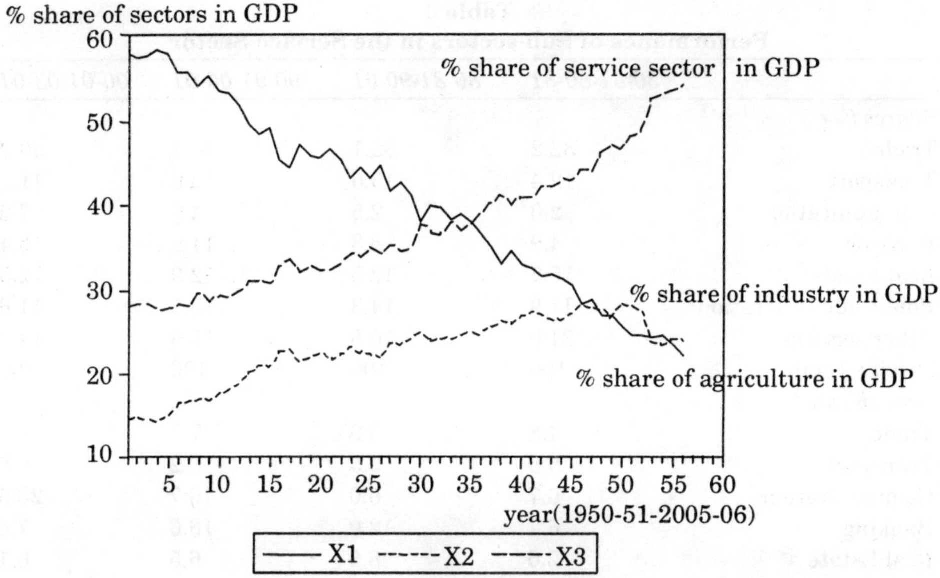

Figure: 1

respectively. The shares in GDP growth rates, the growth rates of sub-sectors and contribution to GDP growth rates of the sub sectors of the service sectors were given in the Table 3 where it was found that the share of trade is the dominant followed by real estate, transport and banking etc. The share of banking and communication grew rapidly during the planning period especially in the reform period. All the sub sectors' growth rates increased during the subsequent period from 1950-51-80-81 to the next decades. Even, most of the sub sectors' contribution to GDP grew slowly but steadily during the said period except in 2000-01-03-04. This exceptional performance of the Indian service sector led to high rate of economic growth. Since, external trade constitutes the lion's share of GDP and its growth and contribution to GDP growth are significantly higher than that of the other sub sectors, then export led strategy may be a synonymous to service-led growth in Indian economy as was seen in East Asia and South East Asian countries in the recent past.

The inter linkage of the sectors can be found out through the Granger Causality Test which explores that the share of industry in GDP does not Granger cause the share of agriculture in GDP and vice versa during the period 1950-51-2005-06. In the similar jurgon, share of service sector in GDP does not Granger cause the share of agriculture and converse is true during the same period. Lastly, the share of tertiary sector in GDP

Table 3
Performance of Sub-sectors in the Service Sector

	50-51-80-81	*80-81-90-91*	*90-91-00-01*	*00-01-03-04*
Shares (%)				
Trade	32.2	32.1	30.4	30.2
Transport	12.4	13.6	12.0	11.1
Communication	2.0	2.5	4.0	7.0
Banking	4.9	8.3	11.9	13.4
Real Estate	15.7	12.5	12.9	12.0
Public administration	11.9	14.3	13.2	11.6
Other services	21.0	16.6	15.6	14.9
Service Total	100	100	100	100
Growth rate %				
Trade	4.8	5.9	7.2	8.6
Transport	5.6	5.5	6.2	6.8
Communication	6.7	6.0	16.7	23.5
Banking	6.7	12.0	10.6	7.4
Real Estate	2.6	8.5	6.5	6.1
Public Administration	6.1	6.5	6.1	3.3
Other services	3.3	5.8	7.2	6.2
Service Total	4.5	6.2	7.6	7.9
Contribution to service sector growth %				
Trade	1.5	2.0	2.2	2.6
Transport	0.6	0.8	0.8	0.8
Communication	0.1	0.2	0.4	1.3
Banking	0.2	0.8	1.1	1.0
Real Estate	0.5	1.0	0.9	0.7
Public Administration	0.6	0.9	0.9	0.4
Other services	0.8	1.0	1.1	0.9
Service Total	4.5	6.7	7.6	7.9

Source: Seema Bathla (2006).

does not Granger Cause the share of industry in GDP and vice versa during the same period. All these tests are insignificant and are shown below in Table 4.

Table 4
Granger Casuality Test

	Observation	*F statistic*	*Probability*
X_2 does not Granger Cause x_1	55	0.00374	0.9514
X_1 does nor Granger Cause x_2	55	0.64375	0.426
X_3 does not Granger Cause x_3	55	4.1E-05	0.9949
X_1 does not Granger Cause x_3	55	0.38598	0.53713
X_3 does not Granger Causex_2	55	0.61312	0.43717
X_2 does not Granger Cause x_3	55	0.34453	0.55977

Source: Calculated by author.

Moreover, another inter-sectoral linkage model can be computed through the multiple log regression analysis which states that 1% increase in the share of industry and tertiary sector in GDP per year induced to fall in the share of agriculture in GDP by 0.0711% and 1.397% per year respectively during the study period of 1950-51-2005-06. This relation is highly significant. The strong association between agricultural share, industrial share and service sector share during the specified period is justified by the significant ADF value = -3.610596. The equation is stated below:

$$\text{Log}(x_1) = 8.9001 - 0.071187 \log(x_2) - 1.397025 \log(x_3)$$

$$(128.55)^{*} \quad (-2.1505)^{*} \qquad (-41.788)^{*}$$

$R^2 = 0.99$, DW = 0.68, F = 2874.34, SE = 0.027, ADF = -3.610596*,
* = significant 10% level.

The globalization spread over the growth of multinationals throughout the world economy which influenced the sharp increases in the share of service sector in GDP in most of the countries of Europe, Asia and America. Agriculture sector has been transferred into a subsistence sector in the developing economy especially India where modern technology and industrial growth strategy are solely dependent on the developed economies. Hence the process of inequality started there in among the countries and the intersectoral linkage in the stages of development broke down. The multinationals became the producers and sellers and the developing countries are buyers and the world exchange economy have been flourished. Thus why, the service sector and its growth create hegemony in the world development pattern.

Although in the growth globalization nexus debates, India showed the positive relation when one per cent increase in the degree of openness produces 4.8287% increase of growth rate per year during 1950-51 -2005-06. This relationship is highly significant although there are several indicators of globalization except the degree of openness. In this process too, the share of agriculture in GDP has a negative association with the GDP growth rate which is significant but the positive association between the share of industry in GDP and growth rate of GDP showed insignificant. On the contrary, the correlation between the share of service sector in GDP and the growth rate had found strong and positive association during 1950-51-2005-06 and showed highly significant which states that one per cent increase in the share of service sector in GDP induced increase in growth of GDP in the economy towards 0.862% per year during the specified period. This rate is higher than that of the other sectors which might prove that the share of service sector in GDP and the share of industry in GDP have induced growth positively, on the other hand the share of agriculture in GDP affects growth rate negatively. Hence, the service driven growth is, no doubt, a clear phenomenon in India since long which is unsustainable in context of inter-sectoral linkage for development.

Now, how much the degree of openness affects the sectoral growth pattern can be shown through the following double log regression analysis which explained that one per cent increase in degree of openness index has reduced the agricultural share in GDP by 0.5093% per year during 1950-51-2005-06. And, one per cent increase in the degree of openness has increased the industrial share in GDP and service sector share in GDP by 0.1119% per year and 0.3429% per year respectively during the survey period. It is clear that the openness influenced most significantly in the service sector than that of others. (Table 5) and (Figure 2).

Table 5

Relation between Sectoral Shares and Degree of Openness

$$\text{Log}(x_1) = 2.1807 - 0.5093 \log(x_5)$$
$$(26.86)^* \ (-16.807)^*$$
$$R^2 = 0.884$$

$$\text{Log}(x_2) = 3.502 + 0.11194 \log(x_5)$$
$$(48.718)^* \ (4.171)^*$$
$$R^2 = 0.319$$

$$\text{Log}(x_3) = 4.5921 + 0.3429 \log(x_5)$$
$$(90.013)^* \ (18.007)^*$$
$$R^2 = 0.897$$

$$\text{Log}(x_4) = 2.833 + 4.8287 \log(x_5)$$
$$(0.474)^*(2.150)^*$$
$$R^2 = 0.116$$

$$\text{Log}(x_4) = -1.6148 + 0.8662 \log(x_3)$$
$$(-1.0635) \ (2.0589)^*$$
$$R^2 = 0.0796$$

$$\text{Log}(x_4) = -0.435 + 0.6242 \log(x_2)$$
$$(-0.315) \ (1.409)$$
$$R^2 = 0.0389$$

$$\text{Log}(x_4) = 3.735 - 0.6117 \log(x_1)$$
$$(3.55)^* \ (-2.128)^*$$
$$R^2 = 0.0846$$

Where x_4 = growth rate of the GDP, x_5 = degree of openness, *= significant at least 10% level.

Source: Calculated by author.

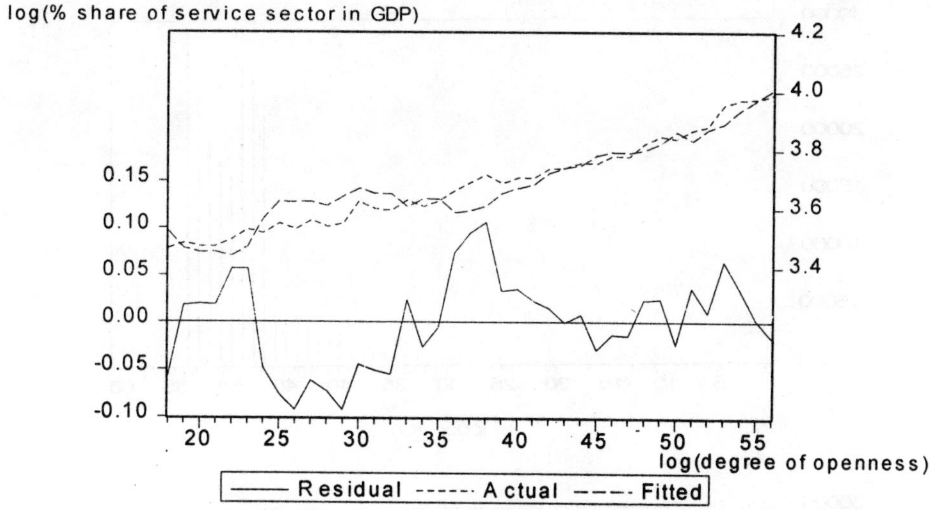

Figure: 2

In India, the exports grew at the rate of 10.44% per year during 1968-2006 in which the exports of primary sector increased at the 11.06% per year and the exports of industrial sector enhanced at the rate of 12.66% per year during 1950-51-2004-05 and the exports of service sector grew at the rate of 16.00% per year during the same period. Thus, exports of services play a significant role in service led growth strategy. Their trend lines are found significant and are given below in Table 6 and the shares are clearly shown in Figure 3.

Table 6
Trend lines of Share of Exports of Sectors

$$\text{Log}(x_7) = 1.079 + 0.1600t$$
(2.95)* (13.84)*
$$R^2 = 0.786$$

$$\text{Log}(x_8) = 4.296 + 0.1106t$$
(43.24)* (31.97)*
$$R^2 = 0.95$$

$$\text{Log}(x_9) = 4.7813+0.1266t$$
(32.163)* (24.46)*
$$R^2 = 0.927$$

Where x_7= share of export of service sector, x_8 = share of exports of primary sector, x_9 = share of exports of industry sector. * = significant at least 10% level.

Source: Calculated by author.

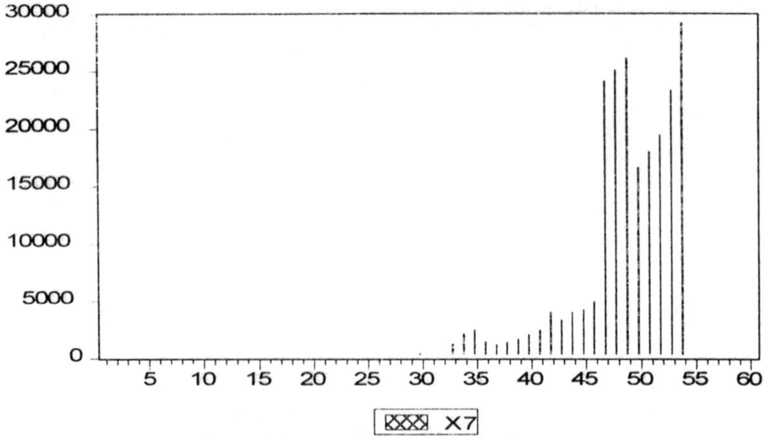
30000
25000
20000
15000
10000
5000
0
5 10 15 20 25 30 35 40 45 50 55 60
X7

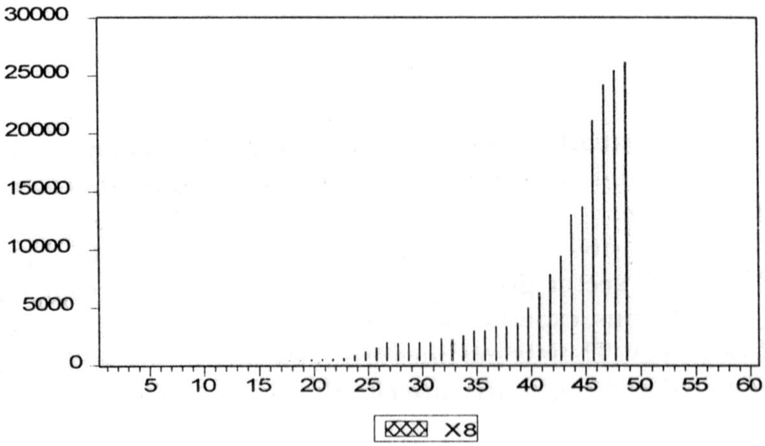
30000
25000
20000
15000
10000
5000
0
5 10 15 20 25 30 35 40 45 50 55 60
X8

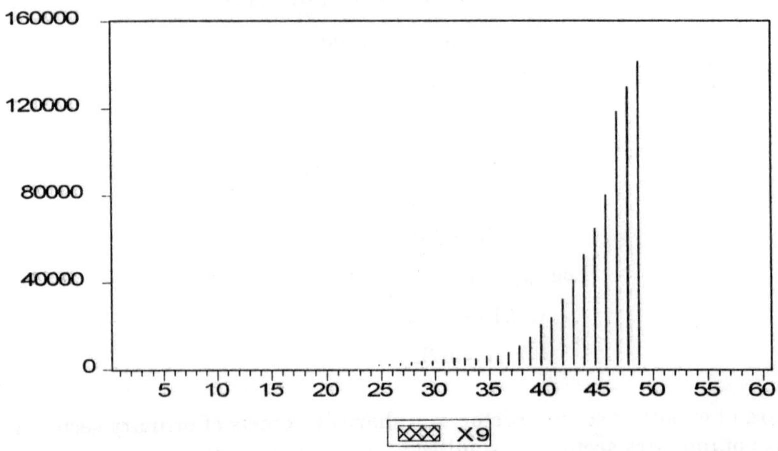
160000
120000
80000
40000
0
5 10 15 20 25 30 35 40 45 50 55 60
X9

Figure: 3

Although the balance of trade of services remained unfavourable to India throughout the planning period and the rate of growth of services imports per year from 1950-51-2004-05 counteracted unfavourably to export-led growth in India. In 1980, India's service exports was 0.760% of the world which increased to 1.090% in 2000 and to 1.22% in 2004 that was 7.78% of USA. On the otherhand, India's service imports was 0.683% of the world in 1980 which enhanced to 1.263% in 2000 and to 1.383% in 2004 that was 10.469% of USA. Hence, service exports are not satisfactory in current account balances although it grew at a higher rate because of the effects of liberalization and globalization. This can be tested through the association between the value of service exports and the degree of openness during 1950-51-2004-05 which states that one per cent increase in degree of openness catapulted 6.28% exports of services per year and was found significant. Again, this service exports has strong association with the share of service sector in GDP which was found by the double log linear model that explained that one per cent increase in the service exports per year leads to increase the share of service sector in GDP by 0.058% per year during 1950-51-2004-05. It is highly significant. The regression equations are given below.

$$\text{Log}(x_7) = 23.486 + 6.2802 \log(x_5)$$
$$(14.04)^* \quad (10.211)^*$$

$R^2 = 0.748$, $F = 104.274$

$$\text{Log}(x_3) = 3.25917 + 0.05809 \log(x_7)$$
$$(141.193)^* (15.503)^*, R^2 = 0.82, {}^* = \text{significant at 10\% level.}$$

During the globalization capital flows under the financial sector reform process has a positive impact on the growth of service sector which implies a significant positive influence on the overall growth of the economy. Thus why, in India, under the reform period the FDI inflows increased the share of service sector in GDP by 0.0644% per year during 1990-2005 which is shown by the following regression.

$$\text{Log}(x_3) = 3.34 + 0.0644 \log(x_6)$$
$$(34.96)^* \ (5.154)^*$$

$R^2 = 0.67$, $F = 26.57$, where x_6 = value of Foreign direct investment in million dollar. * = significant at least 10% level.

This result ultimately satisfies the Levine's (2004) propositions that financial sector development affects economic growth by (i) reducing cost of acquiring information on investment inducing efficient allocation of funds, (ii) enhancing corporate governance, (iii) relaxing cross sectional, intertemporal and liquidity risk, (iv) pooling savings and (v) easing exchange.

Hence, under financial sector reform, free mobility of capital flows, full convertibility of Rupee and the banking sector reform will surely affect service sector positively in increasing the GDP growth rate in the process of globalization.

SERVICE SECTOR AND THE EMPLOYMENT SCENARIO

It was verified from the regression analysis that the growth rate of GDP and the rate of employment has no significant positive relation at all in India during the planning period, on the contrary it showed excessive volatility.

On the other hand, from the elasticity concept, now we can explain the India's employment scenario as given below in the Table 7.

Table 7
Elasticity of Employment in the Sectors of India

	Elasticity of employment					*Total employment*	
	77-78-83	*83-93-94*	*93-94-99-00*	*9th plan*	*future*	*2007*	*2012*
Agriculture	0.45	0.50	0.00	0.50	0.10	233.68	248.47
Manufacturing	0.80	0.69	0.00	0.60	0.00	2.27	2.27
Mining & Quarring	0.67	0.33	0.26	0.25	0.22	53.65	57.91
Electricity	0.73	0.52	0.00	0.50	0.00	1.28	1.28
Construction	1.0	1.0	1.0	0.6	0.6	23.35	28.69
Wholesale & retail trade	0.78	0.63	0.55	0.55	0.5	48.25	56.85
Transport, storage, communication	1.0	0.49	0.69	0.55	0.40	18.2	21.02
Finance, real estate, Insurance	1.0	0.92	0.73	0.53	0.50	6.85	8.54
Community, social science	0.83	0.50	0.07	0.50	0.30	38.65	42.76
All sectors	0.53	0.41	0.15	0.38	0.22	436.18	467.81

Source: Planning Commission.

The above table suggested that the marginal increase in employment elasticity in agriculture justified the increase in employment generation in agricultural sector, but a fall in the employment elasticity in mining and Quarrying, Manufacturing, electricity, construction, wholesale and retailing, transport and communication, finance, real eatate, community and social services etc implied a bleak scenerio in the employment during 1977-78-2000 in India and in future. Taking all the sectors at a time, the employment elasticity has continuously declined unless during 1993-94-1999-00, which means India's GDP growth rate did not increase in the employment growth rate at all. That is globalization may not boost

India's employment growth rate in spite of higher growth rate in the offing.

Yet, the service sector has chief potentiality in generating employment because of rise in productivity and investment. But, it is unfortunate to specify that the decade wise employment growth rates of the three sectors from 60s have been declining rapidly and even negative in the agriculture sector and are much higher in every decades from 1960-61-69-70. It is interestingly to note that the employment growth rates of the three sectors during the pre reform period are much higher than the post reform period and again the growth rate of employment in the service sector in pre-reform period and post reform period showed larger than those of the two sectors.

More specifically, the employment growth rates in the public sector in the post reform period showed a sharp decline compared to pre-reform period. Here, the growth rate of employment in three sectors gradually have been falling decade wise since 60s except in 70s. The employment growth rate of the service sector in every decades are less than the other sectors. On the other hand, the employment growth rates in service sector in the public sector since 60s have been falling up to 80s then increasing and even these growth rates are too higher than the two other sectors. Both the secondary and tertiary sectors showed higher employment growth rate in the post reform period than the pre-reform. This is clearly shown in the Table 8 below.

Table 8
Employment Growth Rate

	60-61-69-70	*70-71-79-80*	*80-81-89-90*	*90-91-00-01*	*pre reform*	*post reform*
Primary	1.41	3.27	1.22	-0.50	1.11	-0.89
Secondary	3.77	2.22	0.82	0.59	0.73	0.54
Tertiary	5.44	2.94	2.21	0.85	2.13	0.73
Public sector						
Primary	4.39	12.86	2.53	-0.75	2.11	-1.17
Secondary	6.01	4.60	2.45	-0.93	2.00	-1.25
Tertiary	4.39	3.05	2.33	0.63	2.20	0.55
Private Sector						
Primary	0.53	-2.96	-0.62	-0.11	-0.15	-0.45
Secondary	2.84	0.91	-0.42	1.79	-0.24	1.92
Tertiary	13.43	2.48	1.51	1.92	1.65	1.89

Source: Seema Bathla (2006).

POLICY ISSUES

For sustainable service led growth the following issues on policies may be considered.

(i) For sustainability of export led growth, the growth of export must be greater than the growth of import and the balance of trade must be positive and should be increasing. Therefore, the policies of incentives to boost export, the export industries, decline of export tax, and free mobility of foreign direct investment to increase domestic as well as foreign demand for industrial production are urgently required. So that the positive trend of current account balance should be maintained in order to gain from foreign trade. The growth of money supply should be positively associated the current account balance that can accelerate the export led growth

(ii) If the export led growth be the complementary to the service led growth strategy then balance between service export and import should be positive and the service sector must be linked to strong industrial base so that the linkage between the two are planned for long term growth. Promotion of foreign direct investment in service sector should be upswing in employment growth pattern with the emphasis on public private partnership.

(iii) As liberalization and globalization are clouded over the world economy so that the service driven growth became the dominant factor of high growth rate in most of the economies and therefore inter-linkage between the sectors did not fit in the sustainable development path. The unequal distribution of income, unequal industrial development, and the capture of market share through multinationals are the prime outcomes of such breakthrough of inter-sectoral-linkage. A good governance can restrict such growth strategies which are responsible to catapult poverty. Hence, service driven growth strategy must be pro-poor, high employment oriented and sustainable.

CONCLUSION

Now, India can be considered as the prototype model of service driven growth where the service sector have high forward linkage and potential productivity gain because service is the input of other sectors too. Recent accelerated growth in the service sector is a big push towards a sustainable development path which is highly a debatable concern. Again, this development model does not explicitly promote merchandise exports and it is hardly called export led growth model. In this big push in service industry must immediately catch up with the fast growing service sector in which industry must have strong base through associated efficiency and productivity gain. Also, as the forward linkage of modern services stimulate the development of industry which in turn has high backward linkage, virtuous self sustaining cycle of broad based rapid economic expansion may ensure, ultimately resulting in higher incomes and a substantial reduction in poverty.

REFERENCES

ADB (2007), Asian Development *Outlook*, 2007.

Bathla, Seema (2006), Intersectoral Growth Linkages in India: Implications for Policy and Liberalized Reforms, Institute for Economic Growth.

Bhanumurthy, N. R. and Arup Mitra (2003), Declining Poverty in India: Decompositions Analysis: D. P. No. 70/2003, Institute of Economic Growth, University of Delhi.

Bhattacharjee, B. B. and S. Kar (2005), The Indian Macro Economy: Prospect for the Future, Institute for Economic Growth, NewDelhi.

B.B. Bhattacharya and Sabyasachi Kar (2007), Macroeconomic Reforms, Growth and Stability, Oxford.

Bhattacharjya, B.B. and C.H. Hanumantha Rao (1986), Agriculture Industry Interrelations: Issues of Relative Prices and Growth in the context of Public Investment, Theme 18, 8th World Economic Congress of the International Economic Association, New Delhi.

Bhattacharjya, B.B. and Arup Mitra (1990), Excess Growth of Tertiary Sector in Indian Economy: Issues and Implications, *EPW*, November 3.

Beck, Thorton, Ross Levine and Norman Loayza (1997), Finance and Sources of Growth. The World Bank Development Research Group.

Chakraborty, S. (1973), Reflections on the Growth Process in Indian Economy, in Writings on Development, Oxford University Press.

Chowdhury, Khorshed and Mamta B. Chowdhury (1995), Sectoral Linkages and Economic Growth in Asia: Evidence from Granger Causality Test, *The Indian Economic Journal*, Vol. 42, No. 4, April-June.

Clerk, C. (1940), The Conditions of Economic Progress. Macmillan.

EPW Research Foundation (2006), National Income Statistics in India, 1950-51-2003-04.

Fisher, A.G.B. (1939), Production in Primary, Secondary and Tertiary, *Economic Record*, Vol. 15.

Johnston, B. F. and J.W. Mellor (1961), The Role of Agriculture in Economic Development, AE R, 78(4):566-593.

Krishna, Raj (1982), Some Aspect of Agricultural Growth: Price Policy and Equity in Developing Countries. *Food Research Institute Studies*, Vol. XVIII, No. 3.

Kuznets, Simon (1966), Modern Economic Growth: Rate, Structure and Spread. New Haven,Yale University Press.

Levine, Ross (2004), Finance and Growth: Theory and Evidence. NBER, WP No. 10766.

Lewis, W.A. (1955), The Theory of Economic Growth. Homewood, III.

Mitra, A. (1977), Terms of Trade and Class Relations: An Essay in Political Economy, London, Frank Cass.

Mundle, S. (1981), Surplus Flows and Growth Imbalances. Allied Publishers, NewDelhi.

Park, Se-Hark and Kenneth S. Chan (1989), A Cross Country Input Output Analysis of Intersectoral Relationship Between Manufacturing and Services and their Employment Implications, *World Development*, Vol. 17, No. 2, pp. 199-212.

Planning Commission (2006), Towards Faster and More Inclusive Growth-Approach in 11th Plan.

————(2001), Report of the Task Force on Employment Opportunity, 2001.

————(2002), Special Group on Targeting 10 Million Employment Opportunity per Year.

Preobrazhensky, E. (1965), The New Economics. Oxford, Clarendon Press.

Rakshit, Mihir (2007), Service-led Growth:The Indian Experience, *Artha Beekshan*, Vol. 15, No. 4, pp. 1-37.

Rangarajan, C. (1982), Agricultural Growth and Industrial Performance in India, Research Report No. 33, International Food Policy Research Institute .Washington D.C.

Ravallion, Martin and Gaurav Datt (1996), How Important to India's Poor is the Sectoral Composition of Economic Growth, *The World Bank Economic Review*, Vol. 10, No. 1.

Tadatern Hayashi (2006), An Outline of the Emerging Services Driven Economic Growth in South Asia–Report on the South Asia Departmental Economists Annual Conference, December 7-8, 2006 by ADB in New Delhi.

UNCTAD (2007), Handbook of Statistics (2007).

UNCTAD (1998, 2005, 2007), World Investment Report, 1998, 2005, 2007.

World Bank (1992, 2006), World Development Reports, 1992 , 2006.

GENDER DISCRIMINATION AND WAGE DETERMINATION OF AGRICULTURAL LABOURERS: A STUDY IN GULBARGA DISTRICT OF KARNATAKA

Vithob B., Y. S. Vaggi** & Mallikarjun Naik****

INTRODUCTION

Indian economy is an agricultural economy, as about 65% of population depends on agriculture sector for their subsistence. Now India's population passed 100 crores, but 71% of population living in rural areas. In rural areas 89.5% of total females are engaged in the agriculture and allied sectors. Agriculture continues to be the mainstay of the Indian economy. Its contribution towards the national GDP is about 25%. In the new millennium with the globalization and liberalization of the economy the challenges in Indian agricultural sector are quite different from those met in the previous decades.

Female labourers constitute overwhelmingly major section of agricultural labour. The remarkable increase in the agriculture labour force in India. In recent years has been one of the most significant social transformations in the history of India. For millions of people born in rural district. There is no chance for escape from agriculture as source of employment.

Female as agricultural labourers participate in several activities such as chilli picking, cotton picking, groundnut picking, sowing, transport and storage, threshing, transplanting, watering, seeding, cutting, plant protection, thinning, harvesting, processing, selling, winnowing etc. Thus by participating in above agricultural activities, they directly or indirectly influence the course of agriculture and animal husbandry.

* Research Scholars, Department of Economics, Gulbarga University, Gulbarga (Karnataka).

** Department of Economics, Gulbarga University, Gulbarga (Karnataka).

*** Research Scholars, Department of Commerce, Gulbarga University, Gulbarga (Karnataka).

Inspite of the fact that, the constitution of India has provided equal rights and privileges for men and women, the women labourers are discriminated in wage payments even in the agricultural operations which are better performed by female labourers. This not only violates the established principle of "equal pay for equal work" but also lowers their income level, which in turn affects adversely their socio-economic states, standard of living efficiency and their productivity (Sharma N.P., 1993). With this background the study has been conducted to examine the issue in Gulbarga district as case study on the basis of following objectives.

OBJECTIVES OF THE STUDY

(1) To study the conditions of female agricultural labourers in India.

(2) To examine the wage difference between male and female agricultural labourers in study region.

(3) To study the labour migration in study area.

(4) To record the suggestions for the improvement of female agricultural labourers pertaining to wage differentials.

METHODOLOGY

The present study has been undertaken at taluka level. This study presents the wages paid to the male and female agricultural labourers in Shorapur taluka in Gulbarga district (Karnataka). The Shorapur taluka having more irrigation facilities from Upper Krishna Project and growing various crops.

Random sampling technique has been adopted to select four villages (2 irrigated and 2 non-irrigated) in the taluka. The primary data has been collected from 150 samples through interview schedules administered among 100 (50 male and 50 female) labourers from irrigated area and 50 (25 male and 25 female) labourers from non-irrigated area.

TYPES OF FEMALE LABOURERS IN AGRICULTURE

There are two types of female labourers in Indian agricultural practices i.e., Casual and Contract gang labour. Casual labour as known as **Dinaguli** as wage for a day. This is an important segment of the hired labour market in India as well as study region. The labourers are hired for a certain period a day, a week or more. This type of labourer are engaged in sowing, manuring, weeding, threshing, transplanting and harvesting etc., and they always ready to work for any employers, who preferred to pay the current market wage. The labour received the payment weekly i.e., on bazaar day or in intervals. Both land less and landed households hire themselves out as casual labours.

The other type of labour hiring system prevalent in the study region is contract gang labour. This practice holds a significant position in the labour market, as known as **"Guttige"** who works in employer's field in a day, no fixation of time, and also called as **Group labourers.** In the study region a group of families from these gang and work together. The payment is fixed on size of land, nature of work and crop, and distance from home, payment will be paid only in cash and there will be no fixation of time for work.

CHARACTERISTICS OF FEMALE AGRICULTURAL LABOURERS

Before any attempts are made to evolve a rational policy for improving the living conditions of a female agricultural labourer who happens to belong to the lowest socio and economic ladder, it is essential to know the distinguishing features of female agricultural labours in India.

(1) Female agricultural labourers are especially coming from villages.

(2) Generally they are unskilled workers carrying on their agricultural operations in traditional ways.

(3) The bargaining power and position of female agricultural labourers in India is very weak.

(4) Female agricultural labour is the most exploited class of people in India.

(5) Female agricultural labourers work as casual and contract gang labour. The nature of employment, wage and the employer-employee relation differ across these groups.

(6) In some parts of India, female agriculture labour are found to be migratory, moving in search of jobs especially at the time of sowing and harvesting in near by areas.

IMPORTANCE OF WOMEN IN AGRICULTURE

Woman is the molder and builder of any nation's destiny. They play a significant role in any economy. They are considered as the backbone of the rural scene. Most of the women perform various types of work for their livelihood and agriculture is considered as the biggest unorganized sector where large number of rural women takes part actively. About 75 per cent of the Indian female population is from rural families, who belonged to the small and marginal farmers and landless agricultural labourers (Census of India, 1991). Though women's primary responsibility is indulging in domestic work, greater emphasis is laid on women's earning in the form of money by working outside the four walls. In India, a significant proportion of the populations are below the poverty Line and it is a fact that labour force participation will increase with poverty, a large Proportions of rural women are under a pressure to participate in the labour force. These Unknown and unacknowledged beings are responsible to keep the economy at a steady Pace and helped the nation to occupy a significant place in the world.

Table 1
Distribution of Female Workers in India (1951-2001)

(In thousands)

Year	*Total Female Population*	*Cultivators*	*Agricultural Labourers*	*Industry and Service*	*Total Female Workers*
1951	173,543	18,368 (45.3)	12,694 (31.3)	9,477 (23.3)	40,539 (100)
1961	212,467	33,103 (55.7)	14,171 (23.9)	12,128 (20.4)	59,402 (100)
1971	263,900	9,266 (29.6)	15,794 (50.5)	6,238 (19.9)	31,298 (100)
1981	321,357	14,932 (33.2)	20,768 (46.2)	9,273 (20.6)	44,973 (100)
1991	402,813	22,871 (34.5)	28,833 (43.6)	14,485 (21.9)	66,189 (100
2001	495,738	41,299 (41.51)	50,093 (50.35)	8,083 (8.14)	99,475 (100)

Note: Figures do not include those of Jammu & Kashmir.
Figures within parentheses denote percentage of women workers.

Source: 1. Towards Equality: Report on the Committee on Status of Women, Government of India, Ministry of Social Welfare, New Delhi 1974, pp. 153-158.
2. Census of India, 1981 Series India, Primary Census Abstract, General Population, Part 11B (i), pp. 7-8.
3. Census of India, 1991 Series 1; Paper 3; Provisional Population Totals: Workers and Their distribution.

The association of women in agriculture is an age-old practice. The 1991 census data indicates that 43.6 per cent of women are working, as agricultural labourers 34.5 per cent are cultivators, but it is increased to 50.35 and 41.51 respectively in 2001 census. Though rural farm labourers work under severe limitations, their contribution towards agricultural production and development is noteworthy. Apart from the job they do outside the household, the unpaid activities in the domestic sphere go unnoticed and un-rewarded. Women workforce outside the four walls is larger in rural areas than in urban India. Women in rural areas help to grow at least about 50 per cent of the world's food. They work in all aspects of cultivation including planting, weeding, harvesting, sowing, threshing, etc.

According to the census reports, there is an increased participation of rural women in economic activities beside doing household duties, though participation of women in agriculture contribute a lot for the economic growth and progress of the country, their problems are shown least concern.

In India female agricultural labourers are not homogeneously distributed all over the country, their percentage varies in different regions due to demographic, technological, ecological and sociological reasons. This may be clearly seen from the following table.

Table 2
Distribution of Female Agricultural Labours in Different States in India (2001)

Name of the states	*Total Agricultural labourers*	*Female Agricultural labourers*	*% of the female agricultural labourers*
Andhra Pradesh	11850113	7191188	60.68
Assam	2509526	437630	17.44
Arunachal Pradesh	171565	7972	4.65
Bihar	7205937	4652672	64.57
Gujarat	5721030	2515045	43.96
Haryana	2376211	543088	22.85
Himachal Pradesh	1266666	37288	2.98
Jammu & Kasmir	940081	50760	5.40
Karnataka	6854752	3455460	50.40
Kerala	1925009	505086	26.24
Maharastra	12695748	6121358	48.21
Madhya Pradesh	8669974	3769434	43.48
Manipur	381802	55895	14.65
Mizoram	118377	5293	4.47
Orissa	4200930	2390685	56.90
Panjab	1749465	363685	20.79
Rajastan	8496356	1449004	17.05
Sikkim	91543	8322	9.10
Tamil Nadu	7175171	3897586	54.32
Uttar Pradesh	11799397	5184385	43.94
West Bengal	5821973	2244803	38.55

Source: Provisional Population Totals, paper 3 Census of India 2001.

Table 2 reveals that, distribution of female agricultural labourers in India, among all the states Bihar state has the highest female agricultural labours i.e., 64.57% to the total agricultural labourers in India, and followed by Andhra Pradesh i.e., 60.68%. The lowest female agricultural labours in Himachal Pradesh, Mizoram and Arunachal Pradesh (2.94%, 4.47% and 4.65%) respectively. Karnataka has got fifth place having female agricultural labourers in India i.e., 50.40% to the total agricultural labourers.

AVERAGE YEARLY WAGE EARNINGS, EMPLOYMENT PER WORKER AND PER CAPITA IN RURAL INDIA

The NSSO 55th round survey conducted in 1999-2000 found that employment has been decreased marginally in rural areas. Employment for females came down by 3% in rural India compared to last survey conducted in 1993-94 (refer the below table).

Table 3
Estimated Average Yearly Wage and Employment Earnings Per Capita and Per Workers in the 54th and 55th NSSO Survey (1999-2000) in Rural India

Particulars	*1993-94*	*1999-00*
Female Population (000)	317950	344640
Female work force (000)	104290	195000
Average number of working days (in a year)	241	246
Average daily wage earnings of female casual labour	15.15	18.27
Yearly wage earnings (RS in crore)	38078	46315
Earning per workers (RS)	3651	4494
Earning per capita (RS)	1198	1344
Growth rate of earnings per worker (% annum)	–	3.52
Growth rate of earnings	–	1.95

Source: 55th NSSO New Delhi, 1999-2000.
Note: Inflation adjustment for rural India has been made by reference to consumer price. Index on agricultural labourers (CPIAL base 1986-87 = 100).

Bihar state is topped the female work participation in agriculture with 650 finding employment in a population of 1000, with Himachal Pradesh at the last end employing only 380 out of 1000 in rural areas. The above table shows that the estimated average wage earnings and employment per worker and per capita in rural India.

The survey further shows that in the year 1999-2000 the self employed secured for 57% of were casual labour and 3% of females were regular employees, but it is compared to study region, lot of difference between irrigated and non-irrigated areas, i.e., 75.6% in irrigated and 68.89% females employed in non-irrigated areas as casual labour. In all surveys between 1972-2000 self-employed people in the rural areas were more than regularly employed.

WAGE DIFFERENTIALS

The general wage rate for casual labourers in study region between Rs. 45 to 50 for male and Rs. 20 to 15 for female labourers depending upon the situation. The peak season the wage rate is generally Rs. 50 for male and Rs. 25 for female labours, but in slack season wage rate would go down to Rs. 40 for male and Rs. 15 to 20 for female labours for seven to eight hours per day, wages in kind still prevalent. Which to some extent protects the real wages in inflationary situations, but cash payment is becoming more common except harvesting, where wages from generally little part of the crop like, bajra cutting, jawar cutting and groundnut picking inter culture the rate of wage was 1 to 2kg of cereals when paid in kind. For threshing was done on threshers cereals was also given to labour.

In some situation the labourers also shifting to work on contract basis. This enables to them to engage other members of their family in leading women and men to the complete the work in shorter time and they move to other employers. Here separate of the women and men gangs or may be fixed and wage rate is determined basis on size of land, variety of crops and distance from house to land. Transplanting operation is being increasingly subjected to this phenomenon. It was observed that, when transplanting or other such operation was done on contract basis the work was finished quickly as every one among the workers wanted the work to be complete as early as possible. So that they may find some other contract is still paid on traditional basis but in some villages a few labour households preformed it on contract basis or both contract and casual labour.

In the study region, wage rate is improved from fifteen years, due to irrigation is developed in the study region. Here wage rate is different in irrigated and non-irrigated areas as well as male and female labourers indicated in the following table.

Table 4
The Average Wage Rates for
Male and Female Agricultural Labourers (Rs.)

	Casual labour (per day)			*Contract gang labour (per acre)*		
Name of the areas	*Male*	*Female*	*Differential*	*Male*	*Female*	*Differential*
Irrigated						
Hunasagi	45	20	25	600	550	50
Waginagera	40	20	20	550	500	50
Non-Irrigated						
Malanoor	50	25	25			
Lingadalli	45	25	20	—	—	—

Source: Field data.

The above table reveals that, wage rate is differs from village to village. In non-irrigated villages wage rate is higher than irrigated villages, due to, there is less employment days available in only for four to five months in a year. In busy season, the labourers are not available. Hence they paid more. Some times wage rate is fluctuating in irrigated area also in peak season. The wage rate is not equal between male and female labourers. Male labourers were getting more wage rate than female labourers. Differential wage rate is more in non-irrigated area i.e., Rs. 30 per day, due to customary, they accept them, illiteracy, unequal working capacity. Female labourers suffering from differential wage rate in contract gang labour also. Rs. 50 per day wage rate are difference between male and female contract gang labours.

OPERATION WISE WAGE RATE

Majority of jobs allotted to female labourers in study region as well as agricultural sector. It is based on their skill and efficiency. Because of availability of female labour, low wage and sincerity in work. Though, more differentials in wage rate among male and female labourers. The operation wise wage rate differentials in study region indicated in the following table.

Table 5
Operation Wise Wage Rate Among
Male and Female Labourers (Per Day Rs.)

Name of the agricultural operations	*Male*	*Female*	*Wage differentials*
Chilli picking and cutting	60	30	30
Cotton picking and cutting	60	25	35
Ground nut picking	55	25	30
Sowing	60	25	35
Transport and storage	70	30	40
Threshing	55	25	30
Transplanting	-	30	-
Weeding	-	25	-
Cutting	60	25	35
Processing	60	30	30

Source: Field data.

The above table shows that, the highest wage differentials in transport and storage, cotton picking, sowing and cutting Rs 40 and Rs 35 per day respectively. Further the important point to be noted here is that, this discrimination against female labourers is not only in the operations like sowing, seeding, cutting and transport and storage, which requires more physical labour, but also in female labours intensive operations such as weeding and transplanting which are better performed by them.

LABOUR MIGRATION

Lack of adequate employment in native is the main reason for labour migration. In the study region labour migration takes place from only dry land area, because of inadequate employment days. So they go to out side villages or urban areas to seek work for their subsistence and they will come to their native during season. They prefer Rabi and summer seasons for migration. The details about migration indicated in the following table.

Table 6
Details about Labour Migration in Non-irrigated Area

Particulars	*Male*	*Female*
No. of respondents migrating	66.67. (%)	90. (%)
Average days in a year	60	85
Wage rates (per day)	100	40
Average income (Rs)	6000	3400

Source: Field data.

The above table shows that, maximum labourers prefer migration in non-irrigated areas i.e., 66.67% of male and 90% of female labourers. They are migrated two to three months in a year, but wage rate is different between native to migrate area i.e., Rs. 100 for male and Rs. 40 for female, because they are not engage in agricultural activities, most of the labourers prefer to canal work and building construction etc., and they are getting payment on the basis of casual labour. Male labourers earn Rs. 6000 in 60 days and female labourers earn Rs. 3400 in 85 days, after these days they will come to their native and remaining days they are going on unemployed in non-irrigated area.

FINDINGS

After collection of data observed some findings on the problem as mentioned below:

1. Some jobs are reserved to female labours in agriculture viz., Chili, Cotton and Groundnut Picking, Transplanting and Weeding.
2. Daily wage rate of female labours is different between Causal and Contract Gang labours as well as irrigated and non-irrigated area.
3. Operation wise wage rate is different between male and female labourers in agriculture as well as irrigated and non-irrigated areas.
4. Migrant labourers are drawn from only in non-irrigated area.

SUGGESTIONS

From the study it is clear that the rural labour community suffers from a lot of social and economic problems. Hence, a multi proposal and organized effort is needed to solve their problems; some necessary measures may be suggested as follows:

1. For female agricultural labourers there is a need to organize a movement to fight against wage differentials.
2. Policy makers can take consideration of the interests of female agricultural labourers at the time of framing policies for the development and welfare of agricultural labourers.
3. The law enforcement agencies must play a crucial role in implementing laws related to agricultural labourers like equal pay for equal work.
4. Creation of awareness among the masses about the benefits of government programmes.
5. Improvement in better employment conditions.
6. Minimum wage rate should be fixed.
7. There is very much need to increase the Female literacy rate.
8. To abolish the problem of child labour, proper steps should be taken at the earliest.

CONCLUSION

From this study it has been observed that, the conditions of female agricultural labours are better in irrigated area compare to non-irrigated area. Therefore provision of irrigation and adoption of labour intensive cropping patterns may helps to improve the conditions of female agricultural labours. Irrigation has increased employment opportunities, but the wage rates have not increased due to excess supply of labour. Female labour market is becoming more flexible. Even though wage is low, the employment of female labour is showing increasing trend. There is actualization of labour and small and marginal farmers are turning into casual labours. They are loosing their control over productions. The conditions of female labours in non-irrigated areas are miserable. There is a need for comprehensive policy and minimum wage to promote welfare of the rural female labour class in the study region. The Grama panchayat, the government, the NGOs and the people have to work together for the same.

REFERENCES

Devdas, R. P. (1972), "Role of Selected Farm Women in Agricultural Operations", *Indian Journal of Home Science*, Vol. 6, No. 1, p. 25.

Varma Shashi (1982), "Women in Agriculture: A Socio-Economic Analysis", Concept Publishing Co. New Delhi.

Jha Shailendra (1990), "Agricultural Labour: Agricultural Labour Problems and Present Positions", Deep and Deep Publication, New Delhi, pp. 33-43.

Sing M. B. (1990), "Women's Role in Agriculture", The Tribune, 16 March, p.12.

Sarap, Kailash (1989), "Trends in Wage Rates and Living Conditions of Agricultural Labourers in Orissa", *Man and Development*, Vol. II, No. 3, Sept. pp. 113-123.

Subah Singh Yadav and Gujar Ram Kumar (1993), "Poverty Alleviation and Employment Generation", Sharma N. P., "Wage Differentials for Women Agricultural Labourers", Pointer Publishers, Jaipur, pp. 147-153.

Samanta R. K. (1995), "Women in Agriculture Perspective Issues and Experiences", M.D. Publications, New Delhi.

Tripathy, S. N. and Pradhan, K. C. (1996), "Agricultural Labour in India", Discovery Publishing House, New Delhi, pp. 1-7.

55th NSSO New Delhi, 1999-2000.

Government of India (1991), "Committee on the Status of Women in India", Census or India 1981, New Delhi.

Govt. of India (2001), "Professional Population Totals, Paper 3, Census of India, New Delhi.

Socio-economic and Health Problems of the Elderly People in Rural Areas

Basalingamma Halemani & S. A. Kazi**

INTRODUCTION

Ageing is a process of gradual and spontaneous change, resulting in maturation through childhood, puberty, and young adulthood and then decline through middle and late age. One of the reasons for the growth of the Indian society had been because of its multi-generation approach, which means staying of many generations together in one family. This phenomenon is also knows as the joint family system. Old people (Elderly) have been always considered as individuals with a vast repertoire of knowledge and experience. Staying with them and respecting them helps not only in personal growth but facilitates multi-dimensional growth of a person. One of the old sayings stated that those who greet elders and does service to them, they grow in all four dimensions such as Age, knowledge, name and strength. Today much of the problems seen in the society are due to the broken family system. Young couples prefer to stay alone for the reason of getting more independence and doing away with the restrictions. But the repercussion of this system is largely being felt on the younger generation. The elders in the family have always been a medium of cultural transmission, who shares their experiences and knowledge with the younger people. The cultural traditions followed in India have been passed from generation to generation. With the emerging nuclear family system; our younger generations are becoming deprived of this rich cultural transmission. It has been found that emotional expressions and values in young generation have also been affected by the absence of elders in the family.

In India, about it is estimated that there is 77 million of the population is aged. The statistical sources revealed that in India, the grey population

* Department of Social Work, Gulbarga University, Gulbarga, Karnataka State.

has doubled in 25 years. In Karnataka, the population statistics for the year 2001 shows that, of the total 5.28 Crores of population about 40.62 lakhs of population is above 60 years of age (Planning Commission: 2007).

STATISTICAL DIMENSION OF ELDERLY PEOPLE (2001) (AGE CARE FORUM: 2007)

- 77 Million elderly population (projected to 177 Million by 2025).
- 90% with no Social Security.
- 30% of older persons live below the poverty line.
- 33% of older persons live just marginally over the poverty online.
- 80% of older persons live in rural areas.
- 73% are illiterate, and can only be engaged in physical labor.
- 55% of elderly women are widows.
- There are nearly 200,000 centenarians in India.

FROM 1901 TO 2025: 12 MILLION TO 177 MILLION

- 1901-12 Million elderly.
- 1951-19 Million elderly.
- 2001-77 Million elderly.
- 2025-Projected 177 Million elderly.

The aged and elderly people, who had a dominant and important position in the family and community in the past and had contributed to society's well-being with their useful knowledge and experience, are very much a part of the present society. However, with the physical, psychological, socio-cultural and economical changes in old age, the aged people are facing a number of problems due to the occurrence of changes in their roles and status (Gurumurthy: 1996). It is noted that still in many rural areas, the elderly people playing an important role in solving problems and making decisions for the administrative problems. In the twenty first century, the family set-up has changed to nuclear/divided family rather than joint family. Further, the younger people are more attracted towards the cities, where they expect the jobs. But it is noted that the rural elderly people cannot adjust to the metropolitan environment. Hence, in majority of the cases, the elderly people are staying in villages and their children are working in cities.

In many cases, it is found that the elderly people are neglected due to various reasons, such as sickness, unemployed, weakening of the family, poverty, lack of care from younger in the family, feeling of insecurity, loneliness (in case of widows/widowers), etc. The findings of an ICMR survey (Jayakumar: 2004) conducted in elderly persons over 60 years of age, attending geriatric clinics in rural areas is shown below.

Health Ailment	*Percentage*
Visual Impairment	40.00
Locomotive disorder, Joint Muscles	18.70
Neurological Complaints	17.40
Cardio-Vascular diseases	16.10
Respiratory disorder	13.30
Skin Conditions	9.00
Gastro Intestinal/abdominal disorder	8.50
Psychiatric Problem	8.20
Hearing Loss	3.50
Geneto Urinary disorders	88.00

Realizing these problems, the Government of Karnataka formulated different schemes to the elderly people, such as Monthly pension, free medical facilities, concessional transportation facilities, day care homes, etc. But in view of the increasing number of the aged in the society, the facilities available and the budget allocation made are limited. Hence, there is need to study and emphasize the care for the aged has gained importance and urgency because of the alarming increasing in the demographic figures of the aged, an indication of development of a society. Hence, the present study is made to know about the socio-economic, psychological and health problems of the elders in the rural areas.

OBJECTIVES OF THE STUDY

- To look into the living conditions of the elderly in the rural areas;
- To know about the socio-economic conditions of the elderly in rural areas;
- To examine the health and psychological problems of the aged;
- To find the importance of the elderly people in the family and society (village);
- To know about the Government Schemes on elderly people and to examine whether the elderly people aware about these schemes.

SCOPE AND LIMITATIONS

The study covered about 367 elderly people living in different rural areas of Yadgir Taluk in Gulbarga district (Karnataka). In the context of the study, the elderly people are of above 60 years of age. Specifically the elderly people both male and females living in 12 Villages namely, Yaragol, Bandalli, Eleri, Ramasamudra, Kandakur, Honagera, Hattikuni, Dadarkot, Chandaraki, Balichakra, Anpur, and Allipur in Yadgir Taluk in Gulbarga district were interviewed to collect the information. The study covered different aspects such as family life, social status, economic background, psychological and health problems of the elderly etc. Interview and Observation methods are used to collect the data.

ANALYSIS AND INTERPRETATION OF THE DATA

The collected data from the respondents is presented in the following sections:

Age-wise and Gender-wise Distribution of the Respondents

As stated already all the 367 respondents are of above 60 years of age and gender-wise and age-wise distribution of the respondents is shown in the following table:

Table 1
Age-wise and Gender-wise Distribution of the Respondents

Particulars	*Males*	*Females*
From 60-70 Years	90	71
71-80 Years	77	35
81-90 Years	32	28
91-100 Years	13	15
Above 100 Years	02	04
Total	214	153

Nature of the Family

The nature of the family decides the social life of the elders. It is observed from the study that majority of the families are single rather than joint family, as the younger people from these families are working outside their native areas. The nature of the family of the respondents is presented in the following:

Table 2
Nature of the Family

Nature of the Family	*Number of Respondents*	*Percentage*
Joint Family	174	47.41
Nuclear/Single Family	193	52.59
Total	367	100

Family Income of the Respondents

The income and wealth of the elderly refers to feeling of security in their life. High income status refers to there is more feeling of security and comfortable life and vice versa. The monthly income of the respondents is stated as under:

Table 3
Family Income Level of Respondents

Particulars	*Number of Respondents*	*Percentage*
Below Rs. 5000	131	35.69
Rs. 5001 to Rs. 8000	122	33.24
Rs. 8001 to Rs. 10000	64	17.44
Rs. 10001 to Rs. 15000	27	7.36
Above Rs. 15000	23	6.27
Total	367	100

Care and Respect in the Family

It was asked to the respondents, whether they are getting adequate care and respected by the family members such as brothers, sisters, wife/ husband, sons, daughters, daughter-in-laws, grand children, etc. Further, the level of the care and respect is also ascertained by mentioning extent of care and respect in their family. The responses of the elderly people are presented in the following table:

Table 4
Care and Respect in the Family

Level of Care and Respect in the Family	*Number of Respondents*	*Percentage*
High	84	22.89
Greater	77	20.98
Satisfactory	102	27.79
Not-Satisfactory	104	28.34
Total	367	100

Difference of Opinion with the Younger Family Members

It was asked to the respondents whether there are any kinds of differences of opinions of elderly people with the younger family members. It is needed to know about the differences of ideas of the elderly people with the younger generation. The following table disclosed the responses of the elderly people:

Table 5
Difference of Opinions with the Younger Family Members

Particulars	*Number of Respondents*	*Percentage*
Regular	61	16.62
Occasional	74	20.16
Never	232	63.22
Total	367	100

Family Problems and Concerns

It was asked to the elders, what are problems, which made them worry about their solution. They include the daughters' marriage, son/daughter's employment, children education, increase in loans, Health Problems, etc. The responses of the elders are presented as under:

Table 6
Family Problems and Concerns

Kinds of Family Problems / Worries	*Number of Respondents*	*Percentage*
Increase in Loans	202	55.04
Daughters' Marriage	89	24.25
Children's Employment	105	28.61
Health Problems	282	76.84
Any Others	61	16.62
Total	367	100

Mental Depression and Feeling of Insecurity

It was asked to the respondents that whether they are feeling unsecured and depressed. The different studies revealed that due to different problems such as ill health, ill treatment from the family members, more responsibilities and lack of adequate income and economic power, the elderly people are suffering from depression and feeling of insecurity. The responses of the elders covered under the study are presented as under:

Table 7
Whether Mentally Depressed and Feeling Unsecured

Particulars	*Number of Respondents*	*Percentage*
Yes	134	36.51
No	233	63.49
Total	367	100

Health Problems of the Elders

It is noted that most of the elders covered under the study, are suffering from different kinds of problems. Of which, major problems are cardio-vascular problems, Diabetes, Asthma, Ophthalmologic Problems,

Psychiatric Problems, Dental Problems, Cancer etc. The collected data revealed that a few of the elderly people are suffering from more than one health ailment. The collected data presented in the following table:

Table 8
Health Problems of the Elders

Health Problems	*Number of Respondents*	*Percentage*
Cardio-Vascular Problems	81	22.07
Diabetes	153	41.69
Asthma	161	43.87
Ophthalmologic Problems	131	35.69
Cancer	21	5.72
Psychiatric Problems	111	30.25
Dental Problems	147	40.05
Others	56	15.26
None	74	20.16
Total	367	100

Knowledge About the Government Schemes Regarding Elderly Population

There are different schemes and programmes from the Central Government and State Governments. The Central Government Schemes and State (Karnataka) Government Schemes include National Old Age Pension Scheme, Annapurna Yojana, Widow Pension, Tax Concession, Travel Concessions, Day Care, etc. As the present study covered the elders living in rural areas, there are more illiterate elders. Hence, there is need to know about whether the elders covered under the present study know about the Government Schemes, so as to get benefit from these schemes. The information collected is presented in the following table:

Table 9
Knowledge about the Government Schemes

Particulars	*Number of Respondents*	*Percentage*
Yes (Know)	158	43.05
No (Do Not Know)	209	56.95

Honour and Respect in the Society (Village)

It was asked to the respondents, that whether they get honour and respect in their respective villages. Generally it is noted that the elders are more respected in the villages. The elderly population plays a significant role in celebrating festivals, cultural activities, administrative decisions, etc in villages. Hence, the collected data is represented as under:

Table 10
Getting Respect in the Society

Particulars	*Number of Respondents*	*Percentage*
Respected	241	65.67
Not Respected	126	34.33
Total	367	100

SUMMARIES OF FINDINGS

- Present study covered total 367 elderly people consisting of 214 Males and 153 female respondents.
- Of the total respondents 47.41% (174) are living in joint family and a major portion that is 52.59% (193) are living in Single and Nuclear family.
- The monthly income of about 35.69% (131) of the respondents is below Rs. 5000/-, about 33.24% (122) elders stated that their income is between Rs. 5001 to Rs. 8000/- and the remaining respondents stated that their income is above Rs. 8000/-.
- Only 28.34% (104) of the respondents are not satisfactory regarding the level of care and respect in their family. About 22.89% (84) of the respondents stated that their get high care and respect, followed by 20.98% (77) get greater care and respect and about 27.79% (102) elders stated that the level of care and respect is satisfactory in their family.
- It is worth to note that about 16.62% (61) of the elders have regular difference of opinion in their families, about 20.16% (74) of the elders face occasional difference of opinion and a major portion that is 63.22% (232) of the respondents never face any difference of opinion in their families with the younger family members.
- It is emphasized from the study that majority of the elderly people in rural areas are suffering from problems of increase in loans and health problems. Specifically, about 55.04% (202) of the respondents have increase in loans, about 24.25% (89) of the elders have concern about daughters' marriage, and about 28.61% (105) of the respondents have concern over their children's employment, a major portion that is 76.84% (282) have health problems and 16.62% (61) have other problems and concerns.
- Of the total 367 respondents, 134 (36.51%) are suffering from feeling of depression and insecurity.
- Health problems are major as stated by the elders in rural areas. The collected data revealed that the elders covered under the study

have different kinds of health ailments such as Cardio-Vascular Problems (22.07%), Diabetes (41.69%), Asthma (43.87%), Ophthalmologic Problems (35.69%), Cancer (5.72%), Psychiatric Problems (30.25%), Dental Problems (40.05%) and such other problems (15.26%). It is noted that only about 20.16% of the respondents have no health problems.

- It is surprising to note that majority that is 56.95% (209) of the elders covered under the present study do not know about the government schemes and programmes for the elders, whereas only 43.05% (158) of the elderly population know about the schemes and programmes of the governments.
- Compared to urban areas, the elderly people living in rural areas will be more respected. It was found from the present study that majority that is 65.67% (241) of the respondents are respected in their villages, whereas only 34.33% (126) of the respondents are not respected in their villages.

CONCLUDING REMARKS

Generally it is noted that in the rural areas, where there are elders in the family, there is joint family set-up, rather than single and nuclear family. But the study revealed that majority of the elders are living in single families, it is found that the joint family is declined its importance in rural areas. It is noted that majority of the elders are respected, cared and given respect and honour in the family as well as in their villages. It is noted that a huge majority of the elders are suffering from different old age diseases and health ailments. There is need to provide medical aid to the elders. Further, most of the elder respondents do not know about the government schemes and programmes on old aged people. Hence, there is need to educate the elders and increase awareness about the schemes of the governments for the elders. In this regard, the social workers and Non-Governmental Organizations must have to act to increase the awareness about the government schemes among the elders.

REFERENCES

Age Care Forum (2007), Age Care: Overview.

Gurumurthy, K. G. (1996), A Study of the Problems of the Aged and Need for the Social Intervention. (Karnataka-Rural), In Research in Social Welfare. Edited by A. S. Kohli, New Delhi, Anmol Publications, p. 273-286.

Jayakumar, B. (2004), Protecting Old Age, *Kerala Calling,* August, p. 13-15.

Planning Commission, Government of India (2007), Karnataka Development Report, New Delhi, Academic Foundation, p. 171.

Contesting Modernity and Globalisation: Multiculturalism or Polarization; A Comparitive Analysis of the Indian and the British Experience

*Ravi Dalawai**

The seventh day of July 2005, marks a watershed in British history. The bombings in London on that day, not only pulverized the steel frame of the security and intelligence system of one of the most developed nations of the contemporary times, but also the neo liberal contentions that the developed industrial capitalistic Western societies dispassionately adhere to the doctrine of multi culturalism, began to appear as schizophrenic.

The civil society of the greatest imperial power in history, which has been acknowledge for its impeccable quality of assimilation and considered to be impregnable to any attempts to create schisms in the pluralistic structure of the society and induce cultural polarization, was brought down on its knees by a consternation of the prognosis of an inter cultural conflict, that may probably afflict the multi cultural edifice of the British society. With this, the thesis of the compatibility between modernity and multi culturalism also started to appear as a sham. Huntington while propounding his famous thesis, clash of civilizations, has been skeptical regarding the sustainability of the principle of multi culturalism and its ability to concretize relationship among diverse social groups. Hence inter cultural conflicts in the internal and external space of polities cannot be ignored. Dubbing culture and civilization as synonymous, he argues: "Global politics is both multi polar and multi civilizational. Modernization is distinct from Westernization and is producing neither a universal civilization in any meaningful sense and nor the Westernization of non Western societies."[1]

For the purpose of this paper it has been argued that the concept of modernity and globalisation is anti thetical to the concept of multi

* Lecturer, R.P.D. College, Belgaum.

culturalism. The events of July 2005 that occurred in London, seems to provide credence to this conviction. As Kymlicka has cogently argued: "Our relationships to our culture are more on line with our self understanding than the available alternatives."[2] An individuals approach towards a particular cultural fabric and his judgment regarding its merit or drawback will primarily rest upon his personal comprehension, inconsiderate to the general cultural milieu in which he is ensconced.

Hence, even after a lengthy inhabitation, a person may feel exotic to a culture, only because the legacies of which may not have been naturally inherited to him. Thus it has been argued here that despite rapid pace of modernization and globalisation, encapsulating the reason and action of the entire humanity which is global in its sweep and influence. Cultural diversities within the most modern multi cultural societies remain omni present. This indicates that the virtues of modernization have not been elemental even to shake the quest on the part of a few groups for cultural chauvinism aiming at preserving their urge for maintenance of the doctrine of mono culturalism.

The British society which had reached the pinnacle of modernity and zenith of development, experienced a staggering impact, when a few Muslim youths born and brought up in Britain turned out to be religious extremists, who were propelled to articulate militant nationalism and belligerence against the liberal values of multi cultural society in the name of religious revivalism or cultural asseveration which are appareled in narrow religious fundamentalist ideology. What is flabbergasting here, how come men who were a part of such a liberal society entrenched in the virtues of multi culturalism, were fascinated towards cultural chauvinism engrained in Islamic fundamentalism. why modernity failed to condition the minds of these fanatics in a broader perspective, so as to anchor their minds in a mentality of tolerance.

The reaction for this question among the elite class of the developed West is one of reticence. All this indicates to the notion that the virtues of modernity has been unable to detoxicate the traces of virulence of cultural fanaticism which has driven a section of British Muslim youth to experience a sense of cultural alienation within the framework of a liberal multi cultural society. Their feelings exhibits a sense of cultural estrangement foreign to the persuasion of modernity. Their obsession to an idea of cultural chauvinism is eccentric to the traits of modernity.

In this perspective, a dip into the deep and abstruse field of multi culturalism confronts us with the high tides of myriad and complex questions. For Kymlicka: "Thinking about cultural plurality rises a host of important questions about the nature of liberal individualism and equality. At the heart of these questions there is the idea of cultural membership. What does it mean to people to belong to a cultural community. To what extent individuals's interests tied to or their very sense of identity dependent upon a particular culture. And do people have a legitimate interest in continuation of their own culture, even if other cultures are available in the political community."[3] All these questions needs lengthy investigation.

At first cut let us try to understand the three concepts in question and only then, we will be able to comprehend the interconnection between the two variables in the context of this paper. At the outset, multi culturalism basically indicates a harmonious existence of multiple cultures within a single society, with each culture enjoying equal societal space and where domination of any particular culture does not exist. In addition to this, multi culturalism posits equal treatment for all cultures in public sphere irrespective of their demographic disposition. Not only that, the problem of multi culturalism does not just incompass the tyranny of the majority, but also the attitude of the minority.

Balance in a multi cultural society largely depends upon how the minority specially an immigrant minority accommodates within the complex web of a plural society. Unless and until, the minority is totally assimilated into the common cultural framework of that society and the diverse cultures are interwoven into a cohesive cultural configuration, the idea of multi culturalism will be a farce. Gurpreet Mahajan has viewed: "Multi culturalism speaks of equality of cultures and argues that in democracy all cultural communities must be entitled to equal status in the public domain. That is fair treatment as an equal citizen is a matter of right it is not and must not be dependent upon the largeness or the benevolence of the majority community."[4]

There are conflicting viewpoints about the exact time of the beginning of the age of modernity. On the one hand burgeoning of the modern European civilization has been considered to be beginning of the age of modernity. "Marks, Weber, and before them Guizot concurred that the birth of modern Europe meant the emergence of a new civilization. Which altered the relations of forces between the various parts of the cultures or civilizations of the World."[5] on the other hand, some believe that confining the rise of modernity only to the dawn of modern Europe is a myopic viewpoint and modernity should be understood from a broader perspective of other civilizations also. Sudipta Kaviraj opines: "My dissatisfaction with received modernization theories have been driven by nay parochial interest in Indian history, just as that theory was deviced by the need to understand the equally parochial interest of making sense of primarily European history."[6]

However, there has emerged a consensus that modernity began with the age of reason, that is the transpiration of renaissance. With Europe becoming its hub. Anyhow, it was also concurred that "The more modernity expands and spreads to different parts of the world it becomes differentiated and plural."[7] Dipesh Chakravarti holds: "Europe can be provincialised only if we recognize, that although its origins were certainly European, modernity's expansion makes it increasingly leave behind and forget its origins."[8]

Regarding the meaning and definition of modernity, the dissonance is even more intense, with the protagonists of the Western version being in a majority. But there are also scholars such as Huntington who make a clear distinction between modernization and Westernization. Hence it has been understood that modernization cannot just be comprehended within the limited sphere of Westernization, it is broader and more global in character. Another school of thought explains modernity from the perspective of the growth of industrial capitalism. "The problem of modernity is infact considerably wider then the question of the exact manner of the rise of capitalist economy. It involves the relation between capitalist economic transformation and political reforms, cultural patterns and social imaginaries."[9]

Synoptically, modernity on one hand refers to the conditions of an epoch and on the other it is an attitude of human beings and their state of mind under certain circumstances of change and above all it is their ability to adapt to these dynamics. Modernity is a process interspersed over a wider sphere of time and space, characterized by what Kaviraj categorizes as "Urbanization, growth of industrial capitalism, emergence of democracy, sociological individuation and secularization. Modernity is a transition into a recognizable set of institutions from a prior set that were different. Modern processes emerge simultaneously and mature together in a temporary parallel development of capitalism, democracy, individuation, secularization, etc."[10]

One of the crucial offshoots of the process of modernization has been globalisation. It symbolises rapid techno-economic growth, cultural hybridization and time-space compression. Today, it has become the way of life. "However, globalisation is not always compatible with all facets of human life."[11] In view of this, it has been argued that, globalisation and the concept of multiculturalism are antithetical to each other. The advent of globalisation has led to the rapid erosion of traditional socio-cultural values and institutions, which has resulted in multiculturalism to become merely an artificial construct. In the age of globalisation, it may be argued that, traditional bonds between human beings is gradually getting lost in the buzz of corporatisation, capitalistic economic transformation and fierce market competition. Globalisation has led to the dehumanization of the society and hence, the concept of culture itself may be in question. This epistemic question may be answered in the light of the growing terrorist activities round the world. The most significant part of this is that most modern and globalised countries like Britain are becoming cradle for the nurturing of terrorism.

This is because the Western concept of multi culturalism is purely an artificial construct. It has emerged as a result of the growth of liberal democracy and in a liberal democracy, law acts as an artificial instrument in the maintainence of social equality. As a contrast the Indian notion of multiculturalism is an antequity and it is based purely on traditional human values. A sense of mutual co-existence, religious tollerence and strong social values have characterised Indian civilization for thousands of years. Hence, the multicultural edifice in India, seems to be less affected by the spate of globalisation. Indian history is replete with examples of amicable co-existance of diverse cultures within a society. Take for instance, since ancient times, the society has been characterized by harmonious co existence of the Buddist, jaina and the Hindu cultures. "The co presence of different communities within a polity is therefore not a new occurrence. Cultural pluralities has been a hallmark of many societies for a very long time."[12] India provides a classic example to the world, of an ancient civilization that has sustained a multicultural society. Despite, modernization and globalisation, still the traditional bonds in the Indian society is alive. This has facilitated the country to foster a multicultural structure.

"However, the existence of plurality at the societal level does not imply that multi culturalism is a value prevailing in societies. The simultaneous presence of many cultures and communities within the same social space points to a plural social fabric. But it does not betoken the presence of multi culturalism."[13] This is the best expression of the multicultural society in Britain. Although, there exists a parallel existence of several cultures, but it has not led to the development of strong humane bonds between those cultures. There merely is an artificial existence of different cultures, but an organic relationship between those cultures seems not to be found. The result is what we are seeing today, the growing Islamic extremism in the urban youth of Britain. The country is one of the most developed, modernized and globalised, but cultural chasms are also rapidly magnifying and it has rapidly emerged as a safe haven for Islamic extremists.

Then on what factors exactly multi culturalism is premised. Multi culturalism actually "Entails some thing more then the mere presence of different communities or the attitude of tollerence in society. Multi culturalism is concerned with the issue of equality it asks weather the different communities living peacefully together exist as equals in the public arena."[14] This notion has emerged after the idea of democracy has gained currency, because the principle of equality is fundamental for a democracy. hence this development can be attributed to the process of modernization. Thus multi culturalism also became one of the chief characters of modernity in addition to those narrated by Kaviraj. Like all other modern processes, multi culturalism has also been considered to have developed in a particular epoch parallally with the processes of democracy, industrial capitalism, urbanization, sociological individuation and secularization and matured into the age of modernity. Due to this, equality became the fundamental imperative for determining weather the society is multi cultural or not.

But it may be viewed here, this is purely a Western notion because it places the concept of equality prior to that of tollerence. Contradistinguished to this, an Indian notion of multi culturalism is entirely distinct to that of the Western and it is not modern phenomenon but one of the ancient values that is framed in the immaculate quality of tollerence. Religion is the bedrock of this belief system. were as the Western concept of multi culturalism has attained popularity as a social value with the development of liberal democratic society. Which as we already have discussed that it formed the part of processes of modernity. But the Indian idea of multi culturalism is not dependent upon the processes of modernity, it is an ancient value inherited through generations. If in the West multi culturalism is a trait of modernity, Indian version regards multi culturalism as being above modernity. This fundamental difference in the idea of multi culturalism of the West and that of the Indian is the base to compare and contrast the contemporary multi cultural societies of India and Britain.

11th September 2001, trumpeted the beginning of the most paranoic and specteral war fought in the name of culture. The neo liberal contentions of the victory of the Western notion of global capitalism over all other ideological considerations has been torn into pieces with the fall of WTC. The trail of events persists. It was Madrid in 2004 and its latest manifestation being the episodes of terror that struck London in July 2005.

The Anglo-American neo imperialists nurtured the Frankenstein monster of Islamic fundamentalism as a part of their cold war grand strategy, which now seeks to destroy its own creaters. Arundati Ghose observes: "Terrorism has become a global phenomenon. Ironically, the groups and individuals financed and supported by the countries of the West have turned on their hosts."[15] As the fierce battle launched by the Anglo-American alliance against the self declared religious revivalists endures, the internal societies of these States are gradually getting infected by the germs of cultural nationalism injected into it by a section of its civil society who owe that culture by virtue of inheritance.

Now they feel sympathetic towards the members of their own culture who are being targeted by the warriors against terror rather then being harmonized with the multi cultural edifice in which they are born and brought up. Hence Islamic revivalism or protection of Islam from the so called infidels, has become the Mantra for them which has replaced the modernist notions of corporate globalization and liberal multi cultural societies.

By and large, the idea of modernity seems to be hostile to the dogmas of Islamic fundamentalism. Youssef Choueiri indicates: "Modernity in its cultural, political and economic dimensions is assumed by contemprory Islamic fundamentalists to have caused the gradual decline of Islam or its virtual disappearance as an active force in international and State affairs. the institutions and concepts of secularism and liberalism, nationalism, Marxism and democracy are blamed for eroding the religion of Islam leading them to forsake its way of life for other ideologies and Western models."[16] With this Fukuyama's claim that "The triumph of the West and the Western idea is evident in the total exhaustion of viable systematic alternatives to Western liberalism."[17] The idea that gained popularity as end of history appears to have been thrown into thin air by the anti modernist rhetoric of the Islamic Jihadists.

NOTES AND REFERENCES

1. Samuel P. Huntington (1997), The Clash of Civilizations and the Re-making of the New World Order, Simon and Schuster, London, p. 1.
2. Will Kymlicka (1989), Liberalism Community and Culture, Clarendon Press, Oxford, p. 121.
3. *Ibid.*
4. Gurpreet Mahajan (2002), The Multicultural Path: Issues of Diversity and Discrimination in Democracy, Sage, New Delhi.

5. Sudipta Kaviraj (2000), Modernity and Polities in India, Daedalus, Winter.
6. *Ibid.*
7. *Ibid.*
8. Dipesh Chakravarti (2002), Provincialising Europe, Princeton University Press, Princeton, p. 14.
9. Charles Taylor (2004), Modern Social Imagineries, Duke University Press, Durham.
10. Sudipta Kaviraj, *Oppcit.*
11. B. Moon (1996), Dilemmas of International Trade, Westview Press, Boulder.
12. Will Kymlicka, *Oppcit.*
13. Gurpreet Mahajan, *Oppcit.*
14. Will Kymlicka, *Oppcit.*
15. Arundati Ghose (2002), The challenges of terrorism, Mainstream, 40 [23] May 25.
16. Yousaf Choueri (2003), Islam and Fundamentalism, in Roger Eatwell and Anthony Wright ed, Contemporary Political Ideologies, Rawat Publishers, Jaipur.
17. Francis Fukuyama (1992), End of History and the Last Man, Free Press, New York.

Scheduled Caste Women in Higher Education and Policies: A Study of Karnataka

Sindhe Jaganath R. & V. Rama Krishna***

INTRODUCTION

Education is universally acknowledged as one of the key inputs contributing to the process of national development. For development of human resources, investment in education is essential in order to empower people with appropriate knowledge, skills, values and attitudes, to enhance their quality of life, to improve their productivity and to enable them to participate more fully in the development process. In the present context of global economy, access to basic education is considered as a human right.

Education is the most powerful and influential social institution, playing a vital role in the process of importing values, knowledge, considered essential to the social reproduction of individual personalities and entire cultures. In its broadest meaning, education is any process by which an individual gains knowledge or insight, or develops attitudes or skills (Encyclopedia of American International Edition). In our national perception, education is essential for all. This is fundamental to our all round development, material and spiritual. Education is an acculturating role. It refines sensitivities and perceptions that contribute to national cohesion, a scientific temper and independence of mind and spirit–thus furthering the goals of socialism, secularism and democracy enshrined in our constitution. According to Dr. Radhakrishnan, the great Indian philosopher and educationalist, "Education is the process by which we conserve valuable elements in our culture and discard the waste. It is both, a stabilizing influence and an agent for change. What is in simpler societies, done by the family, the religious, political and social institutions today."

* Reader & Chairman, Department of Studies in Sociology, Gulbarga University, Gulbarga-585 106.

** Research Student, Department of Political Science, Gulbarga University, Gulbarga-585 106. *E-mail: rahul_rk2004@yahoo.co.in*

'Dreze and Kingdom' point out those students from scheduled caste households have an intrinsic disadvantage; the probability of these students going to school is relatively low. Education is the influence exercised by adult generations of those that are not yet ready for social life. Its object is to arouse and to develop in the child a certain number of physical, intellectual and moral states which are demanded of him by both the political society as a whole and the special milieu which he is specifically destined that is why, the great patriot, Swami Vivekanand Says, "Give me a few young men and women, who are pure and selfless, I will shake the whole world".

Kothari Commission (1964-1966) observes that "The future of India is shaped in her classrooms". This amply portrays the importance of school life in nation building.

The purpose of education are the same in each society but, are carried out differently, they include, learning to be a productive member of society, passing on culture, selecting, training and placement of individuals in society, change and innovation, social and personal development. According to Encyclopedia of American International Edition, "The function of Education is both social and individual. Its social function is to help each individual to become a more effective member, of society, by passing along with him the collective experience of the past and present

HIGHER EDUCATION

Education especially higher education is the most important instrument for development of human resources. Higher education provides people with an opportunity to reflect on the critical social, economic, cultural, moral and spiritual issues facing humanity. It contributes to national development through dissemination of specialized knowledge and skills. According to the new International Webster's comprehensive Dictionary, "Higher Education is College Education or any education beyond secondary schooling giving advanced opportunities in general or special fields of learning".

Kothari Commission Report (1964-66) stressed that; university should seek and cultivate new knowledge, to engage vigorously and fearlessly in the pursuit of truth and to interpret old knowledge and beliefs in the light of new needs and discoveries. University should provide the right kind of leadership in all walks of life, to identify gifted youth and help them to develop their potential to the full by cultivating physical fitness, developing, the power of the mind and cultivating right interest, and moral and intellectual values".

According to International Encyclopedia of Sociology Vol. I. "Higher Education is a system of organizations providing Education and training beyond high school. While Elementary and Secondary School attendance is required by low in many countries colleges and universities confirm academic degrees or certification to individuals who are voluntarily pursuing further education".

According to Encyclopedia, American International Edition "Higher Education comprises all procedures for conserving, transmitting, and increasing the more complex kinds of knowledge which the majority of a population have neither time nor incentive to master". Higher education includes graduate and post-graduate level educational courses in different field of learning medicine, nursing, engineering, humanities, social science and physical, natural and life sciences. Higher education comes to devote the formal type of study that takes place in a university or college on completion of secondary school preparation. University is playing a vital role in the process of imparting higher education to the pupils.

"Universities are organizations engaged in the advancement of knowledge, they teach, and examine students in a variety of scholarly, scientific and professional fields. Intellectual pursuits in university define the higher prevailing levels of competence in these fields. The universities confer degrees and provide opportunities both for members of their teaching staff and for some of their students to do original research.

WOMEN'S EDUCATION IN INDIAN SCENARIO

Every one has the right to education, which shall be directed to the full development of human resources, human dignity and potential, with particular attention to women. Education should be designed to strengthen respect for human rights and fundamental freedom; including those relating to population and development.

The movements for improving women's status all over the world have emphasized the role of education. It is believed that education will bring about a reduction in the inequalities between sexes and uplift women's subjugated position in the society. The status of women has undergone change from the Pre-Vedic to modern times. The position of women today is not as equal as with the position of women in ancient period it was. Once it was time when the position of women in our society was very high, specially in Vedic Period, women enjoyed equal freedom with men in all matters, social and religious. The educational status of women as almost equal to men. During the Post-Vedic period status of women deteriorated. It further went down in the Mughal period; women's Education was also neglected.

It is said, that at the advent of the British infiltration into India, female education had practically disappeared. Hardly one per cent of the female population in Madras were literate *(Altekar, 1956).*

In 1850s the missionaries introduced the Zenana missions, where in women teachers called on the private homes of the upper-class families and taught their women folk, domestic science and other skills. Moreover, these schools prepared women for their future roles, wives and mothers. By 1854, the number of pupils had gone up considerably.

The efforts of missionaries drew the attention of social reformers, who were committed to eradication of social evils, like sati, child marriage, the ill treatment of widows, etc. Among them, Raja Ram Mohan Roy, Ishwar Chandra Vidya Sagar, Ranade were very important social reformers. More importantly, the British acknowledged the need for women's education, and for the first time in 1854, drew the Woods dispatch" and recommended, that "the government should reward the individual Indians and the voluntary agencies who support girls' education.[1]

The success of the Bethuene School at Calcutta in 1849, an experiment at secular education provided the necessity impetuous for individual, like Frances Sorabji and Pandita Ramabai to start schools for girls. Their belief "Reform a girl and reform the society" guided their endeavor in this direction. By the 1920s reformist and revivalist seeks like Brahmo Samaj, Aryan Samaj in addition to several Muslim and Parsee associations became active in the field of women's education *(Ahmed, 1985).*

The first All–India Women's Educational Conference, held in 1927, not only reiterated demands for equality of educational facilities but also agitated for the education of women on the amelioration of their social position. Distinguished of women on the amelioration of their social position. Distinguished women such as the Late Sarojini Naidu. Mrs, Annie Beasant Lady Aabala Bose, Mrs. P. K. Ray, Rajkumari Amrit Ksit, Mrs. Wannah Sen, Mrs. Pandit, Begum Hamid Ali and several others who won their leadership by constant work and agitation-contributed considerably to the emancipation of women both socially and educationally. The work of Mahatma Gandhi during this period was also of great significance. He advocated the equality of men and women, and his writings on the subject were influential in raising the status of women in India.

Lardy Irwin College, founded in 1932, was a result. It sought to make "Women utilize the advantage of science in their homes and to add to that the loveliness of art" *(Thomas, 1964, p. 317).* Domestic science was introduced in many other institutions as well. In pre-independence India, the percentage of literacy of women increased from 0.2 in 1881-82 to 6.0 in 1964-47. The enrolment of females in Colleges and Universities increased from 6 in 1881-82 to 23207 in 1946-47.

After Independence various laws were enacted to ensure equality, social justice and fraternity, enshrined in the preamble of the constitution. Under our constitution every citizen enjoys safeguard against exploitation and various measures have been taken to ensure the protection and equal opportunity to women. But the noble ideals enshrined in the constitution are hardly followed in practice. They are not aware about the various programmes of social welfare and development, which is actually meant for their improvement. Policies to extend educational opportunities to women have failed to bridge the knowledge gap between men and women, which was emphasized as the main task by the National Committee on Women's Education in 1958.

In the post independence era, various committees and commissions had made detailed recommendations for the development and improvement of women's education in the country. Notable among them were Durgabai Deshmukh Committee 1959, Hansa Mehta Committee 1952, Bhaktvatsalam Committee 1963, National Council for Women's Education 1964, Kothari Commission 1968, The Committee on Status of Women in India 1975, and the National Policy of Education 1968. All these bodies had analyzed and discussed at length the obstacles in the way of women's education and the ways and means to be adopted for its development and progress. Due attention had also been paid for evolving a suitable curriculum for the education of girls of different stages of education.

In the field of women's educating a large number of specialized institutions had also been established. Notable among them are women's college, Baroda; Miranda College, Delhi; Banasathali Vidyapeeth, Jaipur; Laxmi Bai College of Physical Education, Gwalior and SNDT University, Bombay. They are doing commendable work in the field of teaching nursing, social welfare, fine arts, music, cottage industries and physical education etc.

In the International Women's year, 1975, due encouragement had been given to their education, training, freedom and rights. This had helped to develop, expand and progress women's education and made them aware with regard to their rights, responsibilities and obligations.

PROMOTION OF WOMEN'S STUDIES IN UNIVERSITIES

The UGC's programme for promoting women's studies envisages assistance to universities for setting up centers and cells for women's studies. The centers/cells are required to undertake research, develop curricula and organize training and extension work in the areas of gender equity, economic self-reliance of women, girl's education, population issues, issues of human rights and social exploitation. There activities are expected to contribute not only to social awareness and change but also to academic development. However, the Women's Study Centers are not expected to be like other conventional departments of a university, in that, they are not required to run courses that lead to an undergraduate or a postgraduate degree, although they could do so. The following activities were reported by the Women's Study Centers under teaching, research and extension.

UGC REPORT ON FACILITIES FOR WOMEN IN HIGHER EDUCATION (1995-96)

The growth in the number of women students in higher education since independence has been phenomenal. While women constituted only 9.3 per cent of all students in institutions of higher education on the eve of independence, the percentage of women students enrolled in all colleges and universities was 34.1 in 1995-96.[2]

GROWTH IN ENROLMENT OF WOMEN IN HIGHER EDUCATION

The pace of growth has been particularly faster in the last two decades or so. As the data in the table below show, the number of women enrolled, per hundred men, registered a four-fold increase during the period 1950-51 to 1995-96.

Table 1
Women Students Per Hundred Men Students

Year	*Total Women Enrolment (000s)*	*Enrolment per Hundred Men*
1950-51	40	14
1995-96	2191	52

Source: Annual Report of the University Grants Commission for the Year 1995-96, pp. 136-143.

DISTRIBUTION OF WOMEN'S ENROLMENT STATEWISE, STAGEWISE AND FACULTY-WISE

Statewise distribution of women's enrolment shows that, while the enrolment of women as a percentage of total enrolment has gone up in al the states, the extent of this increase has varied across the States. As in earlier years, Kerala (52.4%) continued to lead the other States in terms of women's enrolment as a percentage of total enrolment in 1995-96, followed by Goa and Punjab (51.2%), Delhi (44.6%), Manipur (42.8%), Tamil Nadu and Jammu & Kashimir (39.9% each) and Meghalaya, Nagaland (39.7%) each. Bihar continued to remain at the bottom with women's enrolment only 18.6% of its total enrolment in 1995-96.[3]

STAGE-WISE DISTRIBUTION

Women's enrolment as a percentage of total enrolment has, as Table 2 shows, consistently increased during the period 1986-87 to 1995-96 at all the levels of higher education–graduate, post-graduate, research and diploma/certificate courses.

Table 2
Percentage of Women Enrolment to Total Enrolment, Stagewise

Year	*Graduate*	*Post-Graduate*	*Research*	*Diploma / Certificate*
1986-87	29.9	31.6	31.7	24.4
1995-96	34.1	34.0	39.2	26.6

Source: Annual Report of the University Grants Commission for the year 1995-96.

A noteworthy feature of the general increase in the number of women students in higher education is the uniformity in the incidence of their enrolment at all levels of education.

THE DRIVE FOR TOTAL LITERACY-SOME NATIONAL AND GLOBAL DIMENSIONS

Every time we think about Women and Literacy in Indian or S. Asian context, inevitably the statistical profile overshadows all else. In recent years several global initiatives such as the UN International Literacy Year (ILY); the National Literacy Mission (NLM)' the Total Literacy Campaigns (TLCs); and the Education for All (EFA) initiative have all served to place literacy high on the global and national agendas.[4]

LITERACY AND EDUCATION IN KARNATAKA

Education plays a crucial role in empowering the poor and the marginalized everywhere. Literacy and higher levels of education attainment are associated with an improvement in demographic and health indicators. Access to education enables people to exercise their constitutional and legal rights in a judicious manner. Gender inequality has been known to decline as women's access to education is enhanced. The liberating dimensions of education assume special significance in the context of people who have been denied access to learning and, through learning, economic mobility by oppressive socio-cultural ideologies.

The Scheduled Castes in Karnataka have a long history of receiving strong support from the state, commencing with the benevolent policies of the princely state of Mysore where, in 1919 the Scheduled Castes (known as 'Punchamas') got admission in all schools despite protests from the upper castes. By the 1920s a small but signifi cant number of SCs had entered government service and statistics showed that there were 165 Dalits among a total of 4,234 employees in 1918 (about 3.8 per cent).[5]

After Independence and since its formation in 1956, Karnataka has pursued policies that have encouraged SCs to enter the education mainstream. Despite these pro-active interventions, the performance of SCs is nowhere on par with the general population.

The literacy rate of SCs has been consistently lower than that of the general population. The literacy rate among the Scheduled Castes was 27.62 per cent in 1981; it increased to 38.10 per cent in 1991 and further increased to 52.87 per cent in 2001. The literacy rate for the total population was 46.21 per cent (1981), 56.04 per cent (1991) and 66.64 per cent (2001). The gap between the literacy rate of the general population and the SC literacy rate is being bridged but not as rapidly as envisaged. The gap in 1981 was 19.59 percentage points, which fell to 17.98 in 1991 and declined further to 13.83 in 2001. Scheduled Caste literacy rates have been increasing at a faster pace: between 1981 and 1991 the SC literacy rate increased by 10.48 percentage points and by 14.77 in 1991-2001. The increase in literacy for the rest of the population was 9.83 per cent in 1981-1991 and 10.6 per cent in 1991-2001. The literacy rate of urban SCs in 2001 is 69.27 per cent, which is above the state average.[6]

POLICIES

Education, being the most powerful instrument for empowering women, assumes special priority in the Ninth Plan. Efforts in the Ninth plan will, therefore, be target-oriented in fulfilling the goal of Education for women's Equality as laid down in the National Policy on Education (NPE), 1986 and revised in 1992. Towards this, special attention will be paid to the already identified low female literacy pockets and to the women and the girl children belonging to the socially disadvantaged group viz. SC, STs, OBCs Minorities, disabled, etc. as they still lag behind with the lowest literacy rates ranging between 5 and 10 per cent. While the national average of female literacy stands at 39.3 per cent in 1991.

Women's enrolment in college/universities levels had also increased steadily from 1.69 million (32.3%) in 1991-92 to 2.21 million (35.8%) in 1995-96. The number of girls in science courses constituted about 35.5 per cent of total student's enrolled in 1995-96. During the same year, 34.50 per cent of the total students enrolled in MBBS course were girls. In Engineering and Architecture courses, girls constituted 14.25 per cent. The most popular professional course for girls was teacher training, wherein they constituted nearly 48.47 per cent of those enrolled. Thus the total number of girls in the professional courses was 0.95 lakh in 1995-96.[7]

In the State sector, most of the States/UTs were implementing a number of programmes for welfare and development of women and children in addition to those being implemented by the Centre. The important programmes for women in the State sector include various developmental programmes like employment and income generation programmes, training-cum-production centres for destitute women; mahila mandal/mahila sangams; awareness generation/gender sensitization programmes; special campaigns against dowry, prostitution, child marriages etc., rehabilitation of women in distress; welfare services for women in need of care and protection etc. In addition to these, they also have a major responsibility of implementing various women-specific women-related legislations, besides setting up/ maintaining the mandatory institutions under these Acts. The other major contribution of the States and UTs relates to their coordinating role between the Centre and the NGO sector in implementing the various grant-in-aid programmes, as almost all the women development programmes in the Central sector are being implemented only through NGOs. Along with the centre, most of the State Governments have initiated action in formulating their own State Policies for Empowering Women.[8]

Education of women, occupies top priority amongst various measures taken to improve the status of women, the New Education Policy 1986 emphasizes "gender equality in education"–Education will be used as an agent of basic change in the status of women. In order to neutralize the accumulated distortions of the past, there will be a well-conceived edge in favour of women. The National Education System will play a positive interventionist role in empowerment of women.

In this context the paper will bring the higher education of Scheduled Caste Women in Gulbarga particularly in karnataka. The Gulbarga is situated in north of karnataka, where the district is border to Andhra Pradesh and Maharashtra. Gulbarga District Scheduled Caste Women in Higher Education. The paper will focus the scheduled caste women in higher education in Gulbarga University, Gulbarga.

SOCIO-ECONOMIC PROFILE OF SCHEDULED CASTE WOMEN IN HIGHER EDUCATION

In this paper the respondents age is divided into two categories i.e., 20-24 years of age and 25-30 years of age (in completed Years).

Table 3
Distribution of Respondents by Age

Age group	*No. of Respondents*	*Percentage %*
20-24	131	87.30
25-30	19	12.70
Total	150	100

Source: Annual Report of the University Grants Commission for the year 1995-96.

The data on age reveal that an overwhelming majority of the respondents are from the age group of 20-24 years of age that is about 87 (87.30) per cent of them are from the age group 20-24 and only about 13 (12.70) per cent of them are from 25-30 years of age.

The data indicate the fact that, the scheduled caste women enters into the higher education course immediately after completion of their under graduate course. This fact might be because of governmental support for higher education and awareness of education.

EDUCATIONAL BACKGROUND

Education attempts to maximize the acquisition of technical knowledge among individuals, and prepare for a particular type of occupation. Further, his/her achievements in higher education make them to aspire for a particular type of job or occupation. It can be stated there that, educational level and grades achieved therein have a determinate role to play in shaping the occupational aspirations of individuals.

Educational requirements for seeking a job have increased at all occupational levels. Higher the level of education higher wills the probability that a person will be in higher positions. If not, in professional/ occupational field, definitely the position status of a women enhances in her family atmosphere she will be more respected and will have her role in important family matters. Overall life will be some what better in comparison with women without education/lower level of education.

Date on school background indicate that, only about 17.30 per cent of the respondents had their schooling in rural schools. About, 40 per cent of them had schooling in town and about 42.70 per cent of them had their schooling at cities. In general study reveals that as many as 83 (82.70) per cent of them studied and had their schooling in urban schools. This strong urban background or bias becomes stronger when we observe the data regarding their college education.

Of all the respondents studied, about 62.30 per cent of them had their college education in cities or metropolitan areas and the remaining 36.70 per cent of them had their college education in towns. There was virtually no single respondent from a rural college leading to an assumption that education in urban schools and colleges is rather a pre condition for joining higher education. This might be attributed to the fact that, educational facilities provided in rural areas are poor and needs still improvement.

BASIS FOR SECURING ADMISSION TO HIGHER EDUCATION

The study was carried out in Gulbarga University, Gulbarga. In this university allocation of P.G. Seats are on merit basis, on reservation basis and also it has payment seats during these recent years. To know whether there is any difference in basis for admission to P.G Course question was asked and the data are analyzed in the following table:

Table 4
Basis for Secure Admission to P. G. Course

Basis for secure Admission	*No. of Respondents*	*Percentage %*
Merit	88	58.70
Payment Seat	16	10.70
Reservation	38	25.30
Other quota	08	5.30
Total	150	100

Source: Annual Report of the University Grants Commission for the year 1995-96.

It is significant to note that, more than half of the respondents sought the P.G seat on merit basis that is 58.70 per cent had sought the seat on the basis of merit. Only one fourth of the students that is 25.30 per cent of them sought seat on reservation and only about 5.30 per cent of them sought seat on other quota basis. And here it is significant to note that about 11 (10.70) per cent of them sought the seat on payment basis. It is normally believed that scheduled caste students are ill afforded to get the seats through payment basis. This might be reflecting a trend among scheduled castes people, toward getting their daughters highly qualified in a hope, they may get higher position through education and they consider it as a fruitful investment, which promises good returns in the long run. And it is also significant to note that, more than half of the respondents sought admission on merit basis, which denote the increase in the quality of education among scheduled caste population of this region.

FUTURE PLANS

After completion of P.G courses the post-graduates have many options to do. It is not certain that, they should go for teaching profession. As the main attention and thrust of any university is to engage itself in research and extension. The study intends to understand the aptitude of the respondents with this regard the respondents were asked to mention their plans immediately after completion of their P. G. course. The data so collected are presented in the following table:

Table 5
Future Plans

Future Plans	*No. of Respondents*	*Percentage %*
Join Research	26	17.30
Take up job	107	71.30
Marriage	17	11.40
Total	150	100

Source: Annual Report of the University Grants Commission for the year 1995-96.

The date on future plans indicate that, most aspired future plan of the respondents is to take up a job, to join research comes next that is 17.30 per cent of the respondents would like to continue in research and only about 11.30 per cent of them would like to go for marriage. Tendency among the respondents to take up job might be attributed to their low social profile. Inspite of financial support given by U. G. C. and other funding agencies and lower percentage of them expressing their tendency toward research is the area which should be studied in future research.

Issues and Concerns

The greatest single issue that comes into focus is the wide gap between the Scheduled Castes and the general population almost all human development indicators. Economically, the SC population is highly concentrated in rural Karnataka. They are dependent on agriculture, but since they own only 11.65 per cent of operational holdings, 83.25 per cent of which is un-irrigated, they derive only 15.4 per cent of their income from cultivation. A high 52 per cent of marginal holdings are held by SCs. They crowd the primary sector (78.83 per cent) where remuneration is low and their share of the secondary and tertiary sectors is insufficient, probably because of high levels of illiteracy and a poor vocational skill base. The monthly per capita expenditure of SCs is the second lowest in the state at Rs. 419 for rural and the lowest for urban, at Rs. 593.

CONCLUSION

The paper reveals that as an average post-graduate women student (Scheduled Caste) is 22 (22.36) years old, predominantly urban background, coming from middle class. It is significant to note that, social science faculty is still continues to be predominant, in the choice of faculty. Coming to the educational grades we can see that, most of the respondents have a low grades in matriculation and a tendency toward increasing their educational grades at the graduation level is a good sign, indicating that they make good efforts in order to get P.G. seat and maturity at graduation level and the facilities available at graduation level are attributed to this finding. However, it is significant to note that nearly three fourth of the respondents choose P.G course with the motivation of their parents. Further, it is significant to note that, though all the respondents studied belongs to scheduled caste, only one fourth of them got P.G. admission on reservation basis and nearly 60 per cent of them got admission on merit basis. The future career plans, half of the respondents preferred teaching profession, rather than any other profession and a majority of them have confidence in achieving the career plans.

NOTES AND REFERENCES

1. Prasad, Janardan and Kaushik Vijaykumari (1995), "Women Education and Development (A New Perspective), Kanihka Publishers, Distributors, New Delhi.
2. Joshi Rama J. (1973), "Contemporary Change in the Socio-economic Role of Women in India: Kamala Bhasin, Leslie Swahny Programme of Training for Democracy, Bombay.

3. Karuna Chanana (1993), Accessing Higher Education: The Dilemma of Schooling Women, Minorities, Scheduled Castes and Scheduled Tribes in Contemporary India, Subject Collection Humanities, *Social Sciences and Law*, 26 (1), pp. 69-92.
4. Agrawal S. P. (2001), "Women's Education in India: Present Status, Perspective Plan Statistical Indicators with Global View", Concept Publishing Company, New Delhi, pp. 35.
5. *http://planning.kar.nic.in/khdr2005/English/Main%20Report/9-chapter.pdf*
6. *Ibid.*
7. Sutherland (1988), Margaret, Women in Higher Education: Effects of Crises and Change, Higher–Education, 17, 5, 479-490.
8. Agrawal S. P. (2001), "Women's Education in India: Present Status, Perspective Plan Statistical Indicators with Global View", Concept Publishing Company, New Delhi, pp. 58.
9. Vicenzo, Caterina (2000), "Young Women, Identity and Higher Education in Souther Italy": The Case Study of University of Calabria.

Urban Solid Waste Management
A Case Study of Belgaum Municipal Corporation

*Abhay M. Patil**

INTRODUCTION

From the days of primitive society, humans and animals have used the resources of the earth to support life and to dispose wastes. In those days, the disposal of human and other wastes did not pose significant problems, as the population was very small and the area of land available for the assimilation of such wastes was large. However, today, serious consideration is being given everywhere to this burgeoning problem of solid wastes.

Rapid population growth and uncontrolled industrial development are seriously degrading the urban and semi-urban environment in many of the world's developing countries, placing enormous strain on natural resources and undermining efficient and sustainable development.

Management of solid waste may be defined as that discipline associated with the control of generation, storage, collection, transfer and transport, processing, and disposal of solid wastes in a manner that is in accord with the best principles of public health, economics, engineering, conservation, aesthetics, and other environmental considerations. In its scope, solid waste management includes all administrative, financial, legal, planning, and engineering functions involved in the whole spectrum of solutions to problems of solid wastes thrust upon the community by its inhabitants (Tchobanaglous, 1997).

The importance of proper solid waste management is one of the prime functions of the civic body, as in sanitary management of solid wastes is a cause of much discomfort. Since waste management is the fundamental requirement for public health, Article 48-A of the Indian Constitution establishes the responsibility of the state to manage these wastes properly.

* Lecturer, Department of Geography, R. P. D. College, Belgaum.

OBJECTIVE

The purpose of the Solid Waste Management (SWM) exercise is to help improver poor practices of SWM that prevail in many low income countries where this subject has received scant attention compared to other aspects of infrastructure such as water supply and transport. It is a multi-disciplinary field embracing waste collection, transfer, and disposal and its impact is wide. It is therefore important to take a broad view and not to consider disposal options within the narrow confines of a particular technology.

A SCENARIO OF SOLID WASTE GENERATION IN INDIA

Growing population, fast urbanization, rising incomes and changing consumption patterns combine the waste management problems, and it has global dimensions. Any solid material in the material flow pattern that is rejected by society is called solid waste. Solid wastes arise from human and animal activities that are normally discarded as useless or unwanted. In other words, solid wastes may be defined as the organic and inorganic waste materials produced by various activities of the society and which have lost their value to the first user. As the result of rapid increase in production and consumption, urban society rejects and generates solid material regularly which leads to considerable increase in the volume of waste generated from several sources such as, domestic wastes, commercial wastes, institutional wastes and industrial wastes of most diverse categories. Wastes that arise from a typical urban society comprises of garbage rubbish (package materials), construction and demolition wastes, leaf litter, hazardous wastes, etc.

India is a one of the developing country, and it has 19 per cent of world population but only two per cent of the land area. Simultanerous increasing in population and fast economic growth has posed heavy pressure on its natural resources and the environment. Urbanization is one of the important factors affecting the generation of solid waste. The number of urban population is increasing rapidly, in India, from a mere 10.89% of her total population living in urban areas in 1901; it has reached 27.78% by 2001. It is obvious that, this rapid growth in urban population and urban areas generates more and more solid waste. It is cited by Shankar U and Mathur POM (1998) in their article 'Economic Instrument of Sustainability' that Indian cities produce wastes in the aggregate 100,000-110,000 metric tones, or a per capita average of 0.40-0.42 kgs a day. The National Commission on urbanization (1988), on the basis of sample of 40 cities over 100,000 population found that the mean per capita waste/day to be 0.27 kg. An average Indian generates about 350-400 g/day of solid waste and on an average 82.8% of solid waste generated in metropolitan cities are collected and disposed. On the basis of available data, it is estimated that the nine major metropolitan centres in India are presently producing 23,000 tones of solid waste per day. As per recent estimates, Belgaum city generates about 1,40 tones per day. Out of this 80% is collected and transported out daily. The Table 1 provides comparative details about garbage generated and cleared in nine major Indian cities.

Table 1
Urban Waste Situation in Some Major Indian Cities (1994)

Major cities	*Garbage generated (Tones per day)*	*Garbage cleared (Tones per day)*
Mumbai	5800	5000
Kolkata	3500	3150
Chennai	2675	2140
Delhi	3880	2420
Bangalore	2130	1800
Lucknow	1500	1000
Patna	1000	300
Surat	1250	1000
Ahmedabad	1500	1200

Source: India Today, 31st October 1994.

LOCATION OF THE STUDY AREA

The Belgaum city is situated at 15°51' North Latitudes and 74°51' East Longitude (Figure 1) .The city is 710 meters above the mean sea level. The climatic conditions of Belgaum city are healthy, pleasant and characterized by a general dryness except during the rainy season. The average annual rainfall varies from 776 to 1040 mm. The pleasant equable climate ranges around 14.30°C in winter and 35.40° C in summer. The relative humidity of Belgaum city is about 85 per cent and it is generally higher in monsoon season.

SOLID WASTE IN BELGAUM CITY

'Solid Waste' is the term used to describe non-liquid waste materials arising from the domestic, trade and commerce, industries, public services and agricultural activities. In Indian cities, it is a combination of various heterogeneous waste materials. It is commonly known as garbage, refuse, rubbish or trash.

In this part an attempt is made to know the solid waste (Garbage) generation and sanitation conditions of Belgaum city. Belgaum city is plagued with inefficient and insufficient civil amenities. Not a single

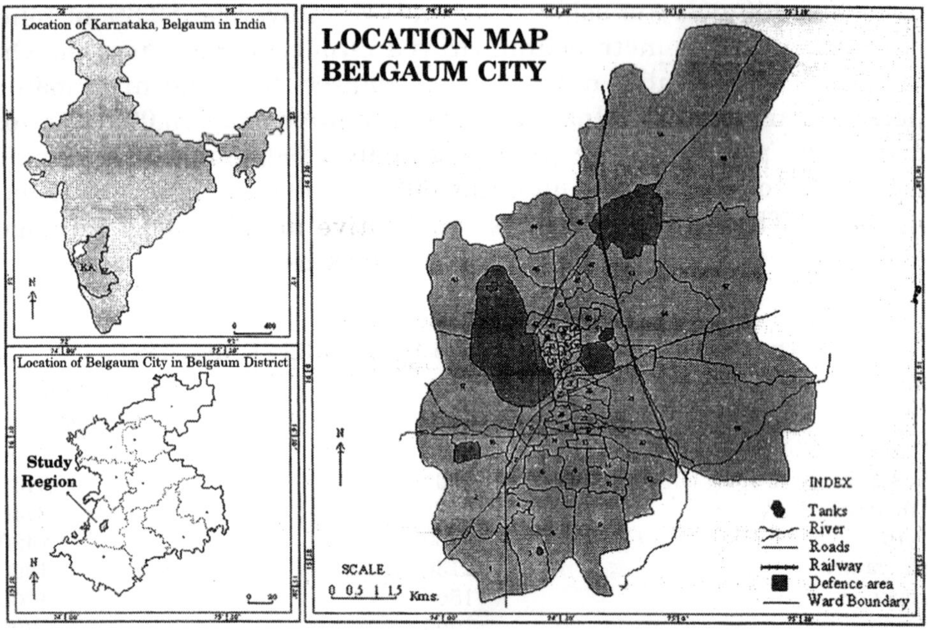

Figure: 1

ward or area of the city is fully cleaned with the growth of city, its trash mainly hazardous plastic, metals, residential wastes, commercial wastes, papers and packaging is growing exponentially. Since the last decade the solid waste is increasing very fast as compared to previous decades, a great threat to the City Corporatoin and Cantonment board as well as city dwellers. Belgaum which had a population of 3,50,352 (including Cantonment) in 1991 now, it reached 423 during 2001 during the same time the city waste has also increased greatly.

In Belgaum city, the generation of amount of garbage is not same in all places but it varied. It is known to every one that the city is not a compact instead it is fragmented. In 1991 each inhabitant use to generate about 210 grams of city waste but it has been increased now at present each urbanite adds 300 grams it is going to be increased further in days to come.

Belgaum City Corporation occupies the center stage but civil issues and problems faced by citizens continue to remain. Garbage management has become a perennial problem and it is intense in city core areas i.e. C.B.D., Central Bustand, Killa Area, Maruti Galli, Court Area and Dharwad Road, J.N..M.C. Area, R.P.D. Corner, Railway station and other busy areas.

Solid Waste generation is more in the city during the festivals. This apart the overflowing drains water and sewage gets mixed up with garbage dumped indiscriminately. Even if the people complain to the city corporation officials, it is not attended to properly garbage is cleared once in every three, four days in the area owing to which accumulation of waste is inevitable. The concerned authority lifts the waste at certain places of the city but waste clearance is not done in a proper manner. Much of the garbage is left behind, it pose an unhygienic conditions in the city area.

Even after the corporation trucks lift garbage it is spilled on the roads during transportation. The people who travel towards Khasbag and K.L.E. Hospital complain that they have to race with waste dumping trucks on their way to work on the busy road, for fear of the waste falling on then. The trucks leave foul smell too on their way to dump sites outside the city. Heaps of uncleared waste is seen scattered in the city like C.B.D., Central Bus Stand, Railway Station, Khade Bazaar, Fish Market, J.N.M.C. Road, R.P.D. Corner, Angol, Vegetable and mutton market areas, Market yard and around Schools, Colleges, Cinema theaters, Hospitals, Temples and residential areas. In addition to unbearable stink, this is hazardous to the health of the residents and may lead to the spread of many diseases, lack of sufficient number of public toilets and latrines has added to problems of sanitation in the entire city.

GENERATION OF SOLID WASTE IN BELGAUM CITY

According to the data collected from the Municipal Corporation and Cantonment Board, the generation of solid waste in Belgaum city and Cantonment is 1,40,000 kg per day. The city corporation and Cantonment are able to lift 1,10,000 kg every day leaving 30,000 kg left behind which creates unhealthy condition of the city. Per capital generation of solid waste in Belgaum city is 0.20 to 0.50 kg per day. The outgrowth however adds a small portion of the waste to the total.

The Table 2 and Figure 2 shows the growth of population as well as solid waste generation is Belgaum city during 1991-2001.

Population has increased sharply during 1991-2001, in Belgaum city. Since the city is well known for industries, commerce medical, hospital, education, administration, and pleasant climate, it has attracted a huge number of the people from its hinterland and surrounding regions, which is leading to generate more and more waste in the city. In addition to this, the growth of industries, commercial establishments and complexes, educational institutions leading to increase in the amount of solid waste in the city. The purchasing and consuming capacity of dwellers of Belgaum city is higher than that of many other cities in Karnataka. This is also one of the reasons for increase in the waste in the city.

Table 2
Belgaum City: The Growth of Population Solid Generation 1991-2005

Period	*Population*	*Solid waste (in Kgs)*
1991	412794	84506
1992	423176	86686
1993	433558	88866
1996	454323	95407
1997	464705	97588
1998	475088	99768
1999	485470	101948
2000	495853	104129
2001	506235	106309

Source: Belgaum City Corporation

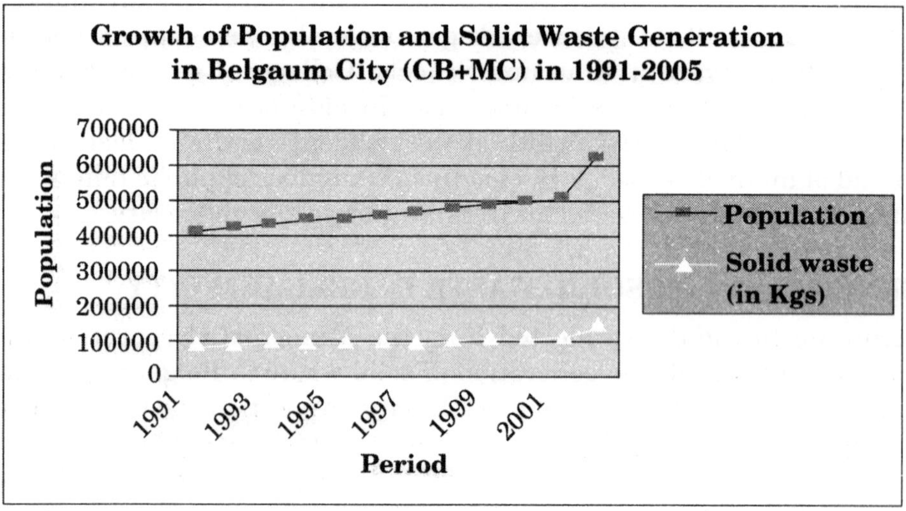

Figure: 2

COMPOSITION OF URBAN SOLID WASTE

Composition is the term used to describe the individual components that make up solid waste stream and their relative distribution, usually based on per cent by weight. Information on the composition of solid waste is important in evaluating equipment needs, systems and management programmes and plans.

The Table 3 and Figure 3a & 3b shows the composition of urban solid waste as weight in percentage.

Table 3
Belgaum City: Physical and Chemical Composition of Solid Waste

Physical Characteristics of Solid Waste		*Chemical Characteristics of Solid Waste*	
Item	*Percentage (%)*	*Item*	*Percentage (%)*
Paper	4.76%	Moisture Content	25.05%
Plastics	0.59%	Organic Matter	22.21%
Metals	0.39%	Carbon	12.55%
Glass	0.34%	Nitrogen	0.61%
Ash and fine dust	39.97%	Phosphorus	0.71%
Total Compostable Matter	39.76%	Potassium	0.73%
Other	14.19%	C/N	20.73%
		Others	17.41%
Total	100%	Total	100%

Source: (City Corporation and Percentage is computed by Author)

Physical Charcteristics of Solid Waste

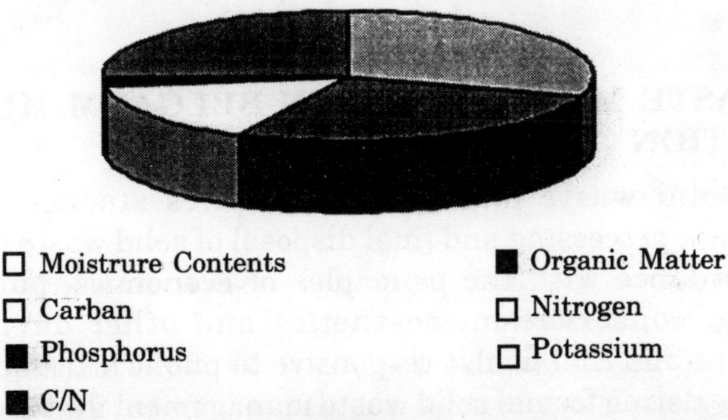

Figure: 3a

Chemical Charcteristics of Solid Waste

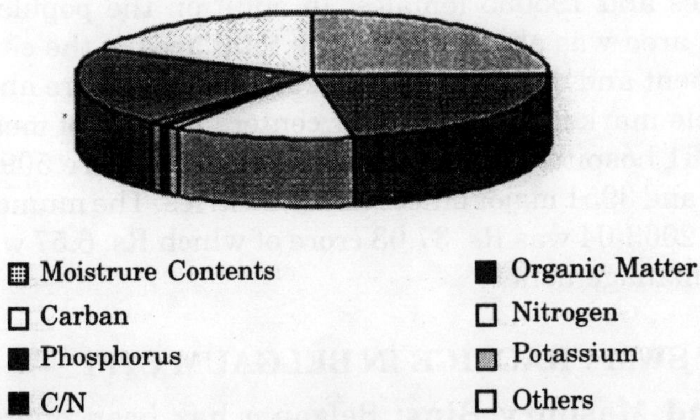

Figure: 3b

PROJECTION OF WASTE GENERATION IN BELGAUM CITY

The waste generation for Belgaum has been project over a planning period of 8 years with a population growth rate of 2% and a waste growth rate of 1%. The data is presented in the Table 4. The waste to be handled in 2010 would be 160 tons per day and in 2015 would be 182 tons per day.

Table 4
Belgaum City: Projection of Waste Generation

Year	*Population*	*Quantity of waste in tons per day*
2001	506235	106309
2005	635400	140000
2010	471528	160000
2015	511488	182000

Source: City Corporation Belgaum.

SOLID WASTE MANAGEMENT IN BELGAUM MUNICIPAL CORPORATION

The term solid waste management implies storage, collection, transportation, processing and final disposal of solid waste in a manner that is accordance with the principles of economics, public health, engineering, conservation, aesthetics and other environmental considerations and that is also responsive to public attitude. We would focus on the existing formal solid waste management system in the area of Belgaum Municipal Corporation.

The Belgaum city corporation has 58 wards (Figure 1) within its municipal jurisdiction accounting for 399653 total population of which 204598 males and 195055 females. In addition the population in the cantonment area was about 55000. The total area of the city including the cantonment and defense area is 94 sq. km. There are about 15 fruit and vegetable markets and 15 major centers for sale of meat and fish. There are 331 hospitals and nursing homes. There are 509 hotels and restaurants and 3951 major offices and industries. The municipal budget for the year 2003-04 was Rs. 37.03 crore of which Rs. 6.57 was spent on solid waste management.

CURRENT SWM PRACTICE IN BELGAUM CITY

- **RCC and Masonry Bins:** Belgaum has been operating on a convention system of solid waste management. The waste generators put the waste into primary collection receptacles consisting of round RCC bins and Masonry bins. Sweeping is undertaken and the sweepings are also transferred to the bins.

- **SWM Staff:** There are about 1237 RCC bins and 16 Masonry bins. The road sweeping is undertaken by Pourakarmikas. There are about 375 Pourakarmikas of whom 309 are deployed for sweeping and other works and 66 are involved in lifting garbage to trucks. There are 15 drivers available. There are totally 22 supervisors and 14 health/ sanitary inspectors. An environmental engineer has been appointed as part of Nimal Nagar Program. One Health officer manages the whole system. There is adequate staff in the city corporation for solid waste management.
- **Privatization:** Out of 58 wards of the city wards have been given out full service contract, which includes sweeping, collection, transport and maintaining the area clean.
- **Biomedical and Industrial wastes:** "The association of Hospitals and Nursing homes Belgaum" has set up hospital wastes management facility and operating the same. The government hospital has its own facility. The biomedical wastes do not enter the municipal system. The city corporation has provided land to the foundry industry to set up a facility to manage their wastes. Only the minor industries non-hazard wastes are transferred to the municipal system.
- **Processing and Disposal:** There are two solid waste (Garbage) dumping sites, one is the Khasabhag and another one is near K.U..P.G Centre, Bhutaramnahatti. (Figure 4).

PROBLEMS OF SOLID WASTE MANAGEMENTS IN BELGAUM CITY

The operational problems crop up in all phases of the solid waste management services namely collection, transportation, disposal were as follows:

Problems in Road Sweeping

The problems faced by road sweepers were:

- Unauthorized parking on public roads.
- Round the clock heavy traffic on same roads.
- Encroachment.

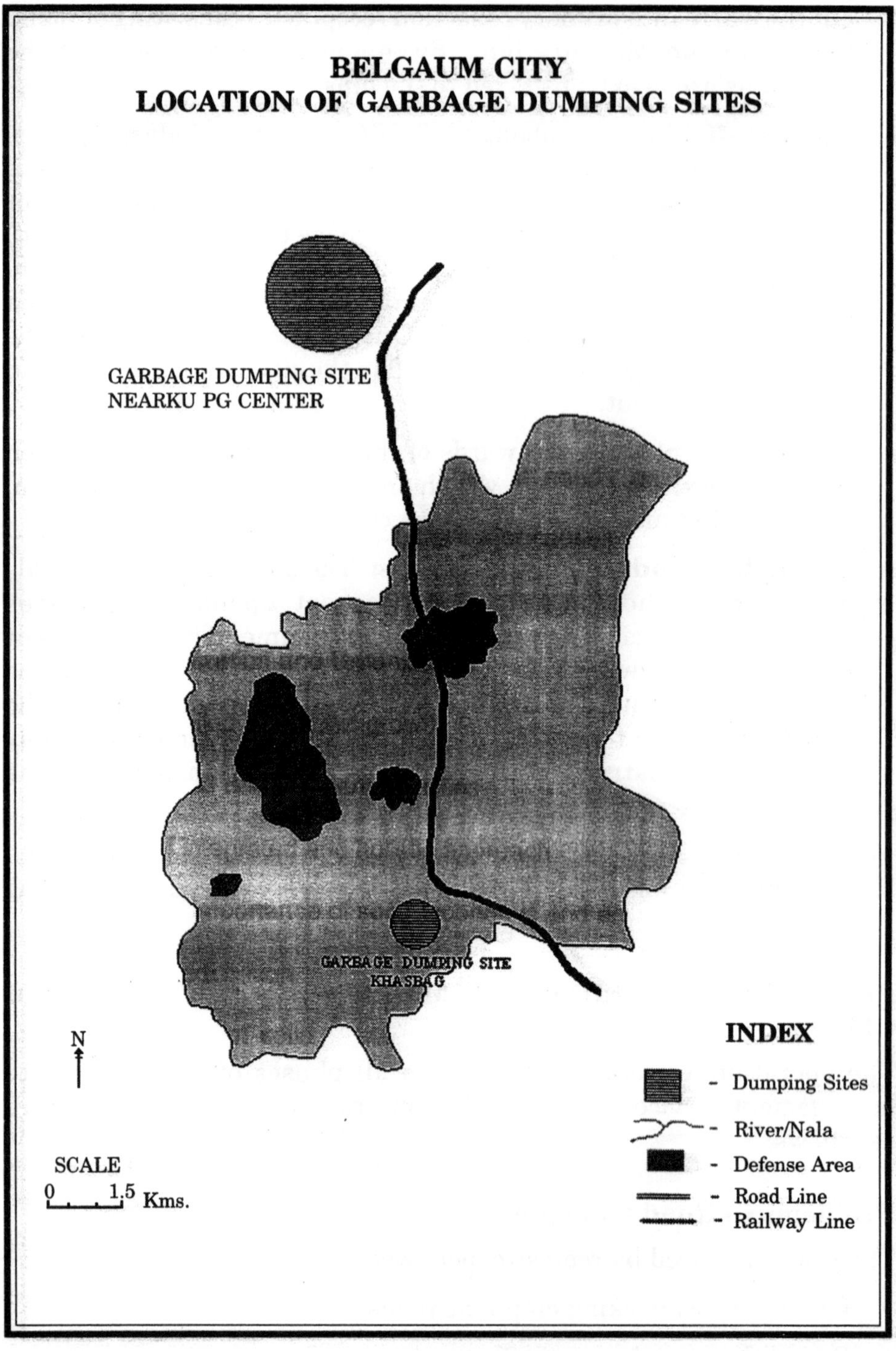
BELGAUM CITY
LOCATION OF GARBAGE DUMPING SITES
GARBAGE DUMPING SITE
NEARKU PG CENTER
GARBAGE DUMPING SITE
KHASBAG
N
SCALE
0 1.5 Kms.
INDEX
- Dumping Sites
- River/Nala
- Defense Area
- Road Line
- Railway Line

Figure: 4

- Using road sides for squatting, urinating, wasting cloths, bathing etc.
- Poor road surface conditions. Due to these problems, road sweeping work is affected adversely in Belgaum city.

Problems in collection of Solid Waste

The problems in the collection of solid waste were:

- People usually prefer that refuse bins are kept for away from their house, shops or commercial establishments.
- Nuisance of stray cattle.
- People do not deposit refuse in the bins, but around and away from the bins and
- Squatting around dust bins.

Problems in Transportation of Solid Waste

- Vehicles are open body vehicles and hence unhygienic in view of possible spill over.
- Big capacity vehicles are unsuitable for small narrow lanes and are economically unsuitable especially where refuse generation is low.
- With limitation on garage and workshop facilities, Municipal fleet, utilization is apparently low and is being gradually raised.

Problems in Disposal of Solid Waste

- The existing disposal sites are not suitable for proper disposal of wastes. New sites have been identified. Proper landfill has to be put into place.
- The existing land fill method is not hygienic from sanitation point of view and hence it is a disadvantageous of operational economy.
- It is difficult to develop and fill sites without such facilities like roads, sanitation, drinking water and lighting.
- The lives of existing dumping sites are fast expiring and new land fill sites are not available nearly. The Corporation has to depend on far away sites, which affects transportation cost.

Mismanagement from the Municipal Authorities

Poor management of Solid waste is a bane of urban society. The problem is severe in urban areas because, people from rural area are migrating at an alarming rate for want of employment and better quality of life. Absence of proper municipal amenities adds to the existing menace. Whenever there are sudden surges of population, municipal authorities are forced to take ad-hoc measures, which compound the problem further. The situation should be turned over for good and it needs an organized and well-thought out approach. In short, the major causes of this dilemma are:

- Burgeoning population.
- Industrialization and Urbanisation.
- Uncontrolled Economic growth.
- Unplanned development activities.
- Lack of integrated and holistic approach.
- Ignoring importance of socio-economic and ecological aspects.
- Lack of education.

The problems of solid waste management are two types, technical and socio-economical problems. With existing technology, management of solid waste activities by trained engineers will solve the first problem. However, to keep the environment clean requires not only the solution of technical problems, but also public acceptance, cooperation and participation. After all, every individual contributes one's mite to generation of solid waste, and one should also be disciplined so as not to pollute his environment. To do this educational techniques should be imported through media like press, radio, TV etc.

SUGGESTIONS

The day-to-day management of solid wastes is a complex and expensive activity. Disposal functions have to be sought for the future, the overall objective being to minimize the adverse environmental effects caused by the indiscriminate disposal of solid wastes. This is of paramount importance to health, environmental protection, natural resources management and sustainable development. Developed countries have adopted sophisticated management practices. Imparting the same in low-income countries is not economically, and technically viable.and socially acceptable. However, the management strategies that are to be adopted for low-income countries like India should ensure maximum safety to the environment.

1. To implement proper Solid waste management, various aspects have to be considered such as:
   - Source reduction
   - Onsite storage
   - Collection and transfer
   - Processing techniques
   - Disposal

The flow Chart 1 shows the interrelationship between the functional elements in solid waste management.

Interrelationship Between the Functional Elements in Solid Waste Management

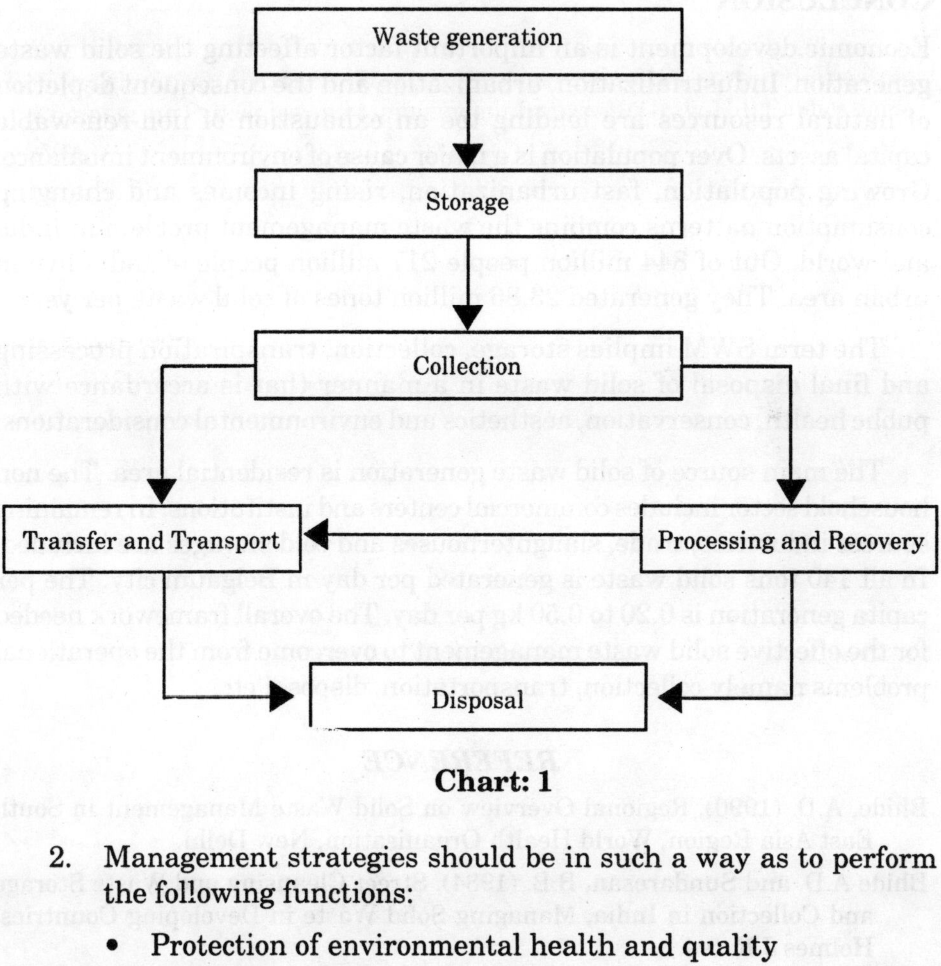

Chart: 1

2. Management strategies should be in such a way as to perform the following functions:
   - Protection of environmental health and quality

   - Supporting the efficiency and productivity of the economy
   - Generation of employment and income

3. Proper incentives should be given to the staff to improve efficiency in the treatment of SWM.
4. Proper maintenance of vehicles and other equipments.
5. Old vehicles should be replaced by new vehicles specifically designed for waste transpiration in order to increase the carrying capacity.
6. The Corporation should involve NGOs and community groups at the managerial and policy making level to strengthen SWM system in the city.

CONCLUSION

Economic development is an important factor affecting the solid waste generation. Industrialization, urbanization and the consequent depletion of natural resources are leading toe an exhaustion of non-renewable capital assets. Over population is a major cause of environment imbalance. Growing population, fast urbanization, rising incomes and changing consumption patterns combine the waste management problem in India and world. Out of 844 million people 217 million people of India live in urban area. They generated 23.86 million tones of solid waste per year.

The term SWM implies storage, collection, transpiration processing and final disposal of solid waste in a manner that is accordance with public health, conservation, aesthetics and environmental considerations.

The main source of solid waste generation is residential area. The non household sector includes commercial centers and institutions. In remaining sources industries, trade, slaughterhouses and cold storages are included. In all 140 tons solid waste is generated per day in Belgaum city. The per capita generation is 0.20 to 0.50 kg per day. The overall framework needed for the effective solid waste management to overcome from the operational problems namely collection, transportation, disposal etc.

REFERENCE

Bhide, A.D. (1990), Regional Overview on Solid Waste Management in South East Asia Region, World Health Organisation, New Delhi.

Bhide A.D. and Sundaresan, B.B. (1984), Street Cleansing and Waste Storage and Collection in India, Managing Solid Waste in Developing Countries, Holmes J.R. (ed.).

Bhuvaneswari Raman, (1994), An Investigation of Non-governmental Organizations, Community Based Organizations and Private Incentives in Indian Cities, Workshop on "Linkages in Urban Solid Waste Management", Bangalore: R-44.

COMIND-sub Committee (1999), Action Plan-Solid Waste Management, IISc, Bangalore.

Earth Summit, (1992), The United Nations Conference on Environment and Development, Rio de Janeiro, Brazil: 184-188.

Environmental Management in Developing Countries (1995), *Waste Management,* Vol. II, Institute for Scientific Cooperation, Tubinger: 92.

Jadhav, H.V. (1995), 'Environmental Pollution', Sterling Publication House, Mumbai.

Karpagam, M. (1999), 'Environmental Economics', Sterling Publishers Pvt. Ltd., Delhi

Koli, P.A. and Mahamuni, V.V. (2005), 'Environmental Economics of Solid Waste Management,' University Book House, Jaipur.

Tchobanaglous, G. Theisen, H. and Eliassen, R. (1997), Solid Wastes: Engineering Principles and Management Issues, McGraw-Hill Publications, New York, USA:52.

MICROFINANCE: AN EFFECTIVE TOOL FOR FINANCIAL INCLUSION

Dinesha P. T. & Jayasheela***

INTRODUCTION

The banking industry has shown tremendous growth in volume and complexity during the last few decades. Despite making significant improvements in all the areas relating to financial viability, profitability and competitiveness, there are concerns that banks have not been able to include vast segment of the population, especially the underprivileged sections of the society, into the fold of basic banking services. Thus, important challenge facing the banking sector is to extend financial services to all sections of society. At this juncture the introduction of "financial inclusion" comes from the recognition that this can serve the interests of both society and the banking system. As a complementary to this, micro-finance[1] can work as a powerful tool to fight poverty became the effective approach of financial inclusion.

Keeping the above facts in view this paper has the following objectives:

- To highlight the nature and extent of exclusion.
- To study the role and importance of microfinance as a strategy of financial inclusion.
- To suggest some policy prescriptions.

NATURE AND EXTENT OF EXCLUSION

Credit is one of the critical inputs for economic development and its timely availability in the right quantity at an affordable cost goes a long

* Junior Research Fellow, Department of Economics, Mangalore University, Mangalagangothri-574 199, Karnataka State, INDIA, *Email: talk2dineshpt@rediffmail.com*

** Reader in Economics and Coordinator, Chair in Rural Banking and Management, Mangalore University, Mangalagangothri–574 199, Karnataka State, INDIA. *Email: jayasheela_mu@yahoo.com*

way in contributing to the well-being of the people especially in the lower rungs of society. Further, access to finance will empower the vulnerable groups by giving them an opportunity to have a bank account, to save and invest, to insure their homes or to partake of credit, thereby facilitating them to break the chain of poverty. But India is lagging behind in this respect so it has become a serious matter of concern.

The Situation Assessment Survey (NSSO, 2003) indicated that out of the total 89.3 million farmer households in the country, 51.4 per cent of households were non-indebted. Further, out of the total 43.4 million indebted households, 20.3 million (46.8 per cent) households had availed financial services from informal sources. The report also shows that 45.9 million farmer households out of the total 89.3 million households do not access credit either from institutional and non-institutional sources. Further, only 27 per cent of the total farm households are indebted to formal sources; in other words 70 per cent of the farmhouses do not have access to formal credit sources. Exclusion is most acute in Central, Eastern and North-Eastern regions–having a concentration of 64% of all financially excluded farmer households in the country.Only 36% of ST farmer households are indebted (SCs and Other Backward Classes- OBC -51%) mostly to informal sources. (GOI, 2008).

There are over 397 million workers in India, out of which 123 million are women workers. Only a small proportion, 18 million, is in the urban areas while 106 million are in rural areas. Not only do a higher percentage of women than men work in the informal economy, women are concentrated in the lower-income segments, working in survival activities or as casual wageworkers or home workers. About 30% of the total workers are poor in India (using the 1999-2000 poverty line at Rs. 336 per capita per month in rural areas and Rs.451 in urban areas). In general a large proportion was poor.

Analysis of the data provided by RBI thru' its Basic Statistical Returns reveal that critical exclusion (in terms of credit) is manifest in 256 districts, spread across 17 States and 1 UT, with a credit gap of 95% and above (GOI, 2008). In these districts, only 10 per cent or less out of 100 persons have access to credit from the fact that the exclusion is large, there is also a wide variation across regions, social groups and asset holdings. The poorer the group, the greater is the exclusion (Rangarajan, 2007).

The inference of these findings is that in spite of a large network of the institutional credit system, it has not been able to adequately penetrate the informal rural financial markets and the non-institutional sources continue to play a dominant role in purveying the credit needs of the people residing in rural areas.

One common measure of financial inclusion is the percentage of adult population having bank accounts. Going by the available data of 2005 on the number of savings bank accounts and assuming that one person has only one account, (which assumption may not be correct as many persons could have more than one bank account) we find that on an all India basis 59 per cent of adult population in the country have bank accounts–in other words 41 per cent of the population is un-banked. In rural areas the coverage is 39 per cent against 61 per cent in urban areas. The un-banked population is higher in the North Eastern and Eastern regions (Thorat, 2007b).

The following table shows that in Northern Region out of 100 persons only 43 persons hold an account in a bank. While coming to the North Eastern Region it is quite low that is just 19. Thus table reveals that access to bank services is low, as well as there exists a large variation across the regions in credit accessibility. Another thing is while compared to the developed world; the coverage of our financial services is quite low. For instance, as per a recent survey commissioned by British Bankers' Association, 92 to 94 per cent of the population of UK has either current or savings bank account (Leeladhar, 2005).

Table 1
Coverage of Banking Services in India

Region	*Current Accounts*	*Savings Accounts*	*Total Population*	*Total No. of accounts*	*No. of acc. Per 100 of population*
North	4215701	52416125	132676462	56631826	43
North East	476603	6891081	38495089	7367684	19
East	1814219	47876140	227613073	49690359	22
Central	2202217	64254189	255713495	66456406	26
West	3178102	49525101	149071747	52703203	35
South	4666014	83386898	223445381	88052912	39
All India	16552856	304349534	1027015247	320902390	31

Source: Situation Assessment Survey 59th Round, National Sample Survey Organisation 2003.

The figures ultimately reveal that there is lack of outreach of banking services to the population, at this juncture micro finance services doing well as a tool of financial inclusion in bringing excluded population to the main stream of formal banking system.

MICRO FINANCE AS AN EFFECTIVE STRATEGY OF FINANCIAL INCLUSION

Financial inclusion is delivery of banking services at an affordable cost to the vast sections of disadvantaged and low-income groups. Although credit is the most important component, financial inclusion covers various financial services such as savings insurance, payments and remittance facilities by the formal financial system to those who tend to be excluded (Mahendra S, 2006).The broad objective of Financial Inclusion is to extend the scope of activities of the organized financial system to include within its ambit people with low incomes. Through graduated credit, the attempts must be to lift the poor from one level to another so that they come out of poverty.

Microfinance through Self Help Groups (SHG) has been highly successful in furthering financial inclusion. The cooperation between the formal banking system and micro-finance organisations has also been encouraging. SHGs are groups of usually women who get together and pool their savings and give loans to members. Members of the group are mostly come under below poverty line so; generally they are excluded from the formal banking habits. Usually there is a Non Governmental Organisation (NGO) that promotes and nurture these groups. National Bank for Agriculture and Rural Development has played a very significant role in supporting group formation, linking them with banks as also promoting best practices. The SHG is given loan against guarantee of group members. The recovery experience has been very good. Banks provide credit to such groups at reasonable rates of interest. However the size of loans is quite small and used mostly for consumption smoothening or very small businesses. In some SHGs, credit is provided for agricultural activities and other livelihoods and could be several times the deposits made by the SHG.

Microfinance has drawn attention to an entire sector of borrowers who had been previously poorly served by the formal financial sector - and MF has demonstrated how to make lending to this sector a viable proposition. The financial inclusion attained through SHGs is sustainable and scalable on account of its various positive features. One of the distinctive features of the SHG-Bank Linkage Programme (BLP) has been the high recovery rate. However the spread of SHGs is very uneven and is more concentrated in southern states. This regional imbalance needs to be corrected and special efforts in this regard may have to be made by NABARD. SHGs also needed to graduate from mere providers of credit for non-productive purposes to promoting micro enterprises. However, there is no need to provide interest rate subsidy to the SHGs. Banks do provide them credit at reasonable rate of interest.

Micro Finance Institutions (MFIs) have been playing an important role in substituting moneylenders and reducing the burden on the formal financial institutions. With the objective of ensuring greater financial inclusion and increasing the outreach of the banking sector, banks have been allowed to use the services of NGO's, SHGs, MFIs and other civil society organizations as intermediaries in providing financial and banking services through the use of business facilitator and correspondent models. Provision for this kind of financial intermediation has opened new and diverse avenues to address the issue of financial inclusion by banks (Mahendra S, op. cit.).

The SHG-Bank Linkage Programme launched by NABARD in 1992 continues to be the predominant Micro-Finance (MF) model in the country. It is a proven method of financial inclusion, providing un-banked rural clientele with access to formal financial services from the existing banking infrastructure. During the year 2006-07 6, 86,408 new SHGs were credit linked with banks as against 6, 20,109 during 2005-06, taking the cumulative number of credit linked SHGs to 29, 24,973. The phenomenal outreach of the programme has enabled an estimated 409.5 lakh poor households to gain access to MF from the formal banking system as on March 2007, registering a growth of 24.2 per cent over the previous year (NABARD, 2007). So, large section of financially excluded population mostly including women came under the formal banking system and microfinance successfully inculcated banking habits among the people.

From the above description it could be stated here that, formation of SHGs in rural areas has kindled new hope of change and development in the status and role of women folk, who are otherwise powerless and marginalized members of the society. Now they are able to grow economically and socially as members have also accepted the changed role of their women folk and most of the time they are supportive to them. In addition they are able to get financial assistance from women folk, which were not possible earlier (Patil, 2006).

POLICY PRESCRIPTIONS

Following are the some of the suggestions for strengthening movement of financial inclusion through microfinance.

- For addressing financial inclusion effectively banking system has to develop a holistic approach in creating awareness about financial products, education, and advice on money management, debt counselling, savings and affordable credit.

- Technology can be a very valuable tool in providing access to banking products in remote areas. According to Prof. M.S. Swaminanthan, the noted agricultural scientist, "SHGs, will however, become sustainable only if they have backward linkages with technology and credit and forward linkages with processing and marketing organisations" (Swaminanthan, 2006). So, technology should be upgraded to bring down the transaction cost, while extending loan, etc...
- The banks need to redesign their business strategies to incorporate specific plans to promote financial inclusion of low income group treating it both a business opportunity as well as a corporate social responsibility.
- In dealing with the needs of rural enterprises and of small and medium enterprises in urban areas, banks have to look for new delivery mechanisms. These must economize on transaction costs and provide better access to the currently under-served. To serve new rural credit needs, innovative channels for credit delivery will have to be found.
- Till now, micro financing has been a grey area in the finance sector as the current laws allow only the entities registered with RBI to raise deposits and lending activities. In view of the rising micro-financing activities in the country, a need has been felt to regulate the unregulated business in this sector and also provide legal framework to facilitate the credit flow in rural areas (Tiwari, 2006).
- Micro-insurance is a key element in the financial services package for people at the bottom of the pyramid. The poor face more risks than the well off. It is becoming increasingly clear that micro-insurance needs a further push and guidance from the Regulator as well as the Government (The Hindu Business Line 2007).
- Government should initiate the SHG programme through state programmes in identified regions where spread of SHG movement is less. There should be machinery in each State to monitor the spread of SHGs.
- The MFIs should be strengthened with the tools of managerial expertise, user-friendly technology and with the principles of good governance and social responsibility.

CONCLUSIONS

Microfinance in India has emerged as a powerful tool for financial inclusion and the 'SHG–Bank Linkage' programme played a predominant role in the financial inclusion of poor. But there is a need to strengthen the SHG-Bank Linkage Programme to fully mainstream it with the commercial banking system. The variations in performance across the regions, both in terms of reach and quality needs immediate attention.

NOTES

1. *Microfinance:* Micro finance is a financial service of small quantity provided by financial institutions to the poor. These financial services may include savings, credit insurance, leasing, money transfer, equity transactions etc. that is any type of financial service provided to customers to meet their normal financial needs life cycle, economic opportunity and emergency.
2. *Micro Finance Institution (MFI):* A MFI is an organization that acts as an interface between the formal credit delivery institutions and credit seekers, with an aim to assist for the socio economic development of poor and marginalized people. The geographical distribution of MFIs is very much concentrated in the Southern India where the rural branch network of formal bank is excellent.
3. *Self Help Group (SHG):* A Self-Help Group (SHG) is a registered or unregistered group of people having homogenous social and economic background voluntarily, coming together to save small amounts regularly, to mutually agree to contribute to a common fund and to meet their emergency needs on mutual help basis. Each group consists of 10-20 members. A group could be exclusively male or female, or even mixed. However majority of SHG's are female groups.

REFERENCES

Fisher, Thomas and M.S. Sriram (2002), *Beyond Microcredit': Putting Development Back into Micro-finance*, Vistaar Publications, New Delhi.

GOI (2008), *Report on the Committee on the Financial Inclusion*, January.

Karmakar, K. G. (2002), Microfinance Revisited, *Financing Agriculture*, Vol. 34, No.2, April-June, pp. 18-22.

Leeladhar (2005), *Taking Banking Services to the Common Man–Financial Inclusion*, at FedBank Hormis Memorial foundation, at Ernakulam on December 02.

Mahendra Dev S. (2006), Financial Inclusion: Issues and Challenges, *Economic and Political Weekly*, Vol. 41, No. 41, October 14-October 20.

NABARD Annual Report, 2007.

Patil, Shobhadevi R. (2006), Role of Self Help Groups in Sustainable Development: An NGO Experience, *Participative Development*, Vol. 5, No 1, Jan-Mar, pp.55-64.

Patnaik, Priti (2006), Nabard to Oversee Micro-lenders, *The Economic Times*, Friday, 27, p. 3.

Rangarajan C. (2007), *Financial Inclusion: Some Key Issues*, Lecture Delivered at Mangalore University, Mangalore, and August 10.

Satish P. (2005), Mainstreaming Indian Micro Finance, *Economic and Political Weekly*, Vol. 40, No. 17, April 23-April 29, pp. 1731-1739.

The Hindu Business Line (2007a), Micro-finance Bill tabled, March 20. Available *at http://www.thehindubusinessline.com/2007/03/21/stories/2007032105170600.htm* (accessed January 30, 2008).

Thorat, Usha (2007a), *Taking Banking Services to the Common Man–Financial Inclusion,* Deputy Governor, Reserve Bank of India at the HMT-DFID Financial Inclusion Conference 2007, Whitehall Place, London, UK, June 19.

Thorat, Usha (2007b), *Financial Inclusion–The Indian Experience* Text of Speech by Deputy Governor, Reserve Bank of India at the HMT-DFID Financial Inclusion Conference 2007, Whitehall Place, London, UK, June 19.

Tiwari, Ravish (2006), Micro-finance Bill Referred to GOM after Objections, *The Indian Express,* Dec 16. Available at *http://www.indianexpress.com/story/18680.html (accessed on January 30, 2008).*

INDEX

A

Administrative Council, 61
Agreement
  On Agriculture (AOA), 95, 96, 97, 103, 109
  On Trade Related Aspects of Intellectual Property Rights, 3, 5
Agricultural
  Activities, 229
  Issues, 95
  Labour, 232
  Labourers, Wage Discrimination, 229
  Industry, 126
  Marketing, 105
AIDS
  Drugs, 58
  Medicines, 58
All India Coordination Research Project (AICRP), 51
Alma Alta Declaration, 191
Alternate Dispute Resolution Mechanism (ADR), 147
Amber Box, 95
American
  Arbitration Association, 154
  Patent Office, 53
Anti-Fatigue Plants, 51
Arbitration, 147-149, 153, 154, 155, 156
  And Conciliation Act, 155
  Tribunal, 150, 152
Art of Healing Wounds, 3
Arya Samaj, 262
Association of National Laws, 22
Australia, 65
Australia Wine Industry, 127
Ayurvedic Healing, 52

B

Bakshi Tekchand, Justice, 81
Bangladesh, 109
Banker's Book Evidence Act, 1891, 23
Banking
  And Communication, 217
  Industry, 289
  Services in India (Easter/North Eastern region), 291
  System, 292
Basmati Rice, 51, 53, 101, 102
  Foreign Exchange Earning, 53
Belgaum, 275, 276, 280
  Generation of Solid Waste, 277
  Municipal Corporation, 273, 286
Below Poverty Line, 232
Berne Convention for the Protection of Literary and Artistic Works,, 6, 50, 134, 150, 170
Bilateral Agreements, 127

Biodiversity, 1, 2
    Preservation of-, 2
Biological
    Diversity Act, 8, 29
    Protection of-, 4
    Resources, (BR), 4-6, 9, 12
Biopiracy, 1, 4, 5, 50, 53, 54
Biotechnology, 5, 140
    Industry, 4
    Patents, 59
Birth/Death Rate, 193
Black Letter Law Traditions, 169
Blue Box, 95
Bombings in London, 251
Border Measures, 117
Brahmo Samaj, 262
British
    India, 80
    Infiltration in India, 262
    Patent Act, 60
    Patent Law, 1852, 80
    Patents and Designs Act (1907), 27
Budapest Treaty, 135
Burgundy (French Region), 127

C

Canada, 65
Canadian
    Copyright Act, 161
    Jurisprudence, 161
Cancun
    Ministerial Conference, 122
    Negotiations, 121
CBR (Crude Birth Rate) in India, 192
China, 105, 192
Chinese Patent Law, 60
CIPR (Commission on Intellectual Property Rights), 142
Civil Criminal Remedies, 33
Clash of Civilization, 251
Code of German Civil Procedure, 151
Colonial India, 213
Committees and Commissions, (C&C), 263
    Bhaktvatsalam Committee, 263
    Committee on Status of Women in India, 263
    Durgabai Deshmukh Committee, 263
    Hansa Mehta Committee, 263
    Kothari Commission, 263
    National Committee on women's Education, 263
    National Council for Women's Education, 263
    National Policy on Education, 263
Computer
    Crimes, 46
    Related Crimes, 17
Contracting Parties, 7
Convention on Biological Diversity (CBD), 2, 5, 7, 8, 12
Copyrights, 6, 20, 28, 49, 118, 150
    Board, 154
    Cases, 160
    Infringement, 166
    Law, 79, 159-171
    Legislation, 161
Credit Cards Frauds, 18
Criminal Sanctions, 28
CSIR (Council for Scientific and Industrial Research), 2, 51, 52

Cultural

Traditions, 241

Transmission, 241

Cyber

Crimes, 17, 45, 46

Security, 47

Space, 17

D

Dalit Workers, 208

Dalits in India, 202-212

Depletion of National Resources, 286

Developed Economies of Asia, Africa and Latin American Countries, 185

Developing Countries, 5, 6, 12, 22, 28, 45, 95, 96, 98, 100, 109, 118, 121, 124, 128, 133, 135, 139, 140, 142-144, 219, 273, 274

Development

Agenda, 144

Programmes 267

Dispute Settlement Body, (DSB), 7

Distinguished Women, (DW), 262

Late Sarojini Naidu—Begum Hamid Ali, 262

District, Gulbarga, 230

DNS Disputes in Indian Courts, 19

Doha Ministerial Declaration, 122

Domain Names System (DNS), 19, 20

Domestic and International Price, 96

Domestic/Export Strategies, 97

Drugs, 50, 55

Drugs Administration, 101

E

Eastern Block, 121

Eastern Book Company Case, 170

Economic

Development, 134, 191, 207, 286

Development of Dalits, 211

Globalization, 133

Growth, 217, 233

Planning, 182

Policy, 96

Reforms, 211

Measures, 209

Movement, 202

Programme, 203

System, 4

Economy, 96, 202

Agricultural, 229

Capitalism, 177

Capitalist, 202

Developing, 219

Developing and Transitional, 113

Indian, 104, 229

Indian Mixed-, 213

Mixed, 202, 203

Political, 148

Service Sector, 213

Socialist, 202

Socio-Economic Development of-, 202

World, 6, 226

Education,

For All (EFA), 265

Secular, 262

Egypt, Slovenia, 113

Elderly People, 241-243, 249

Annapurna Yojna, 247

Day Care, 247

Government Schemes Regarding-, 247

Health Problems, 246
National Old Age Pension Scheme, 247
Tax Concessions, 247
Travel Concessions, 247
Widow Pension, 247
Electronic
Banking Frauds, 18
Transfers, 18
Employment and Income Generation Program, 267
Enforcement Costs, 124
English
Copyright Act, 1842, 28
Jurisprudence and cited cases, 168, 169
European
Board of Appeal, 61
Community, 113, 118
Immigrants, 124
Patent Convention (EPC), 61, 62
Union Members, 117
Union, (EU), 61, 100, 121, 125, 127, 140, 143
Export Credits, 98

F

False Indicators, 116, 117
Family Problems, 246
FDI (Foreign Direct Investment), 143
Federal
Court of Appeal, 161
Food, Drug and Cosmetic Act, 63
Feist in American Supreme Court, 166
Feist Ruling, 161
Female Agricultural Labour, (FAL), 230, 231, 233
Characteristics, 231
Importance, 231
State-wise Strength, 233
Financial Institutions, 293
Fishing Products, 100
Five Year Plan (7th), 182
Five Year Plan (8th), 182
Five Year Plan (9th), 182, 183
Food
And Drug Administration (FDA), 62, 63
Corporation of India, 209
Security, 98
Free Trade
Agreements, (FTAs), 107, 108
Regime, 98

G

Gandhi, Mahatma, 262
GATT (General Agreement on Tariff and Trade), 6, 107-109
Secretariat, 82
System, 135
Gender Discrimination, 229-238
Genetic and Biological Resources, 1, 5
Geographic Indictors, 148
Geographical
Indicators, 113-130
Indicators of Indian Origin, 130
Germany, 151
Germany and Japan, 150, 151
Global
Market, 95
Patent System, 133

Globalization, 177, 183, 252, 255, 257
Gram Panchyats, 238
Granting Patent Requirements, 84, 85
Green Box, 95, 109
Group Labourers, 231

H

Health
  Fundamental Human Right, 191
  Infrastructure, 196
  Infrastructure in India, 191
    Three Tier System of Rural Health, 196
  Status in India, 191, 192
Higher Education, 259-271
  Policies, 259
  Scheduled Caste Women, 259, 268
Horticulture Products, 104

I

Import Substitution and Export Promotion Techniques, 95
Inadequate Building, 194
India
  And Pakistan, 101
  Sri Lanka, Turkey, 113
India's
  Biodiversity Resources, 8
  Planning, 211
  Population, 229
  Service Imports, 223
Indian
  Agriculture, 105, 106
  Agricultural Practices, 230
  Agriculture and WTO, 102
  Aromatic Rice, 54
  Biological Resources, 12
  Copyright Act, 1914, 28
  Dishes, 2
  Evidence Act, 23, 27
  Farming, 104
  Jurisprudence, 169
  Jurisprudence on Originality of Compilation of Facts, 167-168
Laws, 2, 11
    Biological Diversity Act, 2002, 2
    Patent (Amendment) Act, 2005, 2
    Plant Varieties and Protection and Protection-, 2
    Plant—Of Farmers' Rights Act, 2001, 2, 9
  Patent Act, 1970, 28, 56, 57, 58, 81, 83
  Patent System, 80
  Political System, 54
  Service Sector, 216, 217
  Trade and Merchandise Marks Act, 36
  Traditional Knowledge, 50
Indigenous
  Countries, 1, 11, 12
  Remedies on Wounds, 52
Industrial
  Capitalism, 254, 256
  Credit System, 290
  Designs, 6, 49
  Development, 226, 273
  Growth, 219
  Policy and Promotion, D/O, 148
  Property, 49, 50, 79
    Industrial Designs, 79

Patents, 79
Trademarks, 79
Property Protection, 114, 116
Industrialization, 81, 286
Strategies, 96
Industrialized Countries, 6
Infant Mortality Rate, 192, 193
Information, Communication and Technology (ICT), 20, 105
Information Technology, 19, 140, 198
Act, 23
Bill, 27
D/O, 148
Law, (ITL), 17, 19, 20, 27, 46
Communication, 17
Computer System, 17
Digital Electronics, 17
Law Cases, 29
European Court of Justice (ECJ), 29-32
In India, 29-45
Rules, 24
Infrastructure, 187, 191, 192, 195-197
Health Care, 192, 195
Health-in India, 91
Physical, 194
Integrated Circuit Layout Dispute Act, 29
Intellectual Property,
Biodiversity, 54
Disputes and Arbitration, 147-156
In Europe, 116
Law, 21, 22
Legal Regime, 20
Legislation in India, 27
History, 27
Legislation, 23, 28
Protection, 5, 6
Standards, 142
Property Dispute (IPD), 148-154, 155, 156
In India, 1153, 154
Technical Nature, 148
Intellectual Property Rights (IPRs), 6, 17, 18, 19, 27, 49, 113, 133, 142, 147, 152, 155
Administration, 148
And Biological Resources, 2
In India, 20
In Political Systems, 54, 147, 152, 155
Industry, 80
Infringements, 20
Legislation, 80
Management, 106
Protecting of-, 1
Protection, 135
Regime, 2, 8
Standardization, 135
International
Patent Reform, 80
Trade, 79
Trade and Cooperation, 6
Women's Year, 263
Internet Protocol, 19
Inventions, 81-87
Inventions and Designs Act, 27
Islamic
Extremists, 256
Fundamentalism, 257
Jihadists, 257
Revivalism, 257
Iyenger, Justice Rajagopal, 81

J

Jan Swasthya Abhiyan, 195
Japan, 118
Japanese Patent Office, 61
Joint Family System, 241

K

Kani Tribe, 51
Karnataka, Education/Literacy, 266
Kathari Commission, 260
Kefauver Committee of USA, 81
Kerala, 193
Knowledge, Innovation and Practices (KIP), 8

L

Labour
  Casual (Dinaguli), 230, 238
  Contract Gang-, 230
  Hiring System, 231
  Market, 185
  Migration, 237
Labourers, 229
  Female, 229, 230
  Women, 230
Landless Agricultural Labour, 232
Latin American Countries, 124
Law
  Enforcement Agencies, 46
  Society of Upper Canada, 162
Least Developed Countries, (LDCs), 136
Legislation, 21, 22
Liberalization, 95, 96, 183
  And Globalization, 226, 229
  Privatization and Globalization, 202, 203
Life Expectancy, 192, 193
Lisbon Agreement, 116, 117
Literacy, 265
  Female, 267
Lord
  Halsbury, 163
  Mansfield, 163
  Robertson, 163

M

Madras High Court, 58
Madrid Agreement, 116, 117
Mahila
  Mandals, 267
  Sangams, 267
Marine Products, 100
Marketization, 183
Mashelkar Committee, 58, 65
Maternal Mortality Rate, 192
Medium and Small Farmers (MSF), 208
Micro-Finance Institutions, (MFI), 293, 294
Microorganism, 135, 289-295
  Claims, 60
  In China, 60
Microorganism in Japan, 62
Milk Products, 100
Model APMC Act, 105
Modern Legal System in India, 169
Modernity, 254, 257
Modernization, 251, 252, 254-256
Monopolization, 5
Multiculturalism, 251, 253-256
Multilateral
  Trading System, 133
  Training Arrangement, 12

N

National
  Bank for Agriculture and Rural Development, (NABARD), 292
  Biodiversity Authority, 8, 9
  Commission on Urbanization, 274
  Economic Policy, 202, 203
  Education System, 268
  Health Policy (NHP), 195
  Literacy Missions (NLM), 265
  Patent Act, 1920, 81, 82
    Main Features, 81, 82
  Policy on Education, 267
New Economic Policy, 184, 185, 187, 188, 267
Non-Governmental Organizations (NGO), 198, 238, 249, 267, 292, 293
Non-Patentable Inventions Details, 83-84
Non-Tariff Barriers (NTB), 95, 98, 100
North American Free Trade Agreements (NAFTA), 161
North East Region, 291
North-South Antagonism, 113

O & P

OBC in Services, 207
Panchayats, 153
Pandita Ramabai, 262
Paris Convention, 6, 49, 50, 117, 134, 135, 150
Patent
  Act, 2005, 82
  Act, 1970, 10, 90, 154
  Agenda, 86, 143, 144
  And Design Act, 1911, 81
  Bill, 27
  Cooperation Treaty (PCT), 86, 91
  Copyright and Trademarks (PCT), 135, 137-139, 141, 150, 152, 155
    Application, 138
    Contracting States, 139
    System, 139
  Law in India, 64, 79
  Law Standards under WIPO, 134
  Law Treaty (PLT), 136-138
  Obtaining Procedure, 87
  Office in India, 86
  On Pharmaceuticals and Living Organisms, 133
  Protection, 6, 79
  Regulations, 59
  System, 91
Patenting of Microorganism, 61
  In Australia, 63
  In Brazil, 64
  In China, 61
  In Japan, 61
Patents
  And Designs Protection Act, 1872, 27
  On Genes, 141
Performing Arts, 79
Personnel Planning, 195
Plan Expenditure, 205
Planning, 213, 217, 223
  Commission, 182
  Economic, 208
  For Industry, 213
Plant
  Breeder's Rights, 6
  Genetic System, 61
Primary Health Centres, (PHCs), 194-196, 198

Prior Informed Consent, (PIC), 4
Privatization, 96
- Free Market Policies, 183
- Liberalization, Marketization and Globallization (PLMG), 184

Problems, 241-249
- Socio, Economic and Health, 241-249

Procurement Management, 106
Protection of
- Appellations—Registration, 116
- Plant Varieties and Farmers Rights Act, 9
- Wines and Spirits, 118

Protectionism, 125
Protective Technologies, 21
Public Distribution System, 209
Publishing Industry, 171

R

Radhakrishnan, S, Indian Philosopher and Educationalist, 259
RBI Act and Its Details, 24, 27
Reforms, 21, 202
- International, 21
- Legal, 22
- National, 21
- Regional, 21

Regional
- Foods, 126
- Trade Agreements (RTAs), 107, 108
- Trading, 107

Right of
- Broadcasters, 79
- Education, 261

Rights, Commercialization of-, 1
Roy, Raja Rammohun, 262
Rural
- Financial Markets, 291
- Health Care Infrastructure Development, 196
- Women, 232, 233

S

Sabotage of Computer Systems, 18
Sanitary and Phytosanitary Measures, (SPS), 100
- Agreement, 100
- Standards, 100

Scheduled Caste
- Castes in Karnataka, 266
- In Services, 207
- Literacy, 266
- Population, 271

Women in Gulbarga, 268
Scheduled Caste/Tribes/OBC Minorities, 267
Scheduled Tribes in Services, 207
Science and Technology, 18, 53
- Department of-, 2

Sector,
- Agricultural, 50, 213, 216, 229
- Banking, 289
- Health, 193
- Industrial Export, 221
- Service, 214, 224
- Social, 202, 203, 205, 210, 212

Security and Intellectual System, 251
Self-Help Groups, 292, 293, 294
SHGs-Bank Linkage Programme, 292, 295

Shrinking Budget Support, 193

Small

- And Medium Enterprises, 143
- And Marginal Farmers, (SMFs), 104, 232, 238

Smuggling of Plants/Animals, 5

Social Evils, 262

- Sati, Child Marriage, 262

Social

- Justice, 263
- Reformers, 262
- Sector Development, 207
- Sector Expenditure, 205

Socialism, 259

Society (ies), 1

- British, 251, 252
- Indian, 210, 241
- Multicultural, 252, 253
- Plural, 253
- Primitive, 273
- Western, 251

Socio-Economic Development, 208

Software Industry, 22

Solid Waste

- Generation, 277
- Management, 273, 280, 285, 286
    - Current Practice in Belgaum, 280
    - Defined, 273
    - Infrastructure, 283
    - Problems in Collection, 281
    - Problems in Disposal, 283

South

- African Countries, 110
- Asian Countries, 96, 98

Special Safeguards (SSG), 98

Specific Relief Act, 1877, 28

Sri Lanka, 192

State Biodiversity Boards, 8, 9

Structural Transformation, 214

Substantive Patent Law Treaty (SPLT), 139, 140, 142

Swaminathan, MS, Agricultural Scientists, 294

Sweat of Brow Doctrine, 163-166, 169

- British Cases, 167
- Cases, 163-167

Swiss

- Domestic Arbitration, 152
- International Arbitration Convention, 152
- Private Intellectual Law Act, 152

Switzerland, 118, 121, 134, 152, 154

T

TBGRI Kekrala, 51

Tea Board, 116

Techno-Legal Issues, 53

Technology, 103, 198, 219, 294

- Of the Law, 79
- Transfer, 142

Telecommunication Frauds, 18

Terrorists and Crimnals, 18

Texas Camp, 53

Textile and Agriculture, 135

Theft of

- Data, 18
- Intellectual Property, 18
- Marketing Information, 18

Total

- Fertility Rate, 192
- Literacy Campaign, 265

Trade
And Merchandise Marks Act, 154
Liberalization, 96, 107
Restrictions, 125
Trademarks, 20, 22, 28, 49, 115, 116, 118, 121, 150
Act, 1940, 28, 32
Infringement, 22
Rights, 22
Traditional
And Ethno-Medicinal Practices, 53
Biological Resources, 1
Commonwealth Jurisprudence, 162
Folklore of India, 54
Knowledge, 1, 4, 11, 52, 54
Knowledge of Yogic—Health Remedies, 50
Rights, 2
Training-Cum-Production Centres for Women, 267
Transport Facilities, 195
Tribal Families, 51
TRIPS (Trade Related Intellectual Property Rights), 2, 6, 8, 10, 11, 12, 50, 54, 58, 65, 114, 115, 118, 120, 121, 133, 135, 136, 140, 142, 144
Agreement, 28, 55, 82, 83, 91, 101, 113, 114, 116, 122, 127, 136, 141-143
Council, 116, 121
Members, 121
Patent System, 82
Provisions, 118
Standards, 135-137
TRQ (Tariff Rate), 97
Turmeric, 2, 51, 54
Case, 2
In Wound Healing, 52
Patent, 51
Powder, 2, 3

U

UK (United Kingdom), 159, 165, 167, 168
Patent Office, 59
UN (United Nations)
Conference on Environment and Development (UNCED), 7
Developed Programme, 192
General Assembly, 23
International Literacy Year, 265
System, 134
Unani and Ayurvedic System of Treatment, 50
UNCITRAL (UN Commission on Intl Trade Laws), 23
UNCTAD, 28
Unemployment, 177, 188
Criteria, 179
Education, 181
Effects of-, 181
In India, 179
Meaning & Definition, 178
Rates, 181
Social Effects, 187
Trends, 181
Uniform
Dispute Resolution Policy, 22
Patent System, 82
Unorganized Sectors, 185
Urban Solid Waste Management, 273-286
Urbanization, 254, 256, 274, 286
Uruguay Round Agreement, (UR) of GATT, 6, 95, 96, 99

Negotiations, 97
Package, 118
Period, 100
Projections, 100
US, 5, 6, 11, 62, 63, 82, 114, 116, 117, 124, 127, 135, 139, 140, 143, 152, 161, 165, 185, 223
And UK, 65
Based Indians, 2
Companies, 124
Law, 2, 3
Patent and Trademark Organization (PTO), 2, 3, 19, 52, 63
Patent
Act, 152
Codes, 141
Law, 63
System, 52
Patent—Turmeric Wound Healting, 2
Police—Software, 140
Singapore Agreement, 107
US—Australia, 118
US—Latin American Countries, 121
US—Mexico, 113

V

Vedic Period, 261
Vidya Sagar, Ishwar Chandra, 262
Voluntary Retirement Schemes (VRS), 185

W & Z

Wage
Differentials, 235
Rate Operation-wise, 236
Wild Plants, 1
Women
And Child Development, 206
And Literacy in India, 265
Enrolment State-wise, 265
In Higher Education, 264
Studies in Universities, 264
Study Circles, 264
Women's
Education, 261, 262
Educational Status, 261
Enrolment in Colleges/Universities, 267
World Intellectual Property Organization (WIPO), 33, 50, 51, 79, 134-136, 144, 148, 149, 151
Administered PCT, 90
Arbitration
And Mediation Centre, 34
Rules, 151
Assembly Agreement, 136
Conventions, 135
Copyright Treaty, 136
Patent Agenda, 133, 136-138
Patent System, 135
Standing Committee, 139, 140
World Trade Centre, (WTC), 256
World Trade Organization, 6, 7, 8, 28, 95-110, 133, 135, 141
Agreement, 98, 102, 106, 109, 127
Legal Regime, Impact of-, 50
Member States, 128, 129
Reduction Commitment, 110
System, 65
Threat, 104
Zenana Missions, 262